Becoming Eisenhower

ALSO BY MICHAEL LEE LANNING

The Only War We Had: A Platoon Leader's Journal of Vietnam

Vietnam 1969–1970: A Company Commander's Journal

Inside the LRRPs: Rangers in Vietnam

Inside Force Recon: Recon Marines in Vietnam (with Ray W. Stubbe)

The Battles of Peace

Inside the VC and NVA: The Real Story of North Vietnam's Armed Forces (with Dan Cragg)

Vietnam at the Movies

Senseless Secrets: The Failures of U.S. Military Intelligence from George Washington to the Present

The Military 100: A Ranking of the Most Influential Military Leaders of All Time

The African-American Soldier: From Crispus Attucks to Colin Powell

Inside the Crosshairs: Snipers in Vietnam

Defenders of Liberty: African Americans in the Revolutionary War

Blood Warriors: American Military Elites

The Battle 100: The Stories behind History's Most Influential Battles

Mercenaries: Soldiers of Fortune, from Ancient Greece to Today's Private Military Companies

The Civil War 100: The Stories behind the Most Influential Battles, People, and Events in the War between the States

The Revolutionary War 100: The Stories behind the Most Influential Battles, People, and Events of the American Revolution

Double T Double Cross: The Firing of Coach Mike Leach

At War with Cancer (with Linda Moore-Lanning)

Tours of Duty: Vietnam War Stories

Tony Buzbee: Defining Moments

Texas Aggies in Vietnam: War Stories

The VA Cemeteries of Texas

Dear Allyanna: An Old Soldier's Last Letter to His Granddaughter

The Court Martial of Jackie Robinson

The Blister Club: The Extraordinary Story of the Downed American Airmen Who Escaped to Safety in World War II

Hispanic Medal of Honor Recipients: American Heroes

Jewish Medal of Honor Recipients: American Heroes

Patton in Mexico: Lieutenant George S. Patton, the Hunt for Pancho Villa, and the Making of a General

BECOMING EISENHOWER

How Ike Rose from Obscurity to Supreme Allied Commander

MICHAEL LEE LANNING

STACKPOLE
BOOKS

Essex, Connecticut
Blue Ridge Summit, Pennsylvania

STACKPOLE BOOKS

An imprint of The Globe Pequot Publishing Group, Inc.
64 South Main Street
Essex, CT 06426
www.globepequot.com

Distributed by NATIONAL BOOK NETWORK

British Library Cataloguing in Publication Information available

Library of Congress Cataloging-in-Publication Data
Names: Lanning, Michael Lee, author.
Title: Becoming Eisenhower : how Ike rose from obscurity to supreme allied commander / Michael Lee Lanning.
Description: Essex, Connecticut : Stackpole Books, [2024] | Includes bibliographical references. | Summary: "This book tells the story of a young man who pursued the army for its free education but found his calling as an officer, the story of an officer who was initially overlooked but motivated by frustration to make himself the army's indispensable man, the story of how General Eisenhower carried these experiences to Supreme Command and the presidency"— Provided by publisher.
Identifiers: LCCN 2024005886 (print) | LCCN 2024005887 (ebook) | ISBN 9780811773874 (cloth) | ISBN 9780811773881 (epub)
Subjects: LCSH: Eisenhower, Dwight D. (Dwight David), 1890–1969. | Presidents—United States—Biography. | Generals—United States—Biography. | United States—History, Military—20th century.
Classification: LCC E836 .L29 2024 (print) | LCC E836 (ebook) | DDC 973.921092 [B]— dc23/eng/20240521
LC record available at https://lccn.loc.gov/2024005886
LC ebook record available at https://lccn.loc.gov/2024005887

♾️™ The paper used in this publication meets the minimum requirements of American National Standard for Information Sciences—Permanence of Paper for Printed Library Materials, ANSI/ NISO Z39.48-1992.

To my teachers, role models, and mentors

Linda Moore-Lanning

James W. Lanning

James M. Lanning

Alice C. Lanning

H. McKee Andrus

Owen A. Lock

Bernard O. Loeffke

Albert A. Maberry

Corps of Cadets, Texas A&M University

United States Army Ranger School

CONTENTS

INTRODUCTION

The date was June 6, 1944. The mission was Operation Overlord to gain a beachhead on the coast of France that would allow the Allies to establish a footing for recapturing occupied Europe and to push inland to defeat Nazi Germany. The commitment was the full might of the greatest military force ever assembled under one command—the land, air, and sea assets of the United States, the United Kingdom, and their allies. At stake was the outcome of World War II on the European front and possibly the future of the free world.

That outcome ultimately rested on the shoulders of one man—one man who possessed the ability to envision and maneuver this grand-scale attack that would change the direction of the war; one man who had the breadth of military knowledge necessary to grasp the complexities of the multidimensional fronts; one man who had the in-depth, hands-on experience to develop and execute air and ground strategies that would overwhelm the enemy; one man who could parlay his charismatic personality into the respect required for others to follow his commands. The one man was General Dwight David Eisenhower.

While numerous capable generals were ready and willing to step in to lead the fray—many well known and highly respected—who might have been placed in this position of such monumental importance, Eisenhower was the only one who had the unique background and tedious training to orchestrate the European operations with such precision and audacity.

Unlike the flamboyant General George Patton or the arrogant General Douglas MacArthur, General Eisenhower had been a relatively unknown officer before World War II. In virtual obscurity, he was a man who had spent more than three decades preparing—mostly in inglorious ways, in his and others' view—for his destiny. As a young officer, he tried every avenue available to him to get assigned to Europe before the Great War was over; instead, he was selected to be a training instructor and post football coach. As a field grade officer, he tirelessly sought to command troops; instead, he was posted to remote locations to polish his skills in writing and organizing. As a junior general officer, he vied again for troop assignments; instead, he was too valued by his superiors for release from his desk jobs.

Only when the United States was fully committed to war did President Franklin Roosevelt pluck Eisenhower from the upper ranks of the military to make him Supreme Allied Commander Europe.

From this position, Eisenhower issued a message to the troops in the early morning hours of June 6, 1944, that said, in part, "Nothing short of victory is acceptable. Good luck!" Thus did he launch the invasion at Normandy on what became known as D-Day and catapulted his name into the history books as the man who freed Europe.

Who was this fifty-six-year-old man who stepped out of the ranks of obscurity to defeat Adolf Hitler's Nazi war machine? I could not have written more than a paragraph or two from memory about Dwight Eisenhower before he caught my attention while I was completing the first drafts of my book on the early career of General George Patton. I knew, of course, that Eisenhower had come to outrank Patton during World War II and that a plethora of volumes had been written about him both as a general and as a president. Because I had been focusing on the influences that had formed Patton into the soldier he became, I found myself wondering the same about Eisenhower's formative military days.

The idea was not, however, my introduction to General and President Dwight Eisenhower. He is the first U.S. president in my memory from my early boyhood. A closer contact came in 1978. My wife, Linda, and I reported to Fort Leavenworth, Kansas, for a short assignment before I entered the Command and General Staff College. We arrived after midnight in a driving snowstorm and checked into guest quarters in the middle of the post. The next morning, I ventured downstairs from the brick apartment to sunny skies. I noticed a brass plaque next to the apartment's door. On brushing off the snow, I discovered that the quarters had been home to Eisenhower and his wife while he attended the same course some five decades earlier.

After *Patton in Mexico* went to the publisher, I perused some of the Eisenhower biographies and specialty books looking for information about what and who had been for him major influences early on. I found that the bulk of the published works focus almost exclusively on what happened to him from the time he was appointed Supreme Allied Commander Europe until he died years after his time at the White House as the thirty-fourth president of the United States. While some books included a bit of his boyhood background and others mentioned various early chronological events, none closely examined those critical years that Eisenhower spent as a company-grade or field-grade officer—those years when soldiers learn the art and craft of leadership through hands-on experience, the operational procedures necessary to strategize the movements of various-size units, and the finesse of developing networks among all ranks.

In fact, only in Eisenhower's autobiography did I find emphasis on the details of his boyhood and his thoughts and frustrations as he navigated his way from Abilene, Kansas, to the U.S. Military Academy and from there through the challenging years between the world wars. While I was pleased to have the firsthand information, I am always reluctant, as a historian, to depend on the writers of such books to be totally reliable witnesses. I looked further.

My research was basically uncovering a gaping hole in Eisenhower's story—like two bookends standing on either side of a void. Particulars on his family life, childhood, and school experiences were readily available, on the one side, as were the details of his successful years as commander and commander in chief, on the other side. It was the middle—the real story—that held the key to his "becoming Eisenhower." That is what I set out to discover and what I present here in this book as points that are critical to understanding and appreciating the events and people who influenced Dwight Eisenhower.

As I pieced together fragments from scores of sources that mentioned in passing events and incidents from those years between Eisenhower accepting his commission from West Point as a second lieutenant and taking the baton to direct operations in the European theater as a three-star general, I became increasing intrigued. An Airborne Ranger infantry officer with more than twenty years in the army, I am not easily impressed by desk jockeys who work in tidy offices and sleep between clean sheets every night. In my mind, a real soldier is one who spends time with the troops in the field, getting dirty and tired, and who sleeps in the mud when necessary. So I was not predisposed to become an Eisenhower admirer, assuming from his record of administrative assignments that he had avoided duty in the trenches, most likely through taking advantage of whom he knew.

I found studying Eisenhower's life to be an exercise in watching fate at work. When one knows how the story ends, so to speak, reading about Eisenhower's repeated pleas for troop postings and combat assignments is like watching him bang his head against a brick wall because he cannot see that he is not yet at the corner that will eventually lead his life down unimagined pathways. To follow his formative years of military ambition is to watch him bleed and blunder along on all the endless quests that left him so disappointed, when, indeed, to be the leader he would become, he would ultimately call on those very experiences and that very expertise he resented acquiring.

Yet, as the pieces came together, I began to see what looked more and more like a purposeful pattern to his assignments and to his exposure to the formidable officers for whom he worked and under whose mentorship he had developed. Begrudgingly, I came to appreciate and respect the man who was the result of these influences, a man who spent his life "becoming Eisenhower."

Michael Lee Lanning
December 2023

CHAPTER I

Detours to Greatness

DWIGHT DAVID EISENHOWER ARRIVED AT THE BOOT CAMP FOR WEST Point plebes as a young man who had only two real passions. One was to pursue the college degree available to him in exchange for time in service after graduation, which was the only way he could afford this education. The other passion was sports, especially football and baseball, both of which he excelled at playing. Together with his irresistibly affable personality, he was depending on these qualities (and his wits) to move him forward in the world.

Unlike many of his cadet buddies, Eisenhower had given little to no thought to a military career, nor did he come from a military family with generations of service in its lineage. Neither was his presence there the result of family influence, as his had none. Yet this setting provided the ideal background for Eisenhower to come of age. It allowed him to sort out his priorities as to what was important and what was not, to experiment with resisting authority without dire consequences, and to enjoy the rewards of social connections that would lead to lifelong networks.

Eisenhower was a fair-haired boy from America's heartland who had been reared, along with his five brothers, in a hardworking, God-fearing, patriotic family steeped in traditional values. From his earliest days, he charmed those he encountered—from classmates to teachers, from neighbors on his "wrong side" of the tracks to townspeople on the more prosperous side of his small town of Abilene, Kansas. He was a gregarious, amiable person with an easy way around people; a principled, disciplined leader dedicated to his country; an observant, quiet hero with a sense of humor; and a peace-loving fellow determined to steer America through her path to recovery after World War II and the emerging Cold War.

Ike's personality, however, was a double-edged sword. Yes, it made him easy to like, but by making him so acceptable, this trait also made it difficult for him to stand out from the crowd. His agreeable nature made him appear generic and interchangeable. As a result, Eisenhower had to work harder and more diligently than his competitors to gain equal recognition or superiority in his evaluations.

That dedication came only with age and maturity, for Dwight David Eisenhower did not distinguish himself as a West Point cadet, graduating from the U.S. Military Academy as number 61 of 164. Although his class would eventually be known as the one that "the stars fell on"—59 of the 164 rose to the rank of general officer—no one at the time would have predicted that Eisenhower would ultimately outrank them all.

Eisenhower's early years in the army were equally unremarkable. Even though he entered the service during World War I, he remained stateside for its duration despite his best efforts to get to the front. Promoted to captain in the army's World War I expansion, he spent the next sixteen years as a major assigned to desk duty rather than troop command. His only claims to fame as he slowly plodded forward acquiring knowledge and experience were his affable personality—everyone liked him—and his efficient, loyal service to his superiors. He later said, "My ambition in the army was to make everybody I worked for regretful when I was ordered to other duty."

In an exceptional twist of irony, though, his raters at times graded him as only "average" and "good" despite his extraordinary effort and achievements. While those results caused him great disappointment and frustration, they ensured that he found himself in positions where he learned and honed inglorious fundamental skills that would prove essential later in his career. Even when Eisenhower used his social connections to finagle favorable postings, he found himself behind a desk writing letters and preparing documents rather than commanding troops.

The future general's first assignments were a series of less than desirable postings with responsibilities that he thought offered little opportunity for personal or professional growth. His commanders generally sought his skills as a football coach for the post team rather than his military abilities. Eisenhower remained on the sidelines during World War I as he trained troops in the United States rather than joining a combat unit with the American Expeditionary Force in France. Frustrated with his stateside assignments, he vowed, "By God, from now on I am cutting myself a swath and will make up for this." And he did.

As the years passed and assignments changed, Eisenhower worked for and learned from strong leaders, including Frederick Funston, George Patton, Fox Conner, John J. Pershing, Douglas MacArthur, and George Marshall. Each added to Eisenhower's development as an officer and leader, as he continuously displayed a unique ability to get along with all ranks. Ike gained some recognition (at least academically) when he graduated number one in the 1926 class of the Command and General Staff School. He also made an impression as an intelligent, dedicated, efficient subordinate, but, again, no one forecast his future successes.

At fifty years of age and after twenty-five years of service, Eisenhower, with the help of the pre–World War II buildup of the army, finally reached the rank of brigadier general in late 1941. He later admitted that he thought he had reached the pinnacle of his career and would advance no further. Again, no one (especially Eisenhower himself) had any idea that in a mere two years he would assume command of all Allied forces in Europe.

Dwight Eisenhower was the singularly most unlikely candidate for becoming such a powerful figure. No one predicted his destiny as one who would to go from a mid-ranking West Point graduate to a five-star general credited with defeating the European Axis powers to save the Western world from tyranny. Yet he did. No one assumed he had the political moxie to go from glorified military clerk to sitting behind the Resolute Desk in the Oval Office of the White House. But he did.

So how did the unassuming, self-sacrificing, nondescript lad walk out of Abilene, Kansas, as a raw kid and into obscurity as a junior officer who spent more than a decade and a half as a mere major in rank? How did this man end up on the world's stage as a polished leader who would shape history for generations to come? He took not the road less traveled but a road of detours that delivered him to greatness.

CHAPTER 2

"Iron Cutters" to Abilene

THE NAME *EISENHOWER* (TRANSLATING FROM GERMAN AS "IRON CUT-ter," "iron artisan," or "iron hewer") was the remnant of a previous time when surnames reflected occupations. The American branch of the Eisenhower family had long since moved on from any iron workings to become farmers and merchants in Middle America. While the search of his family tree could conceivably trace his heritage back to medieval warriors who fought along with Charlemagne in the eighth century, more recent ancestors of the future five-star general commanding the most powerful armed forces of the twentieth century were, by contrast, descendants of German Mennonites who immigrated to the United States in the 1740s. Adhering to the Bible and personal conscience rather than man or government, the group settled in Pennsylvania for several generations along the Susquehanna and became known as the River Brethren. After the Civil War, the Eisenhowers, along with other River Brethren, followed opportunities westward to Abilene in Dickinson County, Kansas, located twenty miles from the geographic center of the country.

David Eisenhower, Ike's father, was fifteen years old when he accompanied his family on the move west. Although David liked his new home, he took to farming no more in Kansas than he had in Pennsylvania. His father offered him land and money to establish his own farm, as Jacob did with all his children, but David preferred to pursue a career in engineering and mechanics. Instead of working the land, David enrolled in nearby Lane College in September 1883.

Lane, founded by the River Brethren, not only encouraged religious education but also offered its two hundred students classes in the liberal arts as well as vocational training. David studied mechanics and math along with Greek and speech. It was at Lane that David met Ida Elizabeth Stover, whose family had originally immigrated from the same general area of Europe to Pennsylvania in the eighteenth century as had the Eisenhowers.

Ida, full of life, vivacious, and charming, grew up in a family that emphasized and believed in pacifism. Ida's mother died when she was five, and her father soon sent her to live with her maternal grandfather, William Link. Her grandfather opposed her desire for higher education and encouraged her to become a housewife. Instead, Ida left home after high school and made her living cooking for wealthy couples before teaching in a one-room schoolhouse. She did not set aside her Bible study, however, but rather memorized more than one thousand verses. When Ida reached the legal age of twenty-one, she used her inheritance from her now deceased father to join several of her brothers in their move to Kansas.

Ida briefly lived with a brother in Lecompton before entering Lane College to study music and liberal arts. In the fall of 1884, David and Ida began courting. Their relationship was a classic example of the attraction of opposites. David was temperamental, self-absorbed, and stubborn with little sense of humor. By contrast, Ida was vivacious, outgoing, and optimistic. Differences aside, the couple dropped out of Lane and married on September 23, 1885. Both showed their independence, with David making plans to open a business and Ida using the last of her inheritance to purchase a piano—a possession she would treasure for the remainder of her life.

Financed by his father, David opened a general store in Hope. Despite his tenacity, he lacked business skills and took on Milton Good, a former Abilene haberdashery salesman, as a partner. Both the Good family and the Eisenhowers lived in apartments above the store.

The merchant pair never got along well, David finding neither satisfaction nor profit in the retail trade. After eighteen months, he borrowed more money from his father and purchased Good's interest in the business. The November 5, 1886, edition of the *Hope Dispatch* reported their partnership had been dissolved, with Good being released "from all responsibilities of the late firm." However, according to family legend, Good stole the store's cash and left in the middle of the night. It is not known whether David and Ida's son Dwight, who later wrote in support of this story, believed the theft occurred or was deliberately defending his father's reputation. In reality, Good did not flee Hope to parts unknown with the store's money, as the Eisenhowers claimed. Instead, he moved back to Abilene, where he became involved in the town's administration and in 1892 opened a dry goods store.

With Good's departure, David's younger brother, Abraham Lincoln (so named because his father so admired the president), joined in the ownership of the store, which the pair renamed Eisenhower Brothers. Abraham, a Brethren preacher and veterinarian, was as jovial and outgoing as his brother was somber. David lost interest in being a businessman and in October 1888 turned the store over to his brother, who renamed it A. L. Eisenhower and Company.

With no desire to rejoin the family farming businesses, David left Ida (now pregnant with their second son) in Hope and ventured about four hundred miles south to Denison, Texas, a town established in 1872 with the arrival of the Missouri Kansas Texas Railroad, known as the Katy. The Katy was the town's principal employer, and David took a job in the rail roundhouse as an "oil wiper," the man who packed every moving part of the locomotives with grease and then wiped away the excess. In this position, at the bottom of the railroad job hierarchy in prestige as well as pay, David worked mostly twelve-hour shifts.

In April 1889, Ida, with her newborn son, Edgar, and his older brother, Arthur, joined David in Denison. She left her beloved piano behind in Kansas with friends in hopes of someday returning. The Eisenhowers rented a modest wood-frame house near the railroad tracks just east of what is today U.S. Highway 75. On October 14, 1890, Ida—in the midst of a violent thunderstorm—gave birth at home to their third son, whom they named David Dwight in honor of his father and Dwight Lyman Moody, an internationally famed evangelist and religious writer.

There was no formal birth certificate at the time; an entry in the family Bible sufficed, as it did for all the Eisenhower children.

Shortly after this baby's birth, Ida became concerned that her son would be called David Jr. or nicknamed Dave. To guard against this outcome, Ida simply reversed the first two names to Dwight David—something she had done as a young girl with her own original name of Elizabeth Ida.

In 1891, Jacob Eisenhower visited Texas and was appalled at the conditions David and his family were living in. He provided money for them to purchase their own house but, deciding his son lacked financial management skills, insisted that the property be registered in Ida's name. Still, Jacob repeatedly encouraged his son to return to Kansas. When the couple could no longer avoid admitting defeat in Texas, David, Ida, Arthur, Edgar, and Dwight made their way northward—after more than three and a half years in Denison—back to Abilene. There they rented a small shack with virtually no yard until David's brother decided he wanted to leave the area and offered to sell them his two-story house.

Dwight was only ten months old when the family left Texas. He later visited Denison a few times, returning in 1946, when the town acquired and refurbished his parents' old home in his honor; in 1952, as a stop in his presidential campaign; and in 1965, to dedicate the Denison High School Eisenhower Auditorium.

Dwight had no recollection of his brief childhood in Denison and no allegiance to his birthplace. Beyond his listing it as his place of birth and later learning to make recipes his mother acquired there, Texas had no impact on him. For the rest of his life, he often said, "The proudest thing I can claim is that I am from Abilene."

The Abilene in which Eisenhower grew up had unpaved roads and wooden planks for sidewalks, a single policeman as its law enforcer, religion as its dominate influence, and a caste system demarcated by the Union Pacific Railroad tracks, which divided the "haves" on the north side from the "have-nots" on the south.

Among the "have-nots" were Dwight's parents—David and Ida—who focused their priorities as they believed best for their family and as evidenced when Dwight reflected on his childhood, writing, "Mother and Father maintained a genuine partnership in raising their six sons. Father was the breadwinner, Supreme Court, and Lord High Executioner. Mother was tutor and manager of our household." He added, "I never heard a cross word pass between them. . . . [T]hey never argued over family, social, or economic" affairs. At the same time, he continued, "they were not demonstrative in their love for each other, but a quiet, mutual devotion permeated our home. This had a lasting effect on all the boys."

David spent most of his time at work as a general maintenance man making minimum wage at a new branch of the Belle Springs Creamery and had little to do with the raising of his six sons. Dwight later observed, "Mother was by far the greatest personal influence on our lives."

Thus, in that setting, and in that family, Dwight spent his formative years. Both David and Ida hoped for a girl as their family grew, but each new birth brought another son, with the arrival of Roy in 1892, Earl in 1898, and Milton in 1899. A seventh baby, Paul, born in 1894, died at the young age of ten months from diphtheria.

The boys all had chores both outside and inside the home. Ida, with no daughters, made the boys help with the cleaning, laundry, and cooking as well as caring for the animals and tending the garden. Dwight particularly took to the kitchen and enjoyed cooking for the rest of his life.

In 1898, David bought from his brother Abraham a large two-story wood-frame house with a barn and fruit orchard on three acres located at 201 Southeast 4th Street. Little could anyone have imagined that the property would one day be known as the home of the Dwight Eisenhower Presidential Library and Museum.

At the time, though, the purpose of the purchase was to bring stability to a family that had been seeking its rightful place. The new home and grounds included space for a milk cow, chickens, ducks, and pigs. A large garden plot provided fresh vegetables as well as enough to be canned for winter consumption. Ike later recalled that potatoes were the most prolific crop, appearing on the table for nearly every meal. A horse pulled a garden plow as well as the family wagon. Except for having to purchase flour, sugar, salt, other spices, and lamp oil, the Eisenhowers were basically self-sufficient.

In addition to making them responsible for the family garden, David and Ida allotted each son a piece of ground on which to grow his own vegetables to sell to Abilene residents. Dwight did particularly well with his plot and made spending money peddling primarily corn and cucumbers. He also prepared and sold tamales made from a recipe his mother brought back from her sojourn in Texas. During the summers, he picked apples, assisted in the wheat harvest, and worked in a coal yard.

Dwight worked two summers riding the lead horse of a team that cut down the wheat stalks. He lost the job when his boss decided the boy had become too large and replaced him with a lighter rider. Undeterred, the young Eisenhower applied for a job riding along with livestock on the railroad from Abilene to Hutchinson, only to be turned down for not being big enough. The frustration he felt at being too big for one job and too small for another made a lasting impression.

As a maturing Eisenhower son, he summarized his lesson, writing, "This may have been my first lesson that human relations are governed by neither fixed rules nor logic. One side in a different opinion may be blind to what the other considers obvious decency and common sense. For years I had been taught that it takes two to start a quarrel. Now, I saw that in any organized effort there may be as many disagreements about policy and practice as there are participants."

Although Ike's father never liked his job at the creamery, the elder Eisenhower was at least pleased not to be digging in the dirt on a farm, which he had hated passionately as a boy. He stayed on at the creamery for more than twenty years before leaving for a similar handyman-maintenance position at the local natural gas plant. Although he rose to general manager at the plant, he never parlayed his status into an official position or office in the city of Abilene.

With six boys growing up in a small home, it is no wonder that sibling rivalries often surfaced that led to wrestling matches and bloody fist fights. While Edgar, older by one year, provided the most opposition to the quick-tempered Dwight, conflicts were not limited to these two. But despite these quarrels, all six brothers looked out for each other. The most serious incident between them came as an accident rather than as a result of anger. In 1902, four-year-old Earl watched as his older brother

Dwight used a knife to whittle a wooden toy. When he took a break, Dwight carefully placed the knife on a windowsill that he thought was out of Earl's reach. When Dwight turned his back, Earl managed to climb on a chair, reached for the knife, and then fell with the sharp blade penetrating his left eye. Dwight remained remorseful for the rest of his life for not watching more carefully over his brother.

Despite their scuffles, the brothers remained close. Dwight later wrote, "In spite of boyish frictions, the household and even life outside was exceptionally happy." He explained, "Though our family was far from affluent, I never heard a word even distinctly related to self-pity. If we were poor—and I'm not sure that we were by the standards of the day—we were unaware of it. We were always well fed, adequately clothed, and housed."

Religion was important in the day-to-day life of the Eisenhowers. Meals began with prayers, and after supper each boy read a passage from the family Bible. However, David and Ida began to distance themselves from formal services because of the church's failure to provide sufficient solace on the death of their son Paul. Of more significant impact was the Eisenhowers' independent thinking and their personal Bible study.

Ida joined a small sect called Bible Students that grew to later be known as Jehovah's Witnesses. David dabbled in mysticism before giving up organized religion for good. Despite their changes of interpretation, the Bible remained the center of their religious beliefs and practices.

Regardless of the devoutness of their parents and the enforced Bible study of their youth, none of the six Eisenhower sons followed any religious organization in their adulthood. After West Point, with its mandatory chapel attendance, Dwight did not attend or belong to a church until it became politically advantageous to join the Presbyterians during his presidential campaign in the 1950s. Although he did not attend church services for many years, the lessons he learned around the family table about right and wrong, good and evil, remained at the center of his values.

In addition to his religious lessons, Dwight learned much from his extended family that influenced his development. He recalled in his book *At Ease*, "My earliest memory involves an incident that occurred two or three months before my fifth birthday." While visiting his mother's sister in Topeka, Dwight recounted, he encountered a flock of geese in his aunt's and uncle's yard. In repeating the story, Ike wrote, "The male resented my intrusion from our first meeting and each time thereafter he would push along toward me aggressively and with hideous hissing noises so threatening my security that five-year-old courage could not stand the strain. I would race for the back door of the house, burst into the kitchen, and tell any available elder about this awful old gander."

Dwight, curious to explore new surroundings, ventured several more times into the yard only to be sent running in tears back to the kitchen by the territorial gander each time. His uncle decided to come to the aid of his nephew. He took an old broom, cut off the straw, and handed the stick to Dwight with instructions on how to defend himself. Ike later wrote:

> The gander remained aggressive in his actions, and I was not at all sure that my uncle was very smart. More frightened at the moment of his possible scolding than I was of aggression, I took what was meant to be a firm, but was really a trembling, stand the next time the fowl came close. Then I let out a yell and rushed toward him, swinging the club as fast I as could. He turned and I gave him a satisfying smack right in the fanny. He let out a most satisfactory squawk and ran off. This was my signal to chase him, which I did.

Eisenhower continued by relating the influence of this first memory: "From then on, he would continue his belligerent noises whenever he saw me (with the stick). He kept his distance and I was the proud boss of the back yard. I never made the mistake of being caught without my weapon. This all turned out to be a rather good lesson for me because I quickly learned never to negotiate with an adversary except from a position of strength."

Another lesson learned as a boy influenced his later life. He recalled that both parents "were against quarreling and fighting" and "deplored violence," but, he wrote, "I did discover one day that my father was far from being a turn-the-other-cheek type."

Dwight arrived home one afternoon chased by a schoolmate. His father asked, "Why do you let that boy run you around like that?"

"Because if I fight him, you'll give me a whipping, whether I win or lose," responded Dwight.

"Chase that boy out of here," said his father. Dwight recalled in *At Ease*:

> That was enough for me. I turned around and it was the suddenness of my counterattack, rather than any fighting prowess, that startled my tormentor, who took off at a rapid pace. I, being faster, was more than overjoyed when I caught him, threw him down to the ground, and voiced threats of violence. He seemed to take these most seriously. In fact, I promised to give him a thrashing every day unless he let me alone. I was rapidly learning that domination of others in this world often comes about or is sought through bluff. But it took me some years to learn that pounding from an opponent is not to be dreaded as much as constantly living in fear of another.

Dwight's temper surfaced often to various degrees. His first real lesson in controlling his anger, as well as feelings of hate, came from his mother. In *At Ease*, he wrote that when he was ten, his parents would not allow him to accompany his two older brothers on Halloween for "trick or treating." He stated, "I have no exact memory of what happened immediately afterward, but I was completely beside myself. Suddenly my father grabbed my shoulders to shock me back into consciousness. What I had been doing was standing by an old apple tree trunk and pounding it with my bleeding fists, expressing resentment and rage. My father legislated the matter with the traditional hickory switch and sent me off to bed."

"Perhaps an hour later," he continued, "my mother came into the room. I was still sobbing into the pillow, my feelings—among other things—hurt, completely abused and at odds with the entire world. Mother sat in a rocking chair by the bed and said nothing for a long time. Then she began to talk about temper and controlling it. Eventually, as she often did, she drew on the Bible, paraphrasing it, I suppose. This time she said, 'He that conquereth his own soul is greater than he who taketh a city' (Proverbs 16:32)."

Dwight remembered that his mother had continued, admonishing that "hatred was a futile sort of thing because hating anyone or anything meant that there was little to be gained. The person who had incurred my displeasure probably didn't care, possibly didn't even know, and the only person injured was myself. This was soothing, although she added that among all her boys, I was the one who had the most to learn. In the meantime, she had set about putting salve on my injured hands and bandaging the worst places, not failing to make the point that I had expressed resentment and only damaged myself." He concluded:

> I have always looked back on that conversation as one of the most valuable moments in my life. To my youthful mind, it seemed to me that she talked for hours but I suppose the affair was ended in fifteen or twenty minutes. At least she got me to acknowledge that I was wrong, and I felt enough ease in my mind to fall off to sleep. The incident was never mentioned again. But to this day I make it a practice to avoid hating anyone. If someone's been guilty of despicable actions, especially toward me, I try to forget him.

Dwight's parents and brothers were not the only influences in his early development. The people of Abilene, as well as the town itself, had a lasting impact. Although there were some intermittent conflicts between children who lived on opposite sides of the railroad tracks, either north or south, the citizens of Abilene fostered an environment that was strictly American heartland with an attitude of "wholesomeness." As a boy, as well as on his later return visits to Abilene, Dwight frequently visited the grave site of Thomas "Bear River Tom" Smith, one of his earliest heroes and role models. Smith had been the Wild West sheriff who finally brought law and order to what had been a rough and violent Abilene following the cattle drive days. A former New York City policeman, he had worn Abilene's lawman badge before being killed by two men whom he was attempting to arrest in November 1870. He was replaced by the famous lawman James Butler "Wild Bill" Hickok. In the Abilene City

Cemetery, young Dwight took inspiration from the headstone, which reads:

Thomas J. Smith
Marshall of Abilene
Dead, a Martyr to Duty, Nov. 2, 1870
A Fearless Hero of Frontier Days
Who in Cowboy Chaos
Established the Supremacy of Law

Yet another influence from Abilene was a living role model and mentor who also traced his linage back to the early Wild West days of Abilene. Eisenhower was an eight-year-old when he first met Bob Davis, and the two developed a teacher-pupil relationship that spanned the next decade. Although illiterate, Davis was a great storyteller and instructor. He regaled his admirer with tales about pioneer Abilene, the cattle herds, and the drovers, while teaching the young Eisenhower about hunting, fishing, trapping, and camp cooking.

In addition to field craft, Davis passed along a skill that Dwight did not share with his parents but that would be an important pastime in his adulthood. Davis taught Dwight how to play poker, imparting a grasp of the odds and percentages that made for a successful card player. Dwight became adept with a deck of cards and for many years supplemented his meager military salary with winnings at the poker table.

J. B. Case, another Abilene resident, fascinated Dwight with stories of the Old West and early Kansas. His tales were all the more interesting because he was a first cousin of Mrs. George Armstrong Custer.

While there is no evidence that young Dwight ever ventured farther from home than to visit relatives ninety miles away in Topeka, he was not without influence from the world beyond his family and Abilene. Transients traveling through the Midwest brought excitement and entertainment to the towns they visited. Sometimes they became permanent fixtures. Dwight later wrote, "The splendiferous C. W. Parker Circus, full of glittering performers and the dusty glamor of far-off places, made Abilene its home base."

Another window into the outside world came from Joseph W. Howe, editor of the *Dickinson County News*. Dwight frequently stopped by Howe's office after school to read copies of newspapers from Kansas City and St. Louis as well as from as far away as New York City. Abilene had no public library at the time, so Howe generously lent books from his personal collection to the young Eisenhower. It was through these books that he was first introduced to Hannibal and military history.

Dwight was popular with his classmates as well as his teachers and the townsfolk, who knew him to be energetic and outgoing. The slogan "I Like Ike" did not come into being until his presidential campaign of the 1950s; however, in Abilene everyone did indeed like Ike. Known by his given name as a boy, he did not acquire the nickname "Ike" until high school—and even then, it was not his alone. At Abilene High School, his older brother Edgar was known as "Big Ike" while Dwight was called "Little Ike." It was not until he entered West Point that Dwight became known simply as "Ike."

When Dwight entered school, he found athletics much more appealing than academics, though he earned good grades with minimal effort. He enjoyed all sports, particularly football and baseball. Despite having limited skills, he was a fierce competitor.

He also displayed his budding leadership abilities in organizing sporting events. In 1908, when Abilene High School had no formal football program, Little Ike took the lead in forming the Abilene Athletic Association and assumed its presidency. The association fielded a team on which he played at right end and brother Edgar at full back, competing with teams from the neighboring towns and the local agricultural college.

One game in particular demonstrated Dwight's leadership as well as his lack of racial prejudices. When his teammates objected to playing against an opponent that fielded an African American player, Little Ike lectured his team against racism, threatening to quit the squad and go home if they did not play the game. The team followed his lead and took to the gridiron. At the conclusion of the game, Dwight reinforced his convictions by shaking the black player's hand.

Dwight demonstrated his writing abilities in the 1909 Abilene High School yearbook, *The Helianthus*. He wrote about the efforts to form the association and listed the names and positions of the starting lineup. Commending his fellow students, he wrote that they "supported the team loyally, and time and again the boys surmounted great difficulties, cheered on by the fierce enthusiasm displayed by our rooters." He continued, "We improved the condition of the Association itself, drawing up a constitution, which makes the organization a permanent one, and each year it will be a simple question of electing new officers."

Dwight's conclusion in the article illustrated that he had already developed skills in diplomacy and unification: "Thanking the citizens of the town who have taken such an interest in the High School Athletics, and also our fellow classmates for their loyalty to us, we are yours for future victories on the gridiron by teams of dear old A.H.S."

The work with the Abilene Athletic Association also made Dwight aware that, regardless of what he accomplished in preparation, successful execution depended on the support of the organization's members. He wrote, "Many times since I have come to realize that a fervent speech, or a painstakingly written document, may be worth no more than the good will and patient co-operation of those who say they subscribe to it."

Writing seemed to come naturally to him—an ability that he would find highly sought after once he entered the army. Although his essays were commendable, his handwriting was practically illegible and improved little over the years.

The earliest known surviving writing by Dwight is a letter he composed on February 27, 1905, to his cousin Nettie Stover Jackson in Topeka. The fourteen-year-old wrote mostly about family news but also included a sentence that self-mockingly addressed his confidence as a writer: "I'll bet this writing would take a prize anywhere and spelling too for all of that."

Dwight appreciated and liked other subjects as well as writing. In *At Ease*, he noted, "In grammar school, spelling was probably my favorite subject either because the contest aroused my competitive instincts or because I had learned that a single letter could make a vast difference in the meaning of a word. In time I became almost a martinet about orthography, inclined to condemn as beyond redemption a man who confused principle with principal and the like. Arithmetic came next because of the finality with which an answer was either right or wrong."

In addition to grammar and math, Dwight became extremely interested in military history. Even though Abilene was home to many Civil War veterans, he preferred to study more ancient conflicts, as he thought the War between the States was not yet history. He particularly liked the Punic Wars, and Hannibal became his first military role model. Study of the American Revolution and George Washington, whom he idolized, also occupied much of his time.

Dwight's interest in history was not visionary of his future military service. As he explained in *At Ease*, "For me, the reading of history was an end in itself, not a source of lessons to guide us in the present or to prepare me for the future. Nor did I become all aware that the richness and variety of opportunity in this country would give me, like all of us, a chance to be joined, intimately and productively, with both the past and the future of the Republic. I did not know what opportunities were there for the learning. I read history for history's sake, for myself alone."

The young Dwight talked so much about early wars and military leaders with his classmates that his high school yearbook prophecy predicted he would someday become a history professor at Yale University. Ironically, the prophecy for his brother predicted that Edgar would become a two-term president of United States.

Little Ike rarely dated while in high school. When asked why, he replied that, in addition to being shy, he did not have money, proper clothes, or the time to date. He went on to say that he also was a terrible dancer. Girls, whom he considered friends, all came from south of the tracks and were his neighbors. One of these, Gladys Harding, would later become his first love interest.

During his freshman year, an incident occurred that could have prevented his attending West Point and precluded his destiny as a soldier and president. While racing down a wooden platform one evening, he slipped and fell to one knee. The scrape seemed minor at the time, but a day later the injury became septic, and the infection spread, driving Dwight into delirium. A doctor came several times a day to treat the wound and cut away dead flesh. Finally, he told the family that if the infection spread to his abdomen, it would be fatal. Dwight, in and out of a coma, was conscious when the doctor recommended amputation of his leg. He recalled, "At that time, my ambitions were directed toward excellence in sports, particularly baseball and football. I could not imagine an existence which I was not playing one or both."

On hearing the word "amputation," Dwight became both alarmed and angry. He asked his brother Ed to guard his door and prevent anyone from cutting off his leg. David and Ida understood their son's concern and called in a specialist from Topeka, who painted a belt of carbolic acid around the wound. The drastic, painful treatment stopped and finally cured the infection. Convalescence took more than two months, requiring Little Ike to repeat his freshman year of high school.

The threatened-amputation story is an example of the loyalty and protective attitude among the Eisenhower brothers and the practicality of their parents. In a chapter in *At Ease* titled "Footnotes for Biographer," this incident was used to further define the religious beliefs of his parents. He wrote, "The episode has often been told in biographies or magazine articles. One story said that my parents remained in prayer, day and night, for two weeks. This is ridiculous. My parents were devout Christians and there is no doubt that they prayed for my recovery, but they did it in their morning and evening prayers. They did not believe in 'faith healing.'"

Granddaughter Susan Eisenhower, in her book *How Ike Led*, provides the best summary of his time in Abilene: "In the broadest sense, the keys to Dwight's upbringing can be put in simple terms: his family, his community, and the benefits of living in a country setting that fostered independence, self-discovery, and time to think."

Dwight was anxious to leave Abilene when the time came, but he never forgot his hometown. Even after his World War II command in Europe and his election as president of the United States, he frequently returned to Abilene and maintained correspondence with old friends who kept him up to date with the town's developments. (For additional information on the Eisenhowers' family background, on Abilene, Kansas, and on the Eisenhower ancestral religion, see appendixes A, B, and C.)

CHAPTER 3

West Point

DWIGHT DAVID EISENHOWER GRADUATED FROM ABILENE HIGH School on May 28, 1909, along with twenty-five girls and eight other boys. The larger number of girls was due to the fact that many boys had dropped out of school as soon as they were old enough to find employment. Among those boys was Edgar, known as "Big Ike" (as opposed to Dwight's "Little Ike"), who had himself left school to work for a year before returning to become a member of the Class of 1909.

The commencement speaker made an impression on both brothers. In his writing of more than a half century later, Dwight still recalled the remarks. Henry J. Allen, editor of the *Wichita Beacon*, and later a Kansas governor and a United States senator, said, "I would sooner begin life over again with one arm cut off than attempt to struggle without a college education."

Both Dwight and Edgar were determined to go to college. Edgar made plans to enter the University of Michigan, while Dwight was unsure where he wanted to enroll. Both boys faced the fact that neither had the funds to follow their dream. In *At Ease*, Dwight explained their solution:

> The following summer was busy. Edgar's plans for enrolling at Michigan meant that both of us had to work to gather as much money as possible to get him started. I changed from one job to another, depending on the prospects for an extra dime an hour or an extra dollar a day. Because I did jump about, certain biographers have suggested that I

was going through a period of indecision and had no idea of what I wanted to do. The exact opposite was the truth. Ed and I had it all doped out. He was going to drop out if necessary, to get me started. His choice of Michigan looked good to me and I was ready to join him two years later.

Big Ike headed to Michigan, leaving the younger Eisenhower as the only Ike in Abilene. Although he himself was not in college, he continued to work to pay tuition—his brother's. The town leaders recognized Ike's sacrifice as well as his potential. In the fall, the Dickinson County Young Men's Democratic Club invited him and two others to speak at their annual banquet. The *Dickinson County News* printed the entire speech in its November 18, 1909, issue. Ike began his remarks with a quote: "As the twig is bent so will the tree be inclined." He then focused on the importance of recruiting citizens into political parties at a young age because people rarely change their political affiliations once determined.

While Ike may have felt frustrated that he could not join his brother at university, it was not initially evident how provident his remaining in Abilene would be. In the meantime, he went to work for a small firm that manufactured steel grain bins before taking a better-paying position as an "iceman" at the Belle Springs Creamery. Working twelve-hour days, Dwight helped move three-hundred-pound blocks of ice from the freezer to a room where they were cut into smaller pieces. He then helped load trucks and rail cars and made deliveries to local residences. This included Abilene's largest and most luxurious home—the eleven-thousand-square-foot Seelye Mansion, which today hosts public tours touting, "Dwight D. Eisenhower delivered ice to the Seelye Mansion when he was a young boy." The Seelye sisters told stories about Ike as a man from "the other side of the tracks." "Though far from intriguing, the job did develop muscles," Ike later recalled.

From the position of iceman, he moved on to the creamery's furnace room, where he fed coal into the burners. After a year, he earned a promotion back at the ice plant as second engineer. He now was earning the same wage as his father—though he had no desire to make the creamery a career. He continued to send part of his salary to Edgar, still hoping to join him at Michigan, but the money left over was not sufficient to pay for his own higher education. The answer to his dilemma is where providence came into play when an old high school friend returned to Abilene.

Ike had met Everett Hazlett, son of a doctor, while in his teens. Although Hazlett was from the north side of the tracks, the two boys became friends, especially after several incidents that Eisenhower described in *At Ease*: "He was big fellow, too, but he had been raised in a quiet atmosphere and occasionally a few people, smaller than he, would try to bulldoze him. I felt protective, a sort of obligation to him, and I took it upon myself to tell a few of the so-and-sos to lay off."

Hazlett had left Abilene for his senior year to attend a private school in Wisconsin, where he could prepare for entrance examinations to the U.S. Naval Academy. When he failed the exams, he returned to Abilene to work and to study more for the admission test the next year. It was then that he renewed his friendship with Ike and encouraged him to pursue his own appointment to the Naval Academy. The suggestion proved fateful, for if there had been no military academy for Ike, there would have been no General or President Eisenhower. Ike later wrote, "Our friendship endured to the day of his death in 1958; our correspondence over those forty-odd years would fill a thick volume. . . . Swede Hazlett was one of the people to whom I 'opened up.'"

Hazlett's suggestion immediately appealed to Eisenhower because he found the opportunity for a four-year scholarship most attractive. He recalled, "It was not difficult to persuade me that this was a good move—first, because of my long interest in military history, and second, because I realized that my own college education would not be achieved without considerable delay while I tried to accumulate money."

Ike's parents offered to increase their support toward Edgar's expenses to free Ike to pursue an academy appointment even though they—especially his mother—were not happy with their son seeking a military career. As a sincere pacifist, she did not approve, but she did not waver from her belief that her sons should be the masters of their own fates. When she eventually saw him off at the train station for his departure for West Point, there were tears in her eyes, but she stoically said, "It is your choice."

Eisenhower and Hazlett wrote to the Department of the Navy asking for and receiving copies of previous admission tests. Hazlett had an appointment in hand to the Naval Academy—if only he could pass his exams. Ike wanted to join him and began pursuing his own appointment through Kansas congressmen and senators. When he learned the state's representatives had already made their appointment for the year, he wrote to Kanas senator Joseph L. Bristol on August 20, 1910, saying, "I would very much like to enter the school at Annapolis, or the one at West Point." Along with his letter, Ike enclosed recommendations from one of Abilene's newspaper editors, a banker, the town's postmaster, and the local heads of both political parties.

While waiting for a response, Ike read in the *Abilene Daily Reflector* that, instead of making direct nominations, Bristol was conducting competitive examinations for academy appointments on October 4–5 in Topeka. Ike was fortunate in the senator's selection process because neither he nor his family had any political influence, and it is doubtful that he would have been chosen otherwise. He again wrote the senator and this time received an invitation to take the examination.

In his initial quest, however, Ike faced an insurmountable problem in being accepted to the Naval Academy because the institute required that an entering midshipman be no older than nineteen. Fortunately, West Point allowed a maximum age of twenty-two. Ike found a simple solution. With no birth certificate to prove otherwise, he simply changed the year in which he had been born.

Eight young men reported for the examination, four declaring they would accept appointment to West Point only, the others willing to accept either academy. Ike finished second in the exam ranking. Despite his interest in history, he scored lowest in that area. Not surprisingly, his writing abilities shone, with his highest score being in English.

In *At Ease*, Ike inaccurately reported that the candidate who had outscored him on the test failed his physical exam; in actuality, the young man received a presidential appointment, leaving Ike at the top of Bristol's list. On October 24, the senator wrote to inform Ike of his appointment to the U.S. Military Academy.

Eisenhower made his first venture out of Kansas in January 1910 to take the West Point entrance and physical exam at Jefferson Barracks outside Saint Louis, Missouri. The new surroundings made an impression; he later wrote, "The farm boy was completely unprepared for the sights of the river metropolis."

"Unprepared" but not intimidated, Ike and another future cadet left the barracks one night to see the town. Delayed by foggy weather and streetcar stoppage, the two were late returning and missed curfew. Instead of going through the main gate, they scaled a wall and sneaked undetected into their building. Ike remembered the possibility of being caught and dismissed from consideration for West Point, writing, "So far as I know, no one ever learned of our silly escapade."

Ike successfully completed his physical and, after returning to Abilene, received orders from the secretary of war to report to West Point on June 14, 1911, to join the Class of 1915. On the train ride to New York, he stopped for a brief visit with his brother at Ann Arbor. In Michigan and throughout the journey, he first began to comprehend the size and diversity of the country outside Kansas.

The U.S. Military Academy at West Point, New York, was well into its second century of operation when Plebe Eisenhower arrived. Established in 1802, West Point had produced generations of generals, though they, as Ike would, all started their careers as second lieutenants. During the American Civil War, 445 generals were West Point graduates—294 on the Union side and 151 with the Confederacy. A West Point graduate commanded either one or both sides in every major battle of the conflict.

Upperclassmen met Eisenhower and his 263 fellow plebes on that first day with shouts, orders, and general hazing, which Ike described as "calculated chaos." Plebes, mostly middle-class Protestants with a few Catholics and Jews—no Blacks, Hispanics, or women—marched double time everywhere they went. Physical exertion and mental fatigue were extreme. Ike recalled, "I suppose that if any time had been provided to sit down and think for a moment, most of us would have been on the next train out." He concluded that any thoughts about leaving were put aside with the question, "Where else could you get a college education without cost?"

Near the end of that first day, the plebes were sworn in as cadets of the U.S. Military Academy, taking an oath that has existed in one form or another since the school's founding until today. Ike and his fellow cadets declared, "I do solemnly swear that I will support the Constitution of the United States and bear true allegiance to the National Government; that I will maintain and defend the sovereignty of the United States paramount to any and all allegiance, sovereignty, or fealty I may owe to any State, county, or country whatsoever, and that I will at all times obey the legal orders of my superior officers and the rules and articles governing the Armies of the United States."

In that ceremonial moment, Ike realized that West Point was more than a free education. A half century later, he wrote:

> Whatever had gone before, this was a supreme moment. The day had been one of confusion and a heroic brand of rapid adjustment. But when we raised our right hand and repeated the official oath, there was no confusion. A feeling came over me that the expression "The United States of America" would now and henceforth mean something different than it ever had before. From here on it would be the nation I would be serving, not myself. Suddenly the flag itself meant something. I haven't heard other officers speak of their memories of that moment but mine have never left me. After half a century, I can look back and see a rawboned, gawky Kansas boy from the farm country, earnestly repeating the words that would make him a cadet.

The first three weeks at the Academy for the Class of 1915 were "strenuous," and, according to Ike, "for some it approached the unendurable." Eisenhower found the period, known as Beast Barracks, challenging but noted that being several years older and more mature than most cadets—as well as in excellent physical condition from his work at the creamery in Abilene—made the unusually hot, late summer days manageable. He recalled, "At times the whole performance would strike me as funny and in the semi-privacy of my room, I could laugh a little at myself and at the system. But whenever an upperclassman saw the sign of a smile, the shouting and nagging started again."

Eisenhower quickly adjusted to the system, which he found amusing. He wrote in *At Ease*, "We soon learned that at West Point we were going to do it West Point's way, or we were not going to be there at all."

Plebes were assigned to companies within the Cadet Battalion according to height, putting Ike in Company F with the tallest cadets. Military speech, jargon, and procedures came easily to him—all except the ability to march in step. He had difficulty keeping in tempo with the band music and for several days marched with the "Awkward Squad" until he "could coordinate . . . with the beat."

The cadet companies moved onto the main campus in September. Ike's assigned roommate was Paul Alfred Hodgson from Wichita, and even though they had few things in common except Kansas and an interest in sports, the two would share quarters for the rest of their time at West Point. Hodgson was a dedicated student and disinclined to join Ike in his pranks and rebellious acts against the system. Ike wrote of his roommate, "Paul was a good student and a serious one. I was inclined to be easygoing about studies, but he devoted every moment he could during study periods to improving his academic standing. He always urged me to do the same." Ike later described Hodgson as one of his "oldest and best friends," who always had his "admiration, respect, and deep affection."

While Ike was far from a troublemaker, he did resist some of the strict regulations. He received demerits for not saluting properly, reporting late to formations and chapel, improperly cleaning his room, incorrectly folding garments, failing to always button his jacket, and leaving assigned lessons incomplete. Ike also received more strikes against him for smoking, a habit he picked up at the Academy and kept most of his life. The resulting demerits, after accumulating to a certain number, led to confinement to his room or punishment tours that included walking the area between the barracks back and forth with a rifle on his shoulder. Each excess demerit called for one hour of punishment tour.

In *At Ease*, Ike admitted, "I was, in matter of discipline, far from a good cadet. While each demerit had an effect on class standing, this to me was of small moment. I enjoyed life at the Academy, had a good time with my pals, and was far from disturbed by an additional demerit or two."

Eisenhower preferred walking punishment tours to being restricted to quarters, writing of the confinement option in his autobiography, "This to my mind, was worse than walking tours because it was far from easy to sit in a room on a Saturday afternoon for an hour and contemplate the sin of have a little extra dust on the shelves of my wall locker or not having folded the blanket correctly on my bed. But I never fully reformed."

In an interview with *Assembly*, the magazine of the Association of West Point Graduates, Ike offered additional insight into his experience: "I loved the place while I was there. I had a hell-of-a-good time. I never was in great scrapes at West Point, never went off the post in civilian clothes for example. I was given demerits for smaller offenses. I did not worry about demerits, however, some of my classmates worried over every one."

While Ike never got into "great scrapes," his list of demerits ran to almost ten pages in the Academy's Discipline Ledgers. Despite these demerits, his fellow cadets and tactical officers recognized his leadership abilities. During his second year, he earned the rank of eleventh corporal and served on the color guard in his last two years.

Academically, during most of his time as a cadet, Eisenhower stood in the middle third of his class. He excelled in English and essay writing, while he did not do as well in mathematics and engineering.

Ike understood that academic standing was more important than just prestige because, on graduation, cadets entered the regular army, ranked in the order of their class standing. Number one outranked his fellow classmates and so on down the list. Ike was untroubled by this system, however, as he had more pressing areas of interest in which to participate: sports.

Athletics remained an important part of and goal in his life as the Academy played against some of the top-ranked teams on the East Coast—at that time some of the major powerhouses in the country. Opponents during his plebe year included Rutgers, Yale, Colgate, and, of course, the Naval Academy.

Plebes were eligible for the varsity football team, so both Ike and his roommate tried out. Hodgson made the roster, but Eisenhower did not. Happy for his roommate, Ike nevertheless believed he should have also made the team and described himself as "fit to be tied" (one of his favorite expressions about his temper).

Disappointed at not making varsity but still wanting to play ball, Ike joined the Cullum Hall team, basically the Academy's junior varsity, which had been established several years earlier by future World War II general Joseph W. "Vinegar Joe" Stillwell, Class of 1904. The team played various military schools and small colleges in the area. In the spring, Eisenhower went out for varsity baseball but failed to make the squad, though he at least received encouragement that, if he worked on his hitting, he could make the cut the following year.

Eisenhower made the varsity football team in his second year at the Academy. He excelled on defense, once hitting legendary Carlisle back Jim Thorpe so hard the future Olympian had to call a time-out. But it was as the starting halfback that Ike quickly earned accolades from his teammates as well as the news media. The *New York Times* labeled him the "Kansas Cyclone" and called him "one of the most promising backs in Eastern football." Eisenhower "is developing into a splendid back," wrote the *New York Tribune*. The West Point newspaper reported, "Eisenhower could not be stopped."

But, in fact, Ike could be stopped. In the seventh game of the season, Ike broke through Tuft's defense only to have a defender grab one of his feet. In attempting to escape the tackle, Ike threw his weight against the leg, an action that twisted his knee. Initially, Ike and the football staff thought the injury was minor; he was released from the hospital when the swelling went down. A few days later, while participating in a "monkey drill"—a horsemanship training exercise for mounting and dismounting—Ike crashed to the ground, reinjuring his knee.

In *At Ease*, Ike noted, "In the hospital, the doctors spent four days straightening my leg, a process so painful that I scarcely slept during the ordeal. They put the leg in a plaster cast, but when later I was again released from the hospital and tried to use it, I learned to my dismay that rugged sports were denied to me from then on."

Ike's knee never healed properly and bothered him for the rest of his life. More immediately, it meant the end of this West Point athletic career. He never played another down of football or inning of baseball.

A free education and the opportunity to play sports had been Eisenhower's reasons for attending West Point. With half his motivation now gone, he became so despondent that he considered leaving the Academy, later admitting, "The end of my career as an active football player had a profound effect on me." Only encouragement from his roommate Hodgson and other classmates convinced him to stay.

Ike found alternative ways to remain involved in athletics by becoming a cheerleader, known as a rabble-rouser at the Academy. He also gave inspirational speeches that developed his oratory abilities. Even though not on the team, Ike continued to attend workouts. He so impressed future College Football Hall of Fame coach Charles Daly that he was invited to coach the Cullum Hall junior varsity team. There he achieved a winning record while developing several players to a level of skill at which they could be elevated to the varsity squad. His reputation as a coach soon eclipsed his fame as a player.

Although he did not realize it at the time, both playing and coaching football would influence Ike's future as a military leader because he would find that the principles of teamwork on the gridiron carried over to the battlefield. During World War II, observers noted that Ike's brand of leadership resembled that of a football coach in that he frequently used football terminology in talking to his subordinate officers and in issuing orders. "Get the ball across the goal line," "pull an end run," "hit the line," and "break through" were phrases he often used.

Ike later wrote, "I believe that football, perhaps more than any other sport, tends to instill in men the feeling that victory comes through hard—almost slavish—work, team play, self-confidence, and an enthusiasm that amounts to dedication."

Not all of Ike's football stories were so somber, however. During his long military and political career, he frequently met Tufts graduates who apologized for injuring his leg—so many, in fact, that Eisenhower once humorously questioned just how many men Tufts had on the field that day.

While athletic activities—whether playing, coaching, or cheering—were major influences on Cadet Eisenhower, they were not the only ones to have an impact on him.

Shortly after the end of his time as an active football player, Ike learned an important lesson that greatly steered his remaining days at the Academy as well as his military career. In *At Ease*, he recorded, "An incident—indeed a lesson—that is vivid in my mind is one in which I learned the wickedness of arrogance and the embarrassment that can come about by the lack of consideration of others."

Hazing had not greatly affected Eisenhower as a plebe. He understood that it was part of the system of making plebes into cadets and future officers. Some of this hazing was designed to remind plebes of their inferiority by questioning their previous condition of servitude, or P.C.S. Ike recalled that a plebe from his own state bumped into him while running down the street on an errand for another upperclassman. Ike bellowed astonishment and mock indignation and demanded from the defeated-looking plebe, "What is your P.C.S.?" and added, "You look like a barber."

The humiliated plebe softly replied, "I was a barber, Sir."

Eisenhower recalled, "I didn't have enough sense to apologize to him on the spot and made a joke of the whole thing." When he returned to his quarters, he told his roommate Hodgson, "P. A., I'm never going to crawl [correct harshly] another plebe as long as I live." He concluded, "And never again, during my remaining three years at the U.S.M.A. did I take it upon myself to crawl a plebe."

Other influences stayed with Ike after his graduation. Playing poker was Ike's favorite pastime at the Academy. Using the skills he learned from Bob Davis back in Abilene, he consistently won at the card table.

After his knee injury ended his sports career, Ike took up smoking cigarettes. Although pipes and cigars were authorized during study period, cigarettes were against regulations. Despite the rules, his cigarette consumption increased until he became a three-pack-a-day smoker and continued for years afterward. He did not give up the habit until 1949 when he quit "cold turkey," which, he explained, he did by "giving an order to myself" to stop.

Another habit Ike acquired at West Point was the prolific use of profanity. As the son of a religious family, he had not used or been often exposed to profane words before his arrival at the Academy. By the time he left, he could curse with the best of them.

One would have thought that Ike's pre-Academy appreciation for history would only increase as a cadet. Such was not the case. While he was solidly aware of the Academy's history and was in awe that he occupied barracks and classrooms where Ulyssess S. Grant, Robert E. Lee, and dozens of other generals had been as cadets, he found the West Point curriculum dated and based more on memorization than any deep thought. History classes focused on who commanded what units and where they were located on the battlefield rather than on imparting any real understanding of tactics and impact on future conflicts. As a result, Ike turned away from his reading and study of history and would not resume the practice until years later.

Many of the cadets (including Eisenhower) eschewed intellectual subjects or cerebral interests. Ike took up reading pulp western novels, with Zane Grey being his favorite author. It became a pastime he continued for the remainder of his life. The exploits of the frontiersmen and the honor and honesty of Grey's characters certainly must have made an impression on the young cadet.

As Ike neared graduation, he and his fellow cadets faced the difficult decision of which branch to select for their commissioning and entrance to active duty. Traditionally, those at the top of the class standing chose the Army Corps of Engineers or the field artillery. Other branches, including the coastal artillery and cavalry, were open to those further down the class standing, with the bottom of the class traditionally having the infantry as their only choice. The Class of 1915 also faced the fact that the small army, which totaled fewer than 120,000 men and 4,948 officers, had a limited number of slots for newly minted second lieutenants. Even though skirmishes were occurring between Mexican bandits and the U.S. Army along the Rio Grande border and the conflict in Europe that would soon escalate into World War I was heating up, there were no immediate plans to enlarge the American military.

As a result, potential officers—including West Point graduates—had to pass rigid physical tests. Shortly before graduation, Colonel Henry Alden Shaw, the Academy's chief medical officer, called Ike into his office. Shaw told him that, after reviewing his records concerning his injured knee, the medical board recommended that Ike graduate with a diploma but not be commissioned a second lieutenant.

To the colonel's surprise, Ike, undaunted, replied that the recommendation was all right with him. He went on to explain that in his study of geography, he had developed a curious ambition to go to the Argentine because he wanted to see the gauchos. He thought that Argentina sounded a bit like the Old West and wanted to see the place for himself, thinking he might even live there for a couple of years.

A few days later, Colonel Shaw once again summoned Cadet Eisenhower to his office. Shaw apparently—like nearly everyone—had taken a liking to Ike and told him that after further review, he would recommend to the board that Eisenhower be commissioned in the coastal artillery. Ike was aware that this branch did not interact with the rest of army, as it remained nonmobile in substantial fortifications equipped with heavy guns that guarded the harbors and coastline of the United States. He knew that with a limited budget, the coastal artillery rarely got to fire its heavy guns, instead performing a numbing series of routine training chores. Ike later wrote, "It was a sedentary, immobile sort of life, and other arms of service—sometimes out of envy—referred to Coast Artillery as 'cottages by the sea.'"

Ike turned down the offer. Shaw, who had served in the coastal artillery himself, abruptly ended the interview. Eisenhower was not being flippant, nor was he negotiating. He recalled, "I meant only to react in the formal way expected of a cadet when in the presence of an officer. I didn't think he wanted to discuss things; I thought he wanted to tell me what he had decided." Ike returned to his quarters and wrote to request information on South America and the cost of travel.

Despite Ike's responses, Shaw did not give up. Once more Eisenhower was called to Shaw's office, where the colonel noted that Ike's knee injury had been aggravated by a riding incident. He told the young cadet that if he agreed not to request cavalry, the doctor would recommend his commission in the infantry. Ike immediately accepted and requested the infantry, known as the Queen of Battle, as his branch choice.

Without Shaw, Eisenhower would not have been commissioned. Because of his knee injury, it is unlikely that he would have been drafted for World War I, and he would have been too old to enlist in World War II. Without Shaw's support, graduation day at West Point would have been Ike's last day in uniform. Rather than achieving greatness as a soldier, he might have gone on to be cowboy on the Argentine pampa.

Instead, on June 12, 1915, Dwight D. Eisenhower stood on the Plain of West Point to receive his diploma, the crossed-rifles collar brass of the infantry, and the gold bars of a second lieutenant. Of the 164 graduates, Ike ranked sixty-first overall—ninety-fourth in deportment—with orders to report to the 19th Infantry Regiment at Fort Sam Houston in San Antonio, Texas. Ike had achieved his goal of a free education and now faced a commitment of eight years on active duty to repay the United States of America.

Few, if any, graduates of the "Class the Stars Fell On" would have given any thought to the future successes of the cadet from Abilene, Kansas. The yearbook described Ike "as big as life and twice as natural" and made no mention of his military abilities, rather stating that he excelled at "tea, tiddlywinks, and talk."

Ike himself later admitted, "From the first day at West Point, and any number of times thereafter, I asked myself: What am I doing here? Like the other young men, I sometimes wondered—where did I come from, by what route and why; by what chance arrangement of fate did I come by this uniform?"

Early in his time at West Point, a superior had written that Ike "was born to command." Eisenhower, neither confident in his military abilities nor ambitious with any thought of a career in uniform, later responded to that praise by saying, "The man who wrote that was either a reckless prophet or had relaxed his standards."

Despite his reservations, Eisenhower would find that his four years at West Point had a lasting influence on his future as a soldier. The Academy truly lived up to its mission "to educate, train, and inspire the Corps of Cadets so that each graduate is a commissioned leader of character committed to the values of Duty, Honor, Country and prepared for a career of professional excellence and service to the Nation as an officer in the United States Army."

Conversely, Eisenhower made little impression at West Point other than his athletic and coaching abilities—and the permanent mark he himself made. Near the end of his days at West Point, he scratched "Ike Eisenhower" on the inside sheeting of the Academy chapel's copper roof.

CHAPTER 4

Fort Sam Houston, Texas

RETURNING TO ABILENE AFTER GRADUATION TO AWAIT ORDERS FOR HIS first assignment, Eisenhower observed years later in *At Ease*, "I set out to have a good time and did." He occupied part of his time fishing, hunting, drinking, and playing poker with his friends. Most of his time, especially the evening hours, was spent with the one who became his first true love.

Gladys Harding, the blonde, blue-eyed daughter of a successful local freighting business magnate, had been a high school classmate of Ike's. The two had dated while Ike was on home leave in 1913 and had seen each other briefly in New York City in late 1914, when Gladys was touring with the Apollo Concert Company. Their romance, however, did not blossom until what Gladys labeled in her diary "the Summer Dwight Came Back from West Point."

In this diary, Gladys noted that the couple attended the local movie theater three or four times a week during July and August. Other evenings were spent in the Harding family parlor. Ike made no mention of the romance in his writings, so most of what is known comes from her recordings. These documents were not made public until donated to the Eisenhower Library on June 6, 1992, by Colonel Cole C. Kingseed, an author and chief of military history at West Point, who had purchased the documents from Gladys's estate.

The bundle included a cover note Gladys had written to her son to explain the diary and letters dated June 2, 1957, titled, "Letters from Dwight D. Eisenhower—that I rec'd when we were 'young and happy.'" She had added that the diary and letters were "not to be opened nor publicized in any way whatsoever until after his death (and Mamie's) and also after my death." The Eisenhower Library describes the collection as "a unique, fascinating addition," stating that they "reveal a side of Dwight Eisenhower we do not see in any of his other papers."

The letters and diary offer insights into the relationship that was far more than just a summer romance—at least to Eisenhower. On August 5, Gladys recorded, "D. asked me to marry him." She did not immediately accept or reject the proposal.

Ike's correspondence can only be described as love letters. Some are undated; some were not even mailed, as Ike wrote them late at night after being with Gladys and then personally delivered them the next day. His letters included endearments such as "I have a keener realization of your worth and sweetness—and feel how lucky I am that you give me even a thought."

As the summer passed and the romance blossomed, his letters became even more romantic. On August 18, he pleaded, "More than ever know I want to hear you say the three words more than I ever have. For, girl, I do love you and want you to know it. To be as certain of it as I am." On August 25, he wrote, "Your love is my whole world. Nothing else counts. Your love is my whole world. . . . I love you Gladys," and said he wanted her to be his "true blue wife."

In September, Ike departed for Fort Sam Houston with no answer to his marriage proposal. Gladys put him off by claiming she wanted to pursue her musical career as a pianist. Her decision was influenced by pressure from her father, who strenuously objected to her marrying a soldier, declaring it as "beneath herself" and not of their class. Ike was devastated and hurt. No record exists that indicates the two corresponded again except for a brief "Dear John" letter from Gladys, nor is there any later writing by the two that reveals why they did not marry or continue the relationship. Both Gladys and Ike would marry other people less than a year later, perhaps on the rebound.

On his graduation from West Point, Ike had requested duty in the Philippines, believing he would have no trouble getting the assignment since the Pacific outpost was not considered desirable. He was surprised when he received orders to report in September not to Subic Bay but to the 19th Infantry Regiment at Fort Sam Houston, Texas.

Shortly after arriving, while acting as officer of the day on a Sunday afternoon, the young lieutenant encountered Lulu Harris, the wife of a major, on the post street across from his quarters. Mrs. Harris introduced him to John and Elivera Doud, a successful meat-packing family from Denver, Colorado, with investments in Iowa and Illinois stockyards, who were wintering in San Antonio. With the couple were their daughters, including eighteen-year-old Mary Geneva—known as "Mamie."

There was an instant attraction and intrigue between Mamie and Dwight despite the fact that he had a post-wide reputation as a woman hater—probably because of his avoidance of other women due to his reluctance to accept that his relationship with Gladys was over.

Mamie found Ike extremely handsome, with the most engaging grin she had ever seen. For his part, Ike was likewise struck, later revealing, "The one who attracted my eye instantly was a vivacious and attractive girl, smaller than average, saucy in the look about her face and in her whole attitude."

Ike invited Mamie to make rounds with him as officer of the day. He was surprised when, following a quick conference with her mother, she consented. He would have been even more taken aback if he had known that Mamie detested walking. Born in Boone, Iowa, and six years old before the family moved to Denver, Mamie was pampered and catered to by her family and their many servants. A flirtatious extrovert, she much preferred social events over academic pursuits, attending high school only briefly before dropping out to take dance and piano lessons and to travel with her family. A year before she met Ike, she had attended Miss Wolcott's Finishing School in Denver, which taught young women social skills.

Neither Ike nor Mamie seemed to care that he was six years her senior. Mamie played hard to get for a few weeks before she and Ike began to court regularly. In the meantime, Gladys apparently heard about Mamie and sent Ike a "Dear John" letter shortly after the new year.

With a clear conscience, Ike could now take Mamie to a weekly vaudeville show and to cheap dinners at San Antonio Mexican restaurants on his small salary. Mamie's parents became fond of the young lieutenant and, despite comments from friends that Ike was not of their class, welcomed his courtship of their daughter.

At the time, Fort Sam Houston was considered a premier assignment, with its excellent quarters and facilities located adjacent to the thriving city of San Antonio. Its commander, Major General Fred Funston—Philippine Insurrection Medal of Honor recipient and Cuba veteran—was generally expected to head the American Expeditionary Force (AEF) when and if the United States entered the war in France. Meanwhile, despite the increased violence along the Texas–Mexico border and the broadening of the war in Europe, duty was easy, leaving Ike ample time to woo Miss Doud.

Fort Sam Houston also served as the headquarters for the army's fledging Aviation Section. Ike later recalled, "I liked the idea of flight training and of course the 50 percent more pay held out great and glittering promise." He applied, and while he awaited a response to his application, the head of the local Peacock Military Academy (known as the West Point of Texas) asked Ike to coach the school's football team. Established in 1904 with the mission to be "the most thorough military school west of the Mississippi, governed by the honor system and conducted on the principles of a cultured home," Peacock had West Point graduate faculty members who were aware of Ike's coaching abilities. Although the additional salary would increase Ike's earnings as a second lieutenant by nearly half and such additional employment was authorized, he turned down the offer, believing it would take too much time from his regular duties.

A short while later, General Funston, an old friend of the Peacock headmaster, approached Eisenhower in the Officers' Club, to the amazement of his fellow lieutenants, and asked whether he had turned down the coaching offer. When Ike responded in the affirmative, Funston said, "It would please me and it would be good for the Army if you would accept this offer."

There was but one answer for Eisenhower: "Yes, sir."

Ike led the Peacock Military Academy to a winning season. The next year, he coached San Antonio's St. Louis College (today a part of

St. Mary's University) to not only its first victory in five years but also a season with five wins. Many of the senior officers at Fort Sam Houston thought Ike's coaching abilities placed the army in a good light. For more than a decade, Ike would be much better known for his development of football players and teams than of individual soldiers and their units.

Ike's first officer efficiency report, written by his company commander, did not mention football coaching. While not a resounding endorsement, the evaluation did note, "I consider this officer an able man, and when he has had sufficient experience will be an excellent officer. He is energetic and takes an interest in his work."

Military duties and football coaching took much of Ike's time, but he still found ample opportunity to court Mamie. He seemed to have put Gladys's rejection behind him, or perhaps he found the sophisticated, vivacious Mamie and her upper-class family just too enchanting. Beyond love, Ike very well might have thought Mamie would make a much better army wife than the girl from a small town in Kansas.

Ike approached Mr. Doud for permission to marry Mamie on the same day he learned that he had been accepted into the Aviation Section. He excitedly told the Douds what he thought to be good news before asking for his daughter's hand. Ike's announcement, he said later, "was greeted with a large chunk of silence." Airplanes, with the successful first flight only a dozen years in the past, were viewed by the Douds (as well as the general public) as extremely dangerous. Ike described the family's reaction, noting, "The silence was broken by Mr. Doud himself, who said they had been ready to take me into their family but if I were so irresponsible as to want to go into the flying business just when I was thinking of getting married, he and Mrs. Doud would have to withdraw their consent." Eisenhower departed the Douds' home without their permission for the marriage.

After much thought, Ike came to realize that aviation was just another form of military service. He regretted losing out on the extra pay pilots received but acknowledged to himself that love came first. Ike recorded, "I was ready to give up aviation. Now I would set my sights on becoming the finest Army officer I could, regardless of the branch in which I might serve."

He returned to the Douds' home and announced his conclusion. They welcomed the decision and agreed to the marriage, with one final stipulation that the couple wait until November, when Mamie would be twenty.

On Valentine's Day, 1916, Ike and Mamie became engaged. Although the Douds did not particularly approve of their daughter marrying a soldier, they liked Ike and respected her wishes.

He concluded, "Although everything was smoothed over, it had brought me face to face with myself and caused me to make a decision that I have never recanted or regretted. The decision was to perform every duty given me in the Army to the best of my ability and to do the best I could to make a creditable record, no matter what the nature of the duty."

Ike's choice of Mamie over aviation had far-reaching effects—some obvious, others not. First, he gained a wife who would be his lifelong partner; second, he remained an infantryman. Despite the rapid rise of what would become the Army Air Corps, there was no chance that a little more than two decades later an aviator would have ever been selected to lead the largest army in history.

Eisenhower came to another conclusion after his engagement. Affording a marriage on an army salary would be difficult. To save money, he stopped smoking expensive ready-made cigarettes and rolled his own.

Shortly after the engagement, Pancho Villa and his bandits/revolutionaries raided Columbus, New Mexico, on March 9, 1916, killing nine soldiers and eleven American civilians. The purpose of the attack has never been determined, but Villa likely wanted the U.S. Army to pursue him into Mexico to reinvigorate his revolution against the Mexican government. He may also have initiated the attack to capture much-needed munitions and supplies, as well as to take revenge on a local merchant who had sold him faulty ammunition. Another theory is that German agents paid Villa to attack in hopes that it would draw the United States into a war with Mexico and keep America out of the conflict in Europe.

Regardless of Villa's motivation, President Woodrow Wilson ordered immediate reprisals, instructing General Funston, the officer responsible for the area, to form a force whose mission was "pursuit and dispersion of the band or bands that attacked Columbus, N. M." Funston organized the operation from his San Antonio headquarters and tasked General John

J. "Black Jack" Pershing, commander at Fort Bliss outside El Paso, with executing the objectives of what became known as the Punitive Expedition. American troops crossed the border into Mexico on March 15.

Every officer interested in a future in uniform, including Eisenhower, volunteered to join the expedition. However, six cavalry regiments, four infantry regiments, and several supporting units were already fully manned and assigned to the operation. One the few officers who successfully petitioned to enlist with the expedition was Lieutenant George S. Patton, who joined Pershing as an aide-de-camp and would play an important role in Eisenhower's development in later years.

Villa's attack on the United States from Mexico and the intensity of the simultaneous Battle of the Somme in France prompted the army to finally take actions that would both deter more invasions from Mexicans and train additional troops for their anticipated deployment to Europe. National Guard units from across the country were activated and ordered to the border. Of the forty-three divisions that eventually fought in France, seventeen were veterans of the Punitive Expedition or service along the border.

Although Eisenhower failed in his attempt to join the expedition, the operation nevertheless touched his life both personally and militarily. The Douds, including Mamie, had returned to Denver, but by spring Ike and his fiancée realized that with the activities on the border and the anticipated U.S. entry into the war in Europe, their future together was uncertain. Through correspondence, they decided to move up their wedding date to July 1, instead of waiting.

The Douds, understanding the situation, reluctantly gave permission. Getting authorization for a leave of absence to marry was another matter because the War Department had issued orders that denied leaves or furloughs for any purposes except an emergency. Nevertheless, Ike applied for a twenty-day leave, which his chain of command promptly denied. Undeterred, Ike took his case to the post commander, General Funston, who welcomed him by saying he remembered the lieutenant from their conversation about coaching the Peabody football team. After Ike explained his reasons for moving up his wedding date, Funston considered the request and finally said, "All right, you may have ten days. I'm not sure that this is exactly what the War Department had in mind but I'll take the responsibility."

On July 1, 1916, the U.S. Army promoted Dwight D. Eisenhower to first lieutenant, and at noon on the same day, he married Mary Geneva "Mamie" Doud in the gladiola-filled music room of the Douds' mansion in Denver. Even though only family attended, Ike arrived two hours early and remained standing so as not to crease his dress white trousers before the ceremony. Following the wedding, the Douds' chauffeur drove the couple to a nearby Eldorado Springs thermal resort for a two-day honeymoon. They briefly returned to the Douds' before departing by train for Abilene.

Although the newlyweds arrived in the predawn hours, the Eisenhower family met them at the station. Mamie, amazed by the "ruralness" of Abilene and the austerity of Ike's family home, nevertheless quickly bonded with Ike's mother, although his father remained fairly distant. Mamie won over his siblings by declaring that she had always wanted brothers. Then, after a visit of only eight hours because Ike's leave was about to lapse, the newlyweds boarded a train for San Antonio, traveling along the Katy rail line, where his father had worked many years earlier.

Ike and Mamie were the classic example of the old adage that opposites attract. He was up at daylight or earlier; she preferred to stay in bed until late morning. Ike liked athletics and the outdoors, whether playing with soldiers while on duty or hunting and fishing when not. In contrast, Mamie could be persuaded to take an occasional walk, and that was as much of the outdoors as she cared to experience. Ike cooked their meals, or they frequented the Officers' Club for better fare. Mamie, always attended by servants, did not know how to cook, sew, or even make a bed. When Mamie became pregnant, it was Ike who took needle and thread in hand to let out her dresses. Ike loved the water; Mamie did not like the seashore. Ike had an adventurous streak and longed to fly to Europe; his wife had no desire to go abroad and remained fearful of flying. While Ike was robust, Mamie took to her bed in times of extreme heat or cold. Mamie later joked that the secret to their marriage was that they had absolutely nothing in common.

Before they married, Ike made clear that despite his love for her, the army and country would always come first. Mamie let Ike know that in her mind he would always come first. Although she hated the frequent moves and long separations, she intended to be a dedicated partner, later saying, "He was my husband. He was my whole life."

In a bit of hyperbole, one of Ike's White House speechwriters wrote decades later that without Mamie, General Eisenhower would have been Colonel Eisenhower. Within officers' ranks, the wisdom is that a wife cannot make her husband's career, but she can quickly ruin it. Mamie proved to be the exception. Although helpless in so many household skills, she was extremely adept at entertaining, and in this endeavor she persuaded her father to help the newlyweds financially, even though he had said he had no intention of doing so. Not only did he present the young couple with a generous wedding check, but he also soon gave them an automobile—one of the few owned by an officer on the post—and began sending a monthly gift of $100. This amount, equivalent in today's currency to more than $2,800, nearly doubled Ike's monthly salary and was often the deciding factor for his remaining in the army rather than seeking civilian employment with higher wages.

Mamie claimed credit—at least within the family—for smoothing the edges off her rough-and-ready Kansan and for polishing his manners, which later stood him in good stead in any company. Any complaints about him she kept to herself. Any disagreements remained private.

Mamie, not only the social secretary of the family but also the financial manager, used some of the additional money to make their post housing a gathering place for Ike's fellow officers and their wives. She continued this practice in future moves, and their quarters, no matter their location, became known as "Club Eisenhower." Ike, accompanied by Mamie on a rented piano, led the singing of popular songs—and provided libations of his homemade bathtub gin after the arrival of Prohibition in 1920.

Soon after his return to Fort Sam Houston, Ike was detailed as the post provost marshal. In this position, he accompanied patrols into the seedier areas of San Antonio that contained bars and brothels, where he discovered that some enlisted men really liked to drink and fight and that not all officers were gentlemen. One night, that latter observation became quite personal when a drunken National Guard lieutenant indiscriminately fired two pistol rounds, one barely missing Ike.

Six weeks after their wedding, the couple experienced their first separation when Ike was transferred to 12th Provisional Division to train the 7th Illinois Infantry Regiment garrisoned at Camp Wilson, a tent city on the edge of Fort Sam Houston. The 7th Infantry, a Chicago National Guard unit composed mostly of Irishmen, had been activated along with the general border mobilization. The troops were poorly trained and undisciplined, while their commander preferred drink over command. This combination of factors gave Ike leeway in administration and training. According to Ike, "I wrote all his orders, prepared reports, and other official papers for his signature and became the power behind the Irishman's throne. As I look back on it, it was one of the valuable years of preparation in my early career."

Napolean Bonaparte may well have said that an army marches on his stomach, but he neglected to point out that it crawls on its bureaucracy. The administrative skills Ike learned and honed at Camp Wilson would play an integral part in his advancement through the ranks. Every commander in every headquarters is burdened by massive stacks of reports, letters, and other paperwork. Rare is the officer who desires to sit behind a desk writing, reviewing, and signing documents. A subordinate who can take much of this burden—and one who writes and edits well—is invaluable. Ike's experience at Camp Wilson identified him as one of the few who could manage the administration of a headquarters with ease while making its commander look good.

By December 1916, it had become obvious that the Punitive Expedition would soon be withdrawn from Mexico. Many of the National Guard units, including the 7th Illinois, returned home. Ike's efficiency report for this period noted his abilities in "instructing, drilling, and handling troops" and went on to say, "He has availed himself of his opportunity for improvement. . . . He has high ideals as a man and officer. He needs more experience, but he has the makings of a splendid officer."

With the departure of the 7th, Ike returned to the 19th Infantry Regiment, where once more he considered transferring to the Air

Service, and Mamie once again opposed the idea of her husband going up in "those flimsy crates." Still, Ike did not totally put the idea aside until Mamie announced that she was pregnant.

Early in 1917, the Mexican Punitive Expedition returned home, and the army turned its focus to preparation for entering the war in Europe. General Funston was a favorite of President Wilson, and it was assumed that he would command the American Expeditionary Force when the time came. Ike, due to his previous relationship with Funston, might have been able to secure a job on his staff, but the general died in February, at age fifty-one, of a heart attack. This development opened the way for his subordinate, General Pershing, to assume that command the following summer.

As a part of the general mobilization, Ike, along with several other officers and sergeants from the 19th Regiment, transferred in June to train the 57th Infantry Regiment at Leon Springs, located along the Fredericksburg Road on the edge of San Antonio. Ike assumed the duties of regimental supply officer, wearing silver captain bars, a rank that took up to fifteen years to attain in peacetime. The promotion, shared with all of his West Point classmates, was based not on merit but on the demands of a rapidly expanding army in need of junior officers.

As noted in *At Ease*, Leon Springs had no advantages other than offering a large open area for training and having a well for fresh water. The camp had "not a building or shelter on it of any kind," according to the new captain. With the assistance of several supply sergeants, Ike began to gather weapons, tents, and all other equipment needed by the 3,500 soon-to-arrive soldiers of the regiment. He wrote, "I made friends with every officer from every supply service. I haunted the quartermaster, ordnance, engineer, and medical services, was constantly pleading the case of our new Infantry regiment." When official sources failed to deliver needed supplies, Ike and his noncommissioned officers (NCOs) resorted to bartering among the units.

Ike's duties at Leon Springs amplified his ability to make friends and to attend to the needs of his commander. Ike's closest companion was Captain Walton H. Walker, West Point Class of 1912—veteran of both the Vera Cruz Expedition and the Mexican Punitive Expedition—who would later serve with distinction in both world wars and the Korean conflict.

Colonel David J. Baker, the regimental commander, was, according to Ike, "something of a dyspeptic and fussy about his meals." He constantly complained about the food, especially breakfast, having hired and fired several mess officers before putting Ike in charge of the dining facilities. Ike knew the colonel liked wild game, so he and Walker rode out of the camp to a nearby field where they shot a number of doves. The birds were dressed, cooked, and served to the colonel's table at breakfast time. They added dove to the colonel's menu rotation, which kept the commander in a good mood. Ike noted in his writings, "This was good for everybody; we all enjoyed life more when he was [happy]."

Ike put in long hours, as did the entire regiment, at work that was not without its dangers. While lecturing his company supply officers and NCOs under a tree during a rainstorm on supply in the field, a lightning burst hit him. He recalled, "The next thing I knew I was lying on my back in the mud and an enlisted man was pushing down on my ribs, trying to bring me back from unconsciousness." Other than having "a splitting headache," Ike emerged unharmed.

The training exposed Ike to the lessons in logistics that would stay with him for the rest of his time in uniform. "During the summer months of 1917, our regiment rapidly rounded into form. The training was intense and in most respects enlightening," he recalled.

One of the "enlightening" incidents involved his first major encounter with bureaucratic blundering. When a large crate of entrenching tools and covers—critical items in the trenches of France—arrived at his unit, Ike discovered that they were the old style instead of the improved new ones. He immediately shipped the crate back to the Ordnance Department. Months later, he received a bill for $22.04 for items missing from the shipment. Despite Ike's written explanation and witness statements that the items were never removed from the crate, Ordnance held firm. Ike then sent a check only to again receive a notice that the bill was unpaid. Fortunately, he had kept the cancelled check, which he sent to the Ordnance Department to put an end to the matter. About this episode, he wrote, "More humiliating than costly, in a way, I felt that in that nebulous region called the War Department, I had been found wanting."

Despite such frustrations, by September Ike thought "the regiment was in good shape." He believed that it was one of the best outfits in the whole army, and he was confident that they were destined for overseas duty. Such was not the case. Neither Ike nor the 57th joined the AEF in Europe.

CHAPTER 5

The Great War

EISENHOWER'S EARLY YEARS AS AN OFFICER WERE SUCCESSFUL. PROFESsionally, he had developed training and logistical skills that would serve him well for the rest of career. Personally, he had enhanced his reputation as a superior football coach, and, more important, he had married Mamie.

Ike assumed the next step for him would be to accompany his regiment to France, where he would encounter even more challenges. In time of war, he believed, there was no other place for a professional soldier than the battlefield. He also believed that whatever expertise he had gained at Fort Sam Houston would be honed and enhanced by his participation in combat. The army, however, had other plans for the regiment and for the young Kansan officer. In September 1917, the 57th Regiment was ordered to Houston, Texas, to perform garrison duties at installations around the city, while Eisenhower received orders to report to Camp Oglethorpe, Georgia, as "Instructor, Officers Training."

Ike found the orders "distressing" and attempted to trade assignments with a fellow officer bound for France. The request was promptly disapproved, and he later wrote, "For me this was a hard lesson that if the mills of the gods grind slowly and exceedingly small, the mills of the War Department seemed to grind to no purpose whatsoever."

Both because there were no married officer quarters at Camp Oglethorpe and because Mamie was in the advanced stages of pregnancy, she remained in San Antonio. According to Ike, "We went to the field and lived in trenches, constructed dugouts, and prepared for warfare on the Western Front. I came out of those trenches on the twenty-sixth of

September and found a telegram dated the twenty-fourth, saying that my son had been born. His name was David Doud."

In a return letter to Mamie, he expressed his love for her and their son, whom they would initially call "Little Ike" and later "Icky" (in some sources spelled as Ikey or Ikky), in accordance with the Doud family tradition of using nicknames. In addition to sending his affection, the new father encouraged Mamie to teach Icky the words to the popular song "Down among the Sheltering Palms," which echoed his love, yearning, and desire that they "wait for [him]."

Other than his letters, Ike had no means or opportunity to celebrate the birth of his son. Days at Oglethorpe began at 5:15 a.m. and did not end until 9:00 p.m. "The work was fatiguing but I enjoyed it," he wrote. The few minutes of leisure Ike did have, he spent reading everything available on the infantry tactics being employed in France.

By the end of the year, the War Department determined that it no longer needed the training at Oglethorpe and closed the camp. Ike received orders to report to Fort Leavenworth, Kansas, as "Instructor of Provisional Officers, Army Service Schools."

Captain Eisenhower's efficiency report from Colonel T. M. Anderson, the Oglethorpe commander, was not one to enhance an officer's career, rating Ike as only average, two steps below the highest rating of superior, and stating that he was "a capable and industrious young officer" who would "improve with service." Perhaps Colonel Anderson was a hard evaluator who gave similar reports to all junior officers, or perhaps Ike simply followed orders and did his duties without calling attention to himself.

Ike's orders for travel to Fort Leavenworth allowed sufficient time for him to see his new son and to spend a couple of days with Mamie. While in San Antonio, he encountered Lieutenant Colonel Gilbert Allen, an old friend from the 19th Infantry, who was organizing a machine-gun company for deployment to France. Ike immediately dispatched a telegram to the War Department in Washington, DC, requesting transfer to the unit, only to receive a prompt negative response explaining that his qualities as an instructor were the priority. All he could do was salute smartly and take the next train to Leavenworth.

After Ike had been at his new station only a few days, the post commandant called him into his office to read him a letter from the War Department stating that the adjutant general did not take kindly to junior officers applying for special duty. Effectively, the letter ordered the captain to be quiet and follow orders. According to Ike, "The message was loud and clear. A man at a desk a thousand miles away knew better that I what my military capabilities and talents were; and he did not want to be bothered by any further exercises of initiative on my part."

When the colonel began to add his reprimand, Ike's temper rose as he replied, "Sir, this offense—if it is an offense—was committed before I came under your jurisdiction. If there is punishment to be given out, I think that it should be given by the War Department and not added to by yourself, with all due respect."

The colonel considered Ike's comment and then said, "Well, I think you are right. And I respect you for your convictions."

"The colonel sent me out in a friendly mood," Ike later wrote, "although my views of the War Department continued to be beyond easy conversion to parlor language."

Ike joined the school's Company Q as an assistant instructor. His duties were similar to those of a football coach as he led calisthenics and conditioning exercises, in addition to conducting bayonet drills. Ike's students respected their leader. In a letter to his mother in January 1918, one of those admiring students, Lieutenant Edward C. Thayer, wrote, "Our new captain, Eisenhower by name, is, I believe, one of the most efficient and best army officers in the country."

Also among Ike's charges was F. Scott Fitzgerald, who had dropped out of Princeton University to join the army. Self-described as "the worst second lieutenant in the United States Army," Fitzgerald spent much of his time completing his first novel, *The Romantic Egotist*, rather than devoting himself to military subjects. Although he never made it to the war zone, Fitzgerald would credit the military with having a profound effect on his life in that his transfer from Leavenworth to Alabama led to his meeting his future wife and muse, Zelda.

Ike liked his physical training duties, if for no other reason than they kept him warm during the long, cold Kansas winter. In his off-duty hours, he read everything available related to his newest interest: the introduction of tanks into warfare. He studied the successes and failures of the iron behemoths in the Battle of the Somme and at Cambrai.

Leavenworth provided Eisenhower time for self-evaluation, and his dismay with the army that began at Camp Oglethorpe came to a head a Fort Leavenworth. He wrote, "My mastery of military paperwork, even of rudimentary training methods, hardly seemed a shining achievement for one who had spent seven years (including the four years at West Point) preparing himself to lead fighting men. Some of my class were already in France. Others were ready to depart. I seemed embedded in the monotony and unsought safety of the Zone of Interior. I could see myself, years later, silent at class reunions while others reminisced of battle."

Ike's doldrums transformed into elation like the phoenix from the ashes when he received orders in late February 1918 to report to the 65th Engineers at Fort Meade, Maryland. There he was to assist in the organization and training of the 301st Tank Battalion for deployment to France. Composed of all volunteers, the 301st had high morale—if not a single tank assigned to the unit, which was to receive vehicles on arrival in France.

Ike learned in March that the 301st was to deploy within weeks from the Port of New York, and he was to be in command. Elated, he "worked [his] head off" in preparing for the embarkation, including a trip to New York to coordinate with port officials. He recalled, "Too much depended on our walking up that gangplank for me to take a chance on a slip up anywhere."

Two days after returning to Fort Meade, Ike received another disappointment in assignments. Instead of accompanying the 301st to France, on March 25, Ike was ordered to the Tank Service Camp at Gettysburg, Pennsylvania. "My mood was black," he later recalled, but he "blew off steam in private and then settled down to do the job at hand." Despite his best efforts to have it be different, World War I was not to be Eisenhower's war.

The Gettysburg facility, established a year earlier, had been used to train several infantry regiments before their transfer to Camp Greene, South Carolina. Renamed Camp Colt (in honor of gun maker Samuel

Colt), it consisted of nearly two hundred acres of the Gettysburg National Park and occupied much of the land where the 1863 battle between the North and South had taken place.

In a report requested by the Pennsylvania War History Commission dated August 5, 1920, Ike described what he found when he arrived, recording that the infantry troops had "left behind a considerable number of open sided and floorless kitchens, and a few stables and warehouses."

Shortly before Ike's arrival at the camp, its mission had changed from "no designation" to performance of "preliminary training to fit (tank soldiers) as rapidly as possible to go overseas for their finishing technical and tactical courses at the American training centers in England and France." The mission statement indicated that the soldiers would receive additional training in Europe because, although Camp Colt was to train tankers, it still had no actual tanks for their drills. Both British and French tanks were supposedly on the way; however, nonc had yet arrived. Ike's only compensation for not deploying to France was that his orders named him as the camp commander. Once again, his skills as a trainer had trumped his desire to see combat, which was a still another fateful happenstance that the frustrated soldier could not yet appreciate.

Simultaneous with Ike's new assignment was the announcement that the tank corps, previously under the oversight of the Corps of Engineers, now had its own designation as a separate branch of the army equivalent to the cavalry, infantry, and field artillery. Colonel Ira C. Welborn, a Mississippi native and member of the Class of 1898 at West Point, had been named the overall commander of the tank corps with his headquarters at Camp Meade, Maryland.

The assignment of Welborn to the tank corps was fortuitous for Eisenhower. Welborn—an army hero who at San Juan Hill, Cuba, shortly after graduation from West Point, "voluntarily left shelter and went, under fire, to the aid of a private of his company who was wounded," earning for himself the Medal of Honor, and who had served in the Philippine Insurrection and the Boxer Rebellion—understood traditional combat but knew nothing about tanks and armored warfare. As a result, he mostly left the training and operation of the post to Eisenhower.

Ike arrived at Camp Colt on March 24, 1918, with a small cadre to establish his headquarters in the field near where General George Pickett had made his famous charge during the Civil War. Required to return to Camp Meade to take care of the final details of the 301st's deployment and to meet with Welborn, Ike appointed a captain named Garner, who had been commissioned from the ranks a year earlier, to command the camp during his absence. Before his departure, Ike held a flag-raising ceremony.

During the ceremony, Ike noticed tears streaming down the face of his acting camp commander, an "old, hard-bitten, gray-haired former non-com." As they together continued to watch the flag flapping in the wind, Garner said, without looking at his new boss, "Captain, the last time I was on this ground was many years ago. At that time I was standing before a general court martial which sentenced me to six months in the guardhouse, and then suspended the sentence. Now, I'm a captain in that same army, and I'm standing here as temporary commander of the camp in which I was disgraced."

The incident moved Ike, reminding him how deeply professional soldiers revere the flag and love the army and their country. Ike could only manage a short response, saying, "Look, Garner, I know you'll do a splendid job." But the captain's emotion and remarks made an impression, causing him to later write, "To this day, whenever we stand to salute the flag, the memory is still with me."

Ike returned from Camp Meade with detailed instructions, which he described as follows: "My orders were specific, indeed rigid. I was required to take in volunteers, equip, organize, and instruct them and then have them ready for overseas shipment when called upon. The orders warned that no excuses for deficiencies in their records or equipment would be accepted and that my camp was not only a point of mobilization but of embarkation. This meant that troops sent from Gettysburg would go directly to the war zone without intermediate stops."

Much as he had at Leon Springs, Ike began to requisition the supplies and weapons needed to train his men. He had the tents raised even though there was no wood for flooring. More important, the supply system had no stoves. This issue became particularly critical when a late-season blizzard covered the camp in more than twenty inches of snow. Because no stoves had arrived, Eisenhower went into Gettysburg and neighboring towns with government vouchers to buy every heating device that would fit into a tent so the troops could weather the storm and resume training.

A few days after the sky cleared, Mamie and Icky arrived from San Antonio, finding quarters in a vacant fraternity house at Gettysburg College on Washington Street, just outside the camp's boundaries. Although spacious, the house had no kitchen facilities, forcing the Eisenhowers to cook on hot plates and wash their dishes in a bathtub. Ike had little time for his family, but when he could find a few hours, he gave Mamie tours of the Gettysburg Battlefield, where he knew the location of every unit during the fight. Mamie, never particularly interested in the outdoors, endured the tours to spend time with her husband. She later said Ike "knew every rock on the battlefield."

By the end of March, the camp population had grown to one thousand; it would soon reach nearly ten thousand as train loads of recruits arrived from induction centers at Camp Upton, New York, and Camp Dix, New Jersey. More than six hundred officers from various candidate schools also reported to the camp. According to Ike's report to the Pennsylvania War History Commission, during its nine-month tenure, Camp Colt had trained four heavy battalions with 800 men and 70 officers each, fifteen light battalions with 350 men and 20 officers, and thirty support and administrative companies.

As the camp expanded in scope and population, Ike was ever aware of the needs of the troops. He immediately had temporary wooden buildings erected to serve as a hospital and mess halls. He also established a camp newspaper, *Treat 'Em Rough* (also the camp's slogan), to distribute information and provide an outlet for soldiers' poetry and stories. He frequently penned letters for the paper, as well as issuing memos in this manner. Ike not only believed in seeing to the physical welfare of his charges but also valued communication with the soldiers under his command. The result was that he often gave speeches to his troops, an effective technique he would use to reinforce morale during World War II.

Knowing there was much more time available than just the hours for close-order drill, bayonet practice, and physical exercise, Ike initiated classes in Morse code and motor mechanics. With no manuals yet written on tank warfare or even after-action reports available from the western front, he resorted to organizing his own training curriculum using newspaper reports from France and his "own imagination" while keeping to himself his criticism of the lack of readiness for wartime expansion.

Through Colonel Welborn, Eisenhower acquired a few naval three-pounder swivel guns and machine guns for training at Camp Colt, although there was neither ammunition nor a sufficient backstop at the camp into which they could fire the swivel guns if they had had the shells. Still, Ike developed drills for the guns, especially the machine guns. He later recalled, "A number of machine guns came in and we trained gunners until they could take them apart blindfolded and put them together again. Then someone had the notion of mounting the machine guns on truck trailers or flatbed trucks, and so we were able to train to fire from mobile platforms at both moving and still targets. The only satisfactory place for firing was Big Round Top, a terrain feature that has a prominent place in the history of the Battle of Gettysburg. Its base made the perfect back stop."

Colonel Welborn, impressed by Eisenhower's actions, sent a message to the adjutant general of the army on April 19, 1918, recommending his promotion. Welborn's justification was that the "rank of major is more commensurate with the duties performed by the Camp Commander, and will enable him to better perform those duties." The colonel, acknowledging that General John Pershing recommended that no officer above the grade of captain be sent over with tank units, nevertheless emphasized that making Eisenhower a major would not contravene the general's orders because he was currently camp commander.

On April 23, the adjutant general responded, "Returned. This officer is not eligible for appointment in the National Army."

Undeterred, Welborn again submitted a request on May 27 for Eisenhower's promotion to major, this time writing, "It is urgently requested that an exception be made in this case. He is doing important work, is deserving of promotion, and his duties can be better performed with the increased rank."

The adjutant general responded curtly, saying, "Returned. Disapproved, as it is contrary to present policy."

Not one to give up easily, Welborn again requested the promotion in July, quoting General Pershing's recent order authorizing such advancements. After several days of additional bureaucratic messaging about the availability of a slot for a major, the adjutant general approved the promotion and backdated the rank for Eisenhower to June 17.

On June 6, the first tank—a seven-ton French Renault—arrived at Camp Colt. The *Gettysburg Times* reported that the soldiers "were as happy as playground full of children with a new toy."

Two more Renault tanks arrived over the next few weeks, though they came without their weaponry. About this condition, Ike wrote, "We improvised." He added, "At about the same time, two British officers appeared as advisors. Thus began my connection with the Allies, a word that was to become vitally important to me as the years rolled on. The British officers helped us understand the uses of these new, armored weapons. In their conversations, I heard about a British political figure named Winston Churchill. According to the two officers, this Churchill had a hand in producing the first tanks. They admired him extravagantly. And I must say from their descriptions, he sounded like a good chap."

The significance of the British officers' influence was further revealed decades later in 1943 when Lieutenant Colonel (Retired) Franklin Summers, one of the British advisors at Camp Colt, wrote to Eisenhower asking him to provide a foreword to his book on armor operations, which was about to be published.

In an immediate response—despite the fact that the request arrived only days after the successful Sicily campaign—Eisenhower wrote on August 26, 1943, "No message I have received in recent months has pleased me more than yours. I have often wondered where you were and what you were doing. I assure you that I could not have attempted to write a foreword to your book, except for my very great feeling of indebtedness for the advice and counsel you so kindly gave me years ago in the little town of Gettysburg. I hope I have profited somewhat of it."

Ike began his foreword by describing the debut of "a clumsy, belly-crawling monster" in World War I and crediting the tank with the "hastening of the German defeat in 1918." In praising the armor soldiers of the present, particularly those who contributed to the book, Ike continued, "We owe to them the overwhelming nature of the Allied Tunisian victory—to say nothing of the triumphal odyssey of the British Eighth Army that began at El Alamein and has reached Catania."

No doubt, with the former NCO and now captain Garner likely in mind, Ike presented each new battalion at Camp Colt with an American flag. The September 10, 1918, issue of *Treat 'Em Rough* contained the speech he gave to the 330th Battalion on its formal organization about the importance of the Stars and Stripes. He is quoted as saying, "As members of the American army we are soon to set foot on foreign soil. It behooves us to watch ourselves that no act of ours, however small, shall ever disgrace the unsullied reputation of this flag. Let us, therefore, resolve that at all times and places in whatsoever conditions we may be, we bear ourselves proudly and courageously, conscious of our duties and responsibilities, and of the great honor that fell to us when we were chosen to fight for our country."

In his role as camp commander, Major Eisenhower was learning firsthand the importance of forming and maintaining good relationships not only with Allies, such as the British advisors, but also with the locals, who offered entertainment outlets for his own troops. To that end, he provided the Camp Colt Drum Corps to participate in the Gettysburg Memorial Day celebration, and he encouraged Camp Colt soldiers to field a baseball team to play against the local nine at the town's Fourth of July celebration.

Generally, the local civilians welcomed the soldiers, both out of patriotism and for the profits the camp brought the community. Some of this revenue came from the soldiers' frequent visits to local bars and taverns, which, unfortunately, often resulted in drunkenness and brawling. Although the War Department authorized commanders to place such troublemaker businesses "off limits," Eisenhower initially requested that local saloon keepers take measures on their own not to serve alcohol to soldiers. Most complied, but according to an article in *Treat 'Em*

Rough, one Gettysburg hotel and bar owner continued to sell spirits to servicemen. Ike responded by dispatching military police to surround the establishment, effectively keeping out soldiers as well as civilians.

The hotel owner protested to his congressman. Showing up at Ike's office and assuming he could intimidate a mere army major, he threatened Ike, saying, "We have means—we can go to the War Department. If you're going to be stubborn, I'll have to take up the question of replacing you."

Ike did not like threats. In fit of temper, he responded, "You do exactly that. Nothing would please me better than to be taken out of this job. I want to go overseas. If they take me out of here, maybe I can get there."

An aide to the congressman told Ike as they departed that he should not to pay attention to the threat, as his boss "had to do this because the hotel man [was] a very important supporter." Not wanting a quarrel with his donor, the congressman followed through with his threat and filed a complaint with the War Department. The War Department sent Ike a letter commending him for safeguarding his troops instead of providing the desired relief of command or a reprimand.

That incident was not the last encounter Major Eisenhower would have with an elected official. When one of his cadre was caught cheating at poker with a marked deck by one of his own colleagues, Ike—believing that "good morale within an outfit is usually reflected by good conduct within it"—summoned the offending officer and gave him the choice of either resigning his commission or facing court-martial.

The officer resigned, but only a few days later his father and congressman arrived at the camp, suggesting that Ike withdraw the lieutenant's resignation and transfer him to another post. Ike politely turned down the request, explaining that this move would only pass the problem on to another commander because the man would likely repeat the same offense. The congressman "blustered a bit" before asking that Ike at least remove the words "for the good of the service" from the resignation. Again, Ike refused, saying, "I'm acting as an army officer protecting my command."

Days later, Ike learned that congressmen had more influence than senior officers when the politician successfully persuaded the War Department to withdraw the cheater's letter of resignation and return him to active duty with his lieutenant's bars intact.

By summer, Camp Colt was graduating enough soldiers to dispatch groups monthly to ports for transport to Europe. Ike was extremely proud that "not a single man of ours was turned back from port because of any defect in his instructions, records, or physical condition."

Ike also expressed his pride in an article titled "A Message to the Men" in a July issue of the camp newspaper. He wrote, "To a man making his first visit here is immediately borne the significant attitude of every man and officer in the camp. It means that the Tank Corps, although the baby branch of the service, is a baby in name only—perhaps a baby wild-cat—and the slogan 'Treat 'Em Rough' will prove to be a very appropriate phrase when the kitten has grown a bit more and sharpened his claws for the Boche [German soldiers]."

The smooth operations of the camp, however, drastically altered in September when a group of recruits arriving from Fort Devens, Massachusetts, had several soldiers complaining of headaches that camp doctors attributed to recent typhoid fever inoculations. By the next morning, the soldiers had high fevers and were diagnosed by camp doctors as having the Spanish flu. Ike immediately ordered the sick men isolated and initiated what many years later, in another epidemic, would be called "social distancing." He quarantined the camp and posted military police to prevent anyone from going into town. Every soldier received a daily medical exam, and tents were left open to air out while their floors were scrubbed with disinfectants and kerosene.

More than three hundred Colt soldiers came down with the Spanish flu between September 15 and October 5; of these, 175 died from the disease. As bad as they were, these numbers compared favorably to those at other army installations. When the War Department learned of the relative success fighting the flu at Camp Colt, officials ordered thirty of the camp's medical personnel to other posts to pass along their preventative measures.

Ike regretted the deaths of his soldiers, but he was gratified that the numbers were no worse and that neither he nor his family had contracted the virus. He was happier still to learn that, on Colonel Welborn's recommendation, he was being promoted to lieutenant colonel as of October 14, 1918. His feelings went from happy to ecstatic later that day when he received orders to report on November 18 to the Port of New York for deployment to France in command of the camp's most recent graduates. Welborn offered Ike a promotion to full colonel if he would stay in the United States and continue to train soldiers. Ike declined the offer and even said that he would take a reduction in rank to major if it would ensure his transfer to France. The trainer of soldiers and coach of football players was finally going to war.

The jubilant mood was dampened a few days later by two unrelated events. First, Mamie received word from Denver that her seventeen-year-old sister, Eda Mae (known as "Buster"), was seriously ill with a kidney infection and heart disease. Mamie and Icky departed Pennsylvania on November 10 on a west-bound train, but they had gotten only as far as Chicago when she learned that her sister had died two days before. Mamie continued the journey to attend her funeral.

Buster's death saddened Ike, as he was fond of his sister-in-law and sympathized with Mamie for her loss. But he was facing a loss of his own as well. In his headquarters visiting with a West Point classmate, who likewise had not gone to France, Ike learned the news from France that the armistice ending the Great War had been signed. Now, instead of going to fight, Ike would remain in the United States to assist in the demobilization of the army. When they learned about the armistice, Ike said to his classmate, "I suppose we'll spend the rest of our lives explaining why we didn't get into this war."

Disgruntled with the news, Ike displayed the attitude that would mark the rest of his career. He swore, "By God, from now on I am cutting myself a swath and will make up for this."

CHAPTER 6

Camp Dix, Fort Benning, and across the Country

INSTEAD OF FULFILLING HIS DREAM OF BOARDING A SHIP FOR FRANCE, Ike began the process of demobilizing the troops at Camp Colt. He recalled this time in his autobiography: "No human enterprise goes flat so instantly as an army training camp when war ends. Everything that sustains morale—peril to the country, imminent combat, zeal for victory, a sense of importance—disappears. The only thing that counts for a citizen soldier is his date of discharge. For the officers, the troop's preoccupation with this one objective made maintaining discipline and morale a major task."

Despite Ike's disappointment at missing the greatest war in history and the sadness both he and Mamie felt for the loss of Buster, their tour at Camp Colt had done much to mold the two into the kind of soldier and army wife they would be in the future.

Colonel Ira C. Welborn best described Ike's progress in his recommendation for the Distinguished Service Medal (DSM), the army's highest noncombat award, which had been first authorized on January 2, 1918. Welborn wrote, "As a captain he started with nothing and organized the Tank Corps Camp and Training Center at Gettysburg, received untrained recruits, established schools, started an officers training camp for selected enlisted men, and organized and trained Tank Corps units, keeping the Tank Corps up to the shipping schedule, and administering all the duties in connection with these activities in a highly satisfactory and creditable manner."

Welborn contributed significantly to Eisenhower's development as an officer and a leader, demonstrating by his actions the importance of persistence and allowing the young officer great independence in running the operations of the camp. When the adjutant general declined Welborn's recommendation for Eisenhower's DSM, stating that Ike's service did not justify the award, the colonel did not give up; rather, he rewrote and resubmitted the request. When that, too, was turned down, Welborn appeared before the next War Department board meeting to lobby his case. Once more denied, he did not give up and again submitted the recommendation. Finally, on October 7, 1922, after nearly four years of effort, Welborn succeeded in gaining approval for Ike's DSM. Welborn's professionalism and persistence marked him as Ike's first significant mentor in uniform.

Mamie, still a young woman, had also learned much about her new role as an army wife. As a pampered child, who at age six had asked for and gotten a diamond ring for Christmas, she had wanted for nothing, lived in mansions, and often traveled in a private rail car. Still, she attempted to adapt to the austere life of an army wife, at some times more graciously than others. Although married for less than two years by this time, she had already endured frequent separations from her husband, three moves of their household, inferior living quarters, and a spouse disgruntled at not being sent overseas to join the war.

One achievement Mamie continued to aim for when adjusting to her new environments was to make their various homes, regardless of their size and quality, gathering places for Ike's fellow officers. Her overcoming her dislike of the outdoors enough to accompany Ike on those tours around the Gettysburg Battlefield was another example of her willingness to adjust. In a somewhat radical venture, she even drove one of the first tanks after its arrival at Camp Colt—becoming the first woman in the United States, and perhaps the world, to drive an armored vehicle.

Not all her adaptations, however, were well advised. When she left San Antonio to join Ike in Pennsylvania, Mamie sold all their furniture for 10 percent of its worth rather than move it to their new quarters. She also gave away Ike's two double-breasted suits, which she did not like, assuming he would not notice due to wartime regulations that soldiers remain in uniform even when off military installations. Ike did notice, and that incident led to one of their first real disagreements.

Despite her youth and her background of wealth and privilege, Mamie quickly learned about finances, albeit sometimes through mistakes like those with the furniture and suits. For the rest of their marriage, she was the couple's money manager and, according to Ike, "a very frugal one."

The end of the war did not bring immediate happiness or even reunion for the Eisenhowers. On November 18, the date he had originally planned to depart for France, Ike instead received orders to close down Camp Colt. His instructions included moving his headquarters and the remaining troops to Camp Dix, New Jersey, where they would be discharged, and preparing Dix soldiers arriving back from France for their out-processing. At the same time, he was to retain as many of his original command as possible to form the nucleus of a Tank Corps. That corps—along with the three Renault tanks—would transfer to Fort Benning, Georgia. With no quarters assigned or even assurance about what his duties would be, Ike asked Mamie to remain with her family in Denver. They would not reunite until a year later.

Ike remained concerned about having missed the war and about his future career in uniform. He wrote, "I was older than my classmates, was still bothered on occasion by a bad knee, and saw myself in the years ahead putting on weight in a meaningless chair-bound assignment, shuffling papers and filling out forms. If not depressed, I was mad, disappointed, and resented the fact that the war had passed me by."

Complicating the matter was Ike's awareness that, as a West Point graduate with administrative and training experience, he was readily marketable in the civilian sector. He was tempted to accept a job offer from one of his former lieutenants who owned a manufacturing firm in Muncie, Indiana. However, he turned down the offer after corresponding with Mamie, who later recalled, "I said to him—it was only about twice I interfered—and this time I said, 'Well, Ike, I don't think you'd be happy. This is your life and you know it and like it.'"

Ike heeded the guidance. Although he would receive several more civilian job offers over the years, Mamie's advice remained forefront in his mind as he refused each and every one.

"There was, after all, a brighter side," Ike wrote. "For an officer graduated from West Point less than two years before the United States entered the war, I had been singularly fortunate in the scope of my first three and half years of duty. How to take a cross section of the Americans and convert them into first-class fighting troops and officers had been learned by experience, not textbook. Not to overstate the fact, I had a feeling for the military potential, in human terms, of the United States. My education had not been neglected."

Once he had decided to remain in uniform, Ike quickly completed his missions at Camp Dix. Then Ike and the armored servicemen he had convinced to reenlist in the army for the Tank Corps, along with their three Renaults, boarded a train for Fort Benning, Georgia, in late December.

The journey south confirmed Ike's low opinion of the War Department. Because the army contracted rail transportation based on the lowest rate, troop trains merited only poorly maintained passenger cars and the most circuitous routes. Eisenhower observed that his unit had the lowest priority of passage, ranking behind passenger express trains, milk trains, and slow freights, and their cars had no lights, heat, or hot water. Though he rarely used humor or sarcasm in his writings, Ike did note about this experience that "low flying birds" had priority over his troop train. When he complained to railway officials, they responded, "What do you expect when the government takes over the railways?"

Ike concluded, "The trip lasted for almost four days, each a year long."

Fort Benning was easy duty for Ike and his tankers—mainly because the infantry post reflected the War Department's position on tanks, having no current use for them in postwar austerity and being unsure of their future value. Ike found himself with so much idle time that he was relieved when orders arrived, after only three months at Benning, for him and his tank unit to report to Fort Meade. Even though the army had decided that the Maryland post would become the headquarters for the Tank Corps, in actuality, field maneuvers and training techniques for the machinery remained in the hands of what Ike called "theoreticians."

Once again Ike turned to duties of demobilization while at the same time continuing to seek assignment to a combat unit. On April 24, 1919, he submitted to the War Department a special personal report and statement of preferences for officers of the regular army in which he stated that he desired to remain in the Tank Corps at any station if it was to become a permanent branch. If not, he requested an infantry assignment to the Presidio in San Francisco; Fort Sam Houston in Texas; or Fort George Wright in Washington State.

In the form's section asking about preferences for overseas service, Ike listed Siberia as his first choice, followed by France, the Philippines, and Hawaii. His request of Siberia was not frivolous; the Russian territory was the one final location where fighting continued, with U.S. and Allied troops having been dispatched to Vladivostok and Siberia in August 1918 to assist in transferring forty thousand Czechoslovakian soldiers from the Russian Bolsheviks to the western front. Almost eight thousand U.S. troops remained in Siberia until April 1920, sustaining 187 deaths due to combat, accidents, or disease.

Eisenhower was not surprised when he did not receive a transfer to Siberia; indeed, he knew the special personal report (more commonly known as the "dream sheet") rarely delivered desired assignments because, as the army readily admitted, the "needs of the service" far superseded the desires of the individual. The only negative impact of Ike's request form was his desire to remain in the Tank Corps, as it did little to endear him to his infantry superiors.

Instead of sailing for Siberia, Ike settled into Meade, where Brigadier General Samuel D. Rockenbach, former commander of the American Expeditionary Force Tank Corps, assumed the overall command of the branch from Colonel Welborn. Ike resumed demobilization duties—once again without his family because there were no available quarters at the camp. Mamie and Icky remained in Denver.

Initially, duties were light. Ike and several other officers, bored and fearful of "going to seed," organized night classes in mathematics, history, English, and military tactics to assist junior officers in their application for regular army commissions. Poker and bridge occupied Ike's otherwise free time until the numbers of soldiers returning from overseas for discharge overwhelmed the camp and their routine changed drastically. As a result of the influx, Ike reported, "Most of us were putting in long hours and sleep consumed the rest of the time."

Despite the demands of the job, Ike easily made friends wherever he was stationed. He generally sought out those individuals with different experiences and expertise from whom he could learn. The Oregon-born Major Sereno E. Brett more than met these attributes as a veteran of the Mexican Punitive Expedition and a highly decorated tanker of World War I. He provided Ike with details about duties on the border and the combat he had missed by not going to France.

As demobilization neared its conclusion, the army began experimenting and training for future conflicts. Previously troop movement across country had been by rail transport. No convoy had attempted a motorized move from coast to coast. There were few paved roads outside towns, and these, essentially trails, were often impassable from mud or shifting sands. No one knew whether a military convoy could traverse the country, but the War Department determined it would be well worth the try. In addition to valuable training, the expedition would test the mobility of the military while also serving as a means of maintaining the postwar support for the army. Officially, the First Transcontinental Motor Convoy's mission was "to test various military vehicles, many developed too late for use in the war, and to determine by actual experience the feasibility of moving across the continent."

Before the expedition's departure, the War Department decided that each service branch should attach observers to the convoy to learn from the experience firsthand. Ike and Brett volunteered as soon as they learned of the opportunity. According to Ike, "I wanted to go along partly for a lark and partly to learn."

The convoy began assembling its eighty-one vehicles, consisting of trucks, cars, and motorcycles, and its personnel—24 officers and 258 enlisted men—in the early summer of 1919. Its objective was to traverse the country from Washington, DC, to San Francisco, a distance of 3,251 miles along what was known as the Lincoln Highway (U.S.

30 and Interstate 80 today). More than half that distance, about eighteen hundred miles, consisted of problematic dirt roads and wagon tracks. At least one hundred bridges would have to be rebuilt or reinforced to get the convoy to its destination.

After lengthy speeches by politicians and military leaders, the convoy departed the Capitol Ellipse on the morning of July 7. Ike, again adding a bit of humor and sarcasm in *At Ease*, recalled, "Each had something to say about the role of these road pioneers; not all of them were brief. My luck was running, we missed the ceremony."

Ike and Major Brett, representing the Tank Corps, joined the convoy at its first overnight stop at the fairgrounds in Frederick, Maryland. It had traveled forty-six miles in a little more than seven hours. Over the next two months, the convoy averaged fifty-eight miles per day, approximately six miles per hour. When asked about the slow pace and the effectiveness of motor vehicles in the recent war, Lieutenant Colonel Charles McClure, the convoy commander, mused, "Motor truck transportation saved France, but France had roads."

The Motor Convoy arrived at the Presidio in San Francisco after sixty-two days on the road—only five days behind schedule. Besides the poor condition of the roads and bridges, the convoy had to contend with frequent equipment breakdowns and inexperienced drivers. Even so, the convoy accomplished its mission of reaching its destination and giving evaluators opportunities to assess a wide variety of vehicles, mostly supplied by commercial factories for this field-testing purpose. In their after-action reports, Ike and other observers noted that the service, engineer, and medial units had performed well; members of the newly formed Transportation Motor Corps, however, were judged not to have been properly prepared. Ike wrote, "Lessons from observation of personnel are that officers and men should be thoroughly trained as soldiers before entrusting to them the valuable equipment of the motor train. This will prevent much unnecessary expense due to breakage, speeding, etc., as well as preserve the standard of conduct essential to a good soldier."

First Lieutenant E. R. Jackson, convoy observer from the Ordnance Corps, agreed with Ike, writing in his report, "During the early weeks of the trip, discipline among the enlisted men of the Motor Transport Corps was conspicuous by its absence."

Even so, the caravan accomplished its primary mission of crossing the country as well as its secondary goal of reinforcing and perpetuating civilian support. Its trek from coast to coast passed through 350 towns and villages in eleven states, all of which welcomed the convoy with ceremonies, speeches, picnics, and washtubs of lemonade. It is estimated that fully 9 percent of the American population lived within a ten-mile zone along the convoy route. National attention to the convoy's progress brought praise for the army and money for bridges and roads from the U.S. Congress.

Ike summarized in his report, "The truck train was well received at all points along the route. It seemed that there was a great deal of sentiment for the improving of highways, and from the standpoint of promoting this sentiment, the trip was an undoubted success." In *At Ease*, he wrote:

> One of the byproducts of this trip, whose usefulness was entirely unpredictable in 1919, was the nodding acquaintance I acquired with the face and character of many towns and cities across the east-west axis of the country. We were always, of course, routed through the main streets of each community. Our snail's pace enabled me to observe anything different or unusual. At every overnight stop where there was a town, we were welcomed by a committee and if only to demonstrate that I was not solely an army propagandist, I tried to learn as much as I could about local interests. Much that I learned was quickly forgotten. But enough stayed with me so that decades later, it had its uses.

As insignificant as it might have seemed at the time, Ike's participation in the Motor Convoy would ultimately serve him well. Decades later, he would retrace the convoy's route when campaigning for president, frequently mentioning to his audiences his impressions from his previous visit in 1919. Many years later, Ike would blend his memories of this convoy with his observations of the German autobahn into an innovative concept for American roadways. In 1956, as president, he signed into law the Interstate Highway Act, which became the forerunner of today's highway system.

While a dedicated officer and a serious military student, Ike also possessed a lighter side: he enjoyed harmless pranks. The convoy had been rife with opportunities to replace his helmet with a prankster cap and have some belly-busting laughs at the expense of the inexperienced and unsuspecting.

Half of the eleven pages dedicated to his convoy report in *At Ease* were not about his observations; rather, they focused on the pranks he and Brett pulled on the naive lieutenants—mostly from the east who had never seen the "Wild West"—whom Ike described as "an audience for a troop of traveling clowns." The pair did such mischievous things as going outside the night camps and howling like coyotes to frighten the city boys. Or, by making war cries, they convinced several officers of a pending attack by Indians. The pranksters also exaggerated warnings about huge, aggressive rattlesnakes and spread rumors that Brett was suffering from shell shock, stories that sent the lieutenants scurrying when Brett began hollering and crazily waving his arms.

The highlight of the convoy for Ike came when Mamie met him at North Platte, Nebraska, a reunion they had arranged by mail before the truck train departed the East Coast. When Mamie enthusiastically made plans to meet her husband by taking the train, her father balked at her going alone. He loaded up the family Packard and drove his daughter the 260 miles from Denver to North Platte, a trip that rivaled the trek of the convoy with its similar lack of roads and abundance of weak bridges. But all was well that ended well, and the couple was happily together again for the first time since the previous November—except for Icky, who had been left behind with his aunts because of the hazards of travel.

Ike recalled, "This was a fine interlude and I decided that it would be nice, being in the West already, to apply for a leave with my family at the end of the tour—if indeed we ever reached the end." Mamie agreed with the idea but informed him that quarters or no quarters, she was going to join him at Fort Meade even if they had to live in a tent.

With the conclusion of the convoy, it was time for Ike to rejoin the regular army. But first he traveled to Denver for a four-week leave, near the end of which he accompanied the Douds on their annual journey to San Antonio. Delayed by rain and muddy roads in Lawton, Oklahoma,

Ike and Mr. Doud strengthened their rapport by keeping up with the latest weather reports and the Major League Baseball World Series. Ike and his father-in-law, both of whom considered themselves experts on the sport, spent hours debating why the Chicago White Sox were not faring well against the Cincinnati Red Sox.

Again for Ike, an unexpected and otherwise trivial incident made a major impression. "The stories after each game, narrating the play, were strictly objective. But stark facts and objective reports could not give the whole story," he recalled. Ultimately, the "Black Sox" scandal revealed that several Chicago players had been paid to throw the series. Ike considered it "an all-time low for disloyalty and sellout of integrity."

The scandal did more than disappoint Ike. He later wrote, "I grew increasingly cautious about making judgments based solely on reports. Behind every human action, the truth may be hidden. But the truth may also lie behind some other action or arrangement, far off in time and place. Unless circumstances and responsibility demand an instant judgement, I learned to reserve mine until the last proper moment."

Many years later, poet Robert Frost presented a book of poetry to then President Eisenhower. On the flyleaf Frost wrote what was, and had been, central to Ike's leadership style: "The strong are saying nothing until they see."

CHAPTER 7

Fort Meade and George Patton

AFTER HIS THREE-MONTH ABSENCE, IKE REPORTED BACK TO FORT Meade in July 1919 to find that many changes had taken place since his departure. Senior tank officers from France had returned, and Brigadier General Samuel D. Rockenbach, armor leader on the western front, had replaced Colonel Ira C. Welborn as the commander of the Tank Corps.

Fellow officers described Rockenbach, an 1889 graduate of the Virginia Military Institute, as "solemn," "hard-bitten," "unimaginative," "narrow minded," "stolid," and "pompous." At the same time, they credited him with being even-tempered and hardworking. He was also well connected, being a favorite of (and having served under) General John J. Pershing, who had appointed him the Tank Corps commander in France.

Eisenhower never had the close, warm relationship with Rockenbach that he did with Welborn. Nevertheless, he listened and learned from the general's experiences with the first American tanks on the western front.

At Meade, Rockenbach integrated the men he brought back from Europe with the trainees Ike delivered from Camp Colt to form two tank brigades. Ike assumed command of the 305th Heavy Brigade, which was armed with American-manufactured Mark VIII tanks that had finally come off the assembly line in the early postwar months. Colonel George Patton, West Point Class of 1909, who had served in France with Rockenbach and led the first American tank attack on the western front, commanded the other brigade, the 304th, which was equipped with French Renaults.

Despite Patton being five years older and having entered the regular army six years before Ike, the two quickly formed a close relationship that was both professional and personal. There is no evidence that Ike envied Patton or that the senior lieutenant colonel looked down on the junior. They were simply colleagues and friends who mutually admired each other's insights and appreciation of tank warfare. Neither they nor any of their contemporaries would have speculated that Ike, the noncombat veteran, would someday surpass Patton, the hero of Mexico and France, in both rank and responsibility.

Eisenhower and Patton had much in common. Both had attended the U.S. Military Academy—Patton graduating in 1909 and Eisenhower in 1915—where they played on the football team and graduated in the middle of their respective classes. They shared a profound interest in military history and theory and the writing of Prussian general Carl von Clausewitz. Both officers excelled at (and were prolific in) writing reports as well as articles for professional journals. Both were extremely profane and yet so conservative that neither spelled out curse words in their journals, using the first letter followed by dashes, such as "h----" and "d----."

Both men also struggled with physical challenges. Each, vain about his personal appearance, worried about the loss of his hair. Had it been a competition, Ike would have clearly won. And each man faced his own health issue. Ike suffered from chronic digestive problems and a bad knee, while Patton fought to overcome dyslexia. Patton was also accident prone and, according to him, suffered some type of debilitating accident every two years or so. For example, at Fort Meade, his horse stumbled, throwing Patton forward on his saddle pomme, seriously injuring his groin, a wound requiring a monthlong rehab.

Interestingly, both men had married women from exceptionally wealthy families, a commonality that allowed them to indulge in pastimes that not every officer could afford—owning horses, hunting, practicing marksmanship, and playing poker.

As soldiers, the two officers shared a great pride in serving the army and their country. Their greatest commonality, however, was their belief that mechanization and mobility would characterize the next war. According to Ike, "From the beginning he and I got along famously. Both of us were students of current military doctrine. Part of our passion was a belief in tanks—a belief derided at the time by others."

Patton and Eisenhower were also polar opposites in some ways. Although both were dedicated and ambitious, Patton believed he was destined for stars on his shoulders and great success in future wars; he professed to believe that a soldier's greatest honor would be to die of the last bullet of the last battle, a grand and glorious sacrifice he undoubtably envisioned for himself. Eisenhower, by contrast, wished to be great in his impact but aspired to the more realistic goal of attaining the rank of full colonel.

Perhaps the most striking of all their differences was their backgrounds. The Patton family, hailing from Scotland, boasted of military service and sacrifice in every American war. George grew up in an extremely wealthy family and added to his means with his marriage. Patton had come into his own in the peach-and-magnolia-blossom South and then relocated to the orange and lemon groves of California, where he later claimed never to have wanted for anything. His appointment to West Point came through family political connections rather than competition with fellow cadet candidates.

In contrast, Eisenhower grew up in a family at the opposite end of the spectrum. Ike had never ventured more than a few hundred miles from central Kansas before attending West Point. Although his family was not totally impoverished, it was very much lower on the socioeconomic scale, necessitating that all the sons work outside the home from an early age. By his teenage years, Ike was doing the work of an adult. With the Eisenhower family having no political connections, Ike was left to gain his West Point appointment through a statewide competition. Another difference lay in their family relations. While Patton was close to and adored his father, Ike held his in distant regard.

The common factors and the distinct differences in these men melded to form a strong bond between them that enabled them to work well together. Much of the two officers' time was, of course, spent training their units. They often integrated these activities as they developed procedures and tactics for their tanks. Ike wrote, "We wanted speed, reliability, and firepower. We wanted armor that would be proof against machine guns and light field guns, but not so heavy as to damage mobility."

Field training was not without its dangers, even for lieutenant colonels. Once, while observing a larger tank tow a smaller one, the two officers barely escaped injury when a cable snapped. It whipped through the air, cutting brush and saplings as it passed near their heads. Neither said anything until that night at dinner, when Patton asked Ike whether he had been as scared as he was. Ike responded, "I was afraid to bring the subject up. We were certainly no more than five or six inches from sudden death."

On another occasion, following a lengthy session of firing machine guns to test which weapon would be best to have on their tanks, they ceased fire and went down range to check their targets. Suddenly an overheated .30-caliber machine gun began firing again from behind them in what is called a "cook off." Ike and Patton dove to the flank to get out of the way of the flying bullets and then quickly circled back to twist the belt on the gun so no more rounds could reach the firing chamber.

To further their education—and in preparation for future selection—Eisenhower and Patton requested copies of past tactical battle problems used for instruction at Fort Leavenworth's Command and General Staff School. After working out how they would solve those challenges, they compared their answers to the Leavenworth "school solution" and then integrated tanks into the problem to determine different—always positive—outcomes.

Eisenhower and Patton also continued their practical study of tanks. They disassembled a Renault "item by item until there was no nut or bolt that had not been removed from the mechanism." With parts all over the garage floor, they quickly discovered that taking a tank apart was much easier than putting it back together. After hours of reassembly, they finally had the tank operational again, as Ike proudly noted, "with no pieces left over."

Both Eisenhower and Patton wrote their analyses of armor warfare in their military and branch journals, advancing the advantages of tanks for the future. The reaction they received was not what they desired or expected. Major General Frank L. Sheets, chief of the Infantry Branch, called Ike into his office and told him his ideas were wrong and danger-ous. The infantry chief, who controlled the assignment of every infantry officer, ordered Ike to cease publishing "anything incompatible with solid infantry doctrine." Once again, Ike had harmed, rather than helped, his career by trying to be innovative in anticipating the future of warfare.

According to Eisenhower, Patton received a similar message from the cavalry branch. Neither was pleased with the responses but had no choice other than to salute smartly and comply with the orders. Privately they blew off steam in railing against the orders. Ike wrote, "With George's temper and my own capacity for something more than mild irritation, there was surely more steam around the Officer's Quarters than at the post laundry."

Mamie joined Ike early in his tour at Camp Meade and stayed in a dingy apartment in nearby Laurel. Having left Icky behind with her sisters and then finding that she saw her husband only a couple of nights a week, Mamie decided to return to San Antonio until Ike could find a better place to live.

Patton's wife, Beatrice, moved into a Washington, DC, townhouse. A few months later, the post commander authorized use of a wartime troop barracks for family housing with the stipulation that all renovating, remodeling, and furnishing would be at the expense of the resident. Ike and George, assisted by enlisted men they hired during off-duty hours, went to work and soon had spaces in good-enough shape to send for their wives. Mamie arrived to find freshly painted quarters with an ade-quate kitchen and even a white painted fence around a small yard.

Mamie and Beatrice became friends but were never particularly close. Their differences outweighed their similarities. Both came from wealth, but Beatrice's family fortune far exceeded Mamie's, resulting in her receiving a larger allowance each month than Mamie. Dorothy Brandon, in her biography of Mamie, explained, "The close friendship between Ike and George Patton was never matched by their wives. Mamie's interest in sports was as a spectator at football games; her reading was confined largely to current events, and an occasional novel. Although her family had better than average means, she had not traveled widely like Beatrice Patton, nor had she associated with internationally famous people.

Mamie's orbit was domesticity. Her sparkle, wit, and charm, her laughter, keen card sense and entertaining music, all made her the popular wife of a popular officer." When Mamie insisted that Beatrice's daughters call her by her nickname, Beatrice was somewhat irritated because the familiarity made Mamie seem glamorous and sophisticated to the girls.

At Camp Meade, Mamie was busy becoming "a good army wife." She later expressed regret that she too often returned to her parents' homes in Denver and San Antonio when proper quarters were not available or when other difficulties hindered a comfortable life.

Not long after getting their families settled in Maryland, both Patton and Eisenhower faced major readjustments in their own careers when Congress passed into law the National Defense Act on June 4, 1920. This bill decentralized the procurement and acquisitions process for equipment, weapons, supplies, and vehicles and reorganized the army into the regular army, the National Guard, and the organized reserve. More important, as least for Ike, the act reduced the number of authorized enlisted men and officers, meaning that officers temporarily promoted in large numbers during the World War I demand were to be reduced back to their permanent ranks. On June 30, Ike traded in his lieutenant colonel's silver oak leaf for the silver bars of a captain. Two days later, because of his previous time in grade as a captain, he received permanent promotion to major—a rank he would hold for sixteen years until his next promotion.

George Patton also was reduced in rank, but he, too, was permanently promoted to major on July 1—making him senior to Ike by one day; he would hold this rank for the next fourteen years. Neither Ike nor George was greatly tormented by the rank change because these reductions were occurring throughout the army, with nearly everyone changing the rank insignia on their shoulders overnight. That pay and allowances continued at the old temporary rank made the reduction more acceptable.

The part of the National Defense Act that concerned Eisenhower and Patton more than their rank reductions was that, while establishing the Army Air Service and the Chemical and Finance branches, the law abolished the Tank Corps as a separate branch and placed it back under the infantry command. Thus, Ike rejoined the infantry while remaining at

Fort Meade, and Patton returned to the cavalry, transferring on October 1 to the 3rd Regiment at Fort Myer, Virginia.

Patton certainly had significant influence on Ike and vice versa. Their friendship and professional relationship would endure far into the future. In addition to what he learned from Patton himself, Ike benefited from his friend's professional connections. One evening in September 1919—back before the Tank Corps had been dismantled—Mamie and Ike joined the Pattons for dinner with their guest Brigadier General Fox Conner. Patton and Conner had met during the Punitive Expedition into Mexico and became close while serving on General Pershing's American Expeditionary Force (AEF) staff. A Mississippi-born West Point Class of 1898 graduate, Conner had acted as General Pershing's operations officer (G-3) in World War I, causing Pershing later to write about this subordinate, "Your broad conception of our task and your able counsel in all our organization, as well as your clear vision of the strategy of our operations, stand out vividly in my memory." He had concluded that there was no better man in the AEF.

Conner believed the armistice that ended the Great War would do little to prevent future hostilities, making a second worldwide conflict inevitable. He thought that instead of debating or dissecting the last war, the army should be preparing for the next.

After dinner, Conner said he would like to see the schools the two men had formed and to hear their ideas about tanks. About this interest, Ike wrote, "This was meat and drink to George and me."

During his visit, Conner directed most of his questions at Ike, some calling for only brief answers while others required lengthy explanations. Conner made few comments, but Ike realized that he "was one of the Army 'brains'" and that his interest was not perfunctory. At the end of the day, Connor thanked the two junior officers for their time and departed with no indication that there would be any follow-up. But Ike knew he had made an impression.

A few months later, the general contacted Ike, informing him that he was about to depart for Panama to command an infantry brigade and offering Ike the executive officer position. Ike was ecstatic. With the

Tank Corps on hold or ignored altogether, this was the opportunity to get back to a troop assignment and to learn from one of the army's best.

Ike immediately went to Rockenbach, the Tank Corps commander, to request a transfer to Panama, but the general said Ike could not be spared because he was one of the few experienced field officers in the unit. He did, however, agree to forward the petition to Washington. The War Department, still not happy about Ike's article promoting tanks, turned down the request. Disappointed, Ike once again had no choice other than to salute smartly and "continue the march." It would not, however, be the last he heard from Conner.

In addition to needing to retain Ike's tank expertise, Rockenbach had another motive for saying he "could not be spared": Ike was to coach the post's football team in his off-duty hours. When Ike once again excelled, Rockenbach recognized him for his "splendid efforts," as did other senior officers. Such praise was pleasing to Ike, but he knew that coaching eleven players on the gridiron, as well as training troops and performing staff work, would not lead to higher rank and responsibility. Still, coaching teams with uneven skills and experienced players provided Ike with even more practice in the tactical and strategic arts involved in achieving victories—whether he realized it at the time or not.

Ike and Mamie did their best to make Fort Meade as pleasant as possible despite Ike's disappointment over not joining Conner in Panama. He wrote, "Barracks or not, Mamie, Icky, and I settled down to a fuller family life than we'd ever known."

To add a bit of comfort and color to their apartment, the Eisenhowers began to collect Oriental rugs, acquisitions most other officers could not afford but that brightened the bleak quarters. Ike also found ways to occupy his off-duty time. Remaining a "Kansas boy" at heart, he turned to gardening, which had provided him with satisfaction as a boy. At Fort Meade, he found tilling the soil relaxing—he continued the pastime during future assignments whenever possible. Gardening even occupied his mind during the off season. He wrote, "For years, I read through many a winter's evening with the Burpee's catalogue in my lap." While his plants were growing, he was so diligent in protecting them from birds, rabbits, and other vermin that, later in his career, some of his fellow officers said that he showed the same diligence in winning World War II as he did in protecting his garden.

Ike also spent his off-duty time continuing to read Western books and pulp magazines. He never explained whether he enjoyed the stories because he identified with their "white hat" heroes or simply admired their good-versus-evil themes. Perhaps he used them as escapism from his daily challenges. Whatever the reason, his interest in the "Old West" never wavered throughout his life.

Poker remained an important pastime for Ike while at Fort Meade. Several members of his staff attended the twice-weekly games, at which only bachelor officers or the few married men who could afford to lose their money at the table, like themselves, were usually allowed. There were, however, many willing officers at Fort Meade awaiting discharge with time and money on their hands, and Ike and the local players made exceptions for them and their cash.

Ike was a formidable player, following the old maxim of fourteenth-century Persian poet Hafiz: "If he being young and unskillful / plays for shekels or silver and gold / take his money my son praising Allah / the fool was made to be sold." When a particularly poor player lost all his money one night, Ike pressed the advantage by lending him markers and winning even more. The next morning, the officer reported to Ike's office to ask whether he would accept government bonds to cover his losses. Ike agreed, only to discover they were "baby bonds" that the officer's wife had saved during the time her husband had been serving in France.

The payment depressed Ike, making him "feel like a dog." He approached the other regulars of the game, and they agreed to let the officer "win" back his losses in their next session. At night's end, they had managed to allow the officer to recoup his dignity as well as his cash.

Ike arranged for the officer's commander to issue an order against gambling. He could only laugh to himself when the officer later told him, "Isn't that just my luck—just as I was started on a real winning streak."

The incident changed Ike's mind about the game: "I decided that I had to quit playing poker. It was not because I didn't enjoy the excitement of the game—I really loved to play. But it had become clear that it was no game to play in the Army. Most of us lived on our salaries. Most losers were bound to be spending not only their own money but their families'. . . . [N]ow I felt that it was a bad idea—and from then on I did not play with anybody in the Army."

Ike later wrote, "If Meade was at times frustrating, it was also a school where I gained additional experience in handling men and in studying weapons." It would also be a period when Ike faced great heartbreak and a threatened end to his career in uniform.

Ike doted on his son. During his journey across the country with the Motor Convoy, he had frequently called Mamie to inquire about Icky's growth and whatever mischief he was getting into. After Icky and Mamie joined him at Fort Meade, the boy became the center of Ike's attention. Ike had a small uniform made for his son and took him to his office, to training sites, and to parades. Icky stood cheering on the sidelines during football practices and games. Members of the tank brigade quickly adopted Icky as their mascot.

The final months of 1920, in their improvised quarters at Fort Meade, were some of the happiest and most blissful in the young Eisenhowers' marriage. As Christmas approached, Ike purchased a tree, and Mamie went into Washington, DC, to shop—her purchases including a bright red tricycle for Icky. Since Ike had recently paid off some debts, the couple was finally financially able to employ a housekeeper. He hired a local girl who, unknown to him, had just recovered from scarlet fever. She still carried the disease, however, and Icky became ill a week before Christmas.

Army doctors called in specialists from nearby Johns Hopkins, but they could only confirm the diagnosis and explain that there was no cure. The doctors were straightforward with the parents, stating that those stricken with the disease either "get well or you lose them." The doctors quarantined Icky in the post hospital, where Ike stood outside his son's room to wave at him through the window. Mamie remained in their quarters bedridden with a severe cold and migraines. Both turned to prayer.

Because his brother Milton had survived scarlet fever as a youth, Ike pinned his hopes on his son also being so fortunate. Such was not the case. Neither medical treatment nor prayer was successful. Icky died on January 2, 1921.

Ike's Tank Corps soldiers provided an honor guard to accompany Icky's small casket to the Baltimore rail station. From there his parents escorted him to Denver, where a funeral service was held in the Douds' music room—the very location of Ike and Mamie's wedding. They then buried him in the Douds' family plot, where his two young aunts already lay.

The Eisenhowers returned to Fort Meade to find that friends had already disposed of the Christmas tree and the red tricycle. The couple blamed themselves—and at times each other—for the loss of their son. The guilt each felt added to the blame and placed a greater strain on their marriage. Ike and Mamie became less communicative as they retreated into their own worlds of sorrow. While Icky's death created enormous tension between them, they were able to keep it from tearing the relationship apart. Each year on Icky's birthday, Ike sent Mamie a bouquet of yellow roses—their son's favorite color. Ike handled his sadness by increasing his already grueling work schedule; his contemporaries noted that he seemed hardened and less emotional.

Neither Ike nor Mamie ever talked or wrote much about the death of their son. Mamie later stated, "For a long time, it was as if a shining light had gone out of Ike's life. Throughout all those years that followed, the memory of those bleak days was a deep inner pain that never seemed to diminish much."

Decades passed before Ike recorded his own feelings. In *At Ease* he wrote, "This was the greatest disappointment and disaster in my life, the one I have never been able to forget completely. Today when I think of it, the keenness of our loss comes back to me as fresh and as terrible as it was in that long dark day soon after Christmas, 1920."

The approach of summer marked the sixth anniversary of Ike's service in the army. Although he had gained extensive experience in organizing and training troops, he was still better known to his superiors as an excellent football coach rather than as a field leader. For him, his accomplishments were far overshadowed by his disappointments. In addition to the loss of his son, Ike had missed service in the Great War and had been reduced in rank in the conflict's aftermath. But as bleak as things seemed, they were about to get worse. This time Ike was threatened with court-martial and dismissal from the service.

In June, Ike appeared as a witness in an investigation of a fellow officer who was accused of drawing an allowance for quarters for which he was not authorized. During his testimony, Ike realized that he himself had also received similar funds. He reported himself to the Fort Meade inspector general, who immediately opened an investigation into Ike's receiving unauthorized funds and—his more damaging breach—signing a false official statement.

Eisenhower outlined the incident and explained his actions in a letter to the adjutant general of the army dated June 17, 1921, stating:

> I have been informed by the Camp Inspector, that in his opinion I erroneously drew commutation for quarters for a dependent child from May 12, 1920, to Sept. 1, 1920. The circumstances are as follows: During this period mentioned I was on duty at this camp, which is considered as being in the field. On May 12, 1920, my wife came to this camp to live with me in quarters which were converted barracks. A great deal of labor, and personal expenditure was necessary before this building was rendered suitable for occupancy by an infant. Therefore, for the above mentioned I maintained an abode for Doud Dwight Eisenhower, who was my son. He was brought to this camp to live with me, on Sept. 1, 1920, whereupon I immediately ceased drawing commutation for a dependent. The abode I maintained for my son, who was totally dependent upon me for support, was at 706 Lafayette Street, Denver, Colorado.

Ike's self-confessions and explanation to the adjutant general hit a buzzsaw when the matter arrived in front of army inspector general (IG) Major General Eli A. Helmick, a native of Quaker, Indiana, and a Class of 1888 graduate of West Point. A veteran of the war in Cuba—where he received the Silver Star—and of the conflict in the Philippines, Helmick was a by-the-book officer who had commanded the 8th Infantry Division and the AEF's supply base at Brest during the war. In this position, he had earned the Distinguished Service Medal for exceptionally meritorious and distinguished services to the Government of the United States, in a duty of great responsibility during World War I. As Commanding General, Base Section No. 5, General Helmick has displayed brilliant administrative ability in successfully directing the manifold activities under his supervision. By his energy in expediting the completion of the various engineering projects necessitated by the enlargement of the Pontanezen Camp and the development of Brest as a foremost embarkation camp, he has rendered invaluable services to the American Expeditionary Forces.

Helmick responded to the adjutant general with a letter copied to Eisenhower, bearing a response that Ike had neither expected nor desired. Though the IG had nothing personal against the major, Helmick followed regulations and did what he thought was right. His response summarized the case and concluded:

a. That Major Dwight D. Eisenhower, Infantry, did submit vouchers for and did receive, from the United States, during the period May 12, 1920, to August 31, 1920, the sum of two hundred fifty and 67/100 dollars, well knowing that he was already in receipt of quarters, heat, and light in kind for himself and wife, from the United States, for the same period.

b. That Major Dwight D. Eisenhower, Infantry, did for the period May 12, 1920, to August 31, 1920, sign certificates as follows: I certify that the foregoing account is correct that payment transfer has not been received; that I have not been absent on leave, either sick or ordinary, during the period covered by this voucher, except as above stated, AND NEITHER I, MY FAMILY, NOR ANYONE DEPENDENT UPON ME HAS OCCUPIED PUBLIC QUARTERS, NOR BEEN FURNISHED HEAT AND LIGHT BY THE UNITED STATES DURING THE PERIOD FOR WHICH COMMUTATION OF HEAD AND LIGHT IS CHARGED [Helmick's emphasis] well knowing that his wife was occupying a public building as quarters and that he and his wife were actually receiving an allowance of heat and light from the

United States, in kind, during the entire period for which commutation was charged and received.

The inspector general then made his recommendations—measures that, if accepted, would end Ike's military career and possibly result in stockade time. He recommended that "Major Dwight D. Eisenhower, Infantry, be brought to trial upon charges based upon the facts as developed." He concluded that Ike's pay should be stopped until he repaid the amount "erroneously received."

On July 18, the army deducted the "erroneously received" amount from Ike's pay. His commander, Colonel Rockenbach, attempted to put an end to the investigation by issuing a verbal reprimand to Ike, but General Helmick insisted on strictly following procedures. The corps commander of the area containing Fort Meade also encouraged an end to the investigation, to no avail.

The inspector general continued to push for a court-martial and, on August 25, received the approval "by order of the secretary of war" to proceed. The IG broadened his investigation on November 1, to determine whether Ike had previously lied and falsified other documents, stating in a memo, "Major Eisenhower is a graduate of the Military Academy, of six years' commissioned service. That he should have knowingly attempted to defraud the government in this matter or, as he contends, that he was ignorant of the provisions of the laws governing commutation for dependents are alike inexplicable. Before submitting a recommendation as to whether or not he should be brought to trial on these charges, it is desirable to have a full statement of his pay accounts as to commutation for dependents that may or may not have been drawn by him in the past."

Helmick continued to prepare for the court-martial of Dwight Eisenhower. Although the army operated on regulations, and leaders like Helmick could demand strict adherence, one constant factor overrode this tenet: connections trump regulation, especially when the personalities involved wear a rank on their shoulders that demands their desires be met.

Fox Conner, promoted to regular army brigadier general and assigned as commander of the 20th Infantry Brigade in Panama, still wanted Ike as his executive officer. Conner sent a memo to General Pershing, who had recently assumed the duties of the army's chief of staff, stating his desire to have Eisenhower assigned to him because of his efficiency and because he was due for foreign service. Pershing turned to his staff and to Helmick and basically said, "Make it happen."

Pershing recognized Conner as the army's most able and influential officer. Besides serving together in France, the two military giants were personal friends. When he returned to the United States in 1919, following his welcome home ceremony, Pershing spent his three-week vacation with the Conners at their Adirondack retreat.

Helmick had begun his investigation under Army Chief of Staff General Peyton Marsh, a West Point classmate and friend, but the situation changed when Pershing ordered an end to the matter. In accordance with his code of strict rule following, however, Helmick did not withdraw without seeking a final pound of flesh.

On December 14, the inspector general wrote to the adjutant general, stating, "The 104th Article of War does not confer jurisdiction on commanding officers to administer disciplinary punishment for grave offenses. Therefore, since Major Eisenhower was charged with offenses of the gravest character for which he might not only be dismissed from the service but imprisoned, any action taken by his Commanding Officer under the 104th Article of War, in advance of preferment of these charges, may not legally be made the basis of a plea in bar of trial for the same offenses stated in informal charges."

Having made his statement, which revealed his personal and professional feelings, Helmick continued so as to be in compliance with his directions from General Pershing. He wrote, "The trial of Major Eisenhower is not recommended, however. While he was clearly not entitled to commutation for his son, there are no circumstances connected with his drawing same to indicate an intent to defraud the Government. Major Eisenhower's claims were made without ordinary prudence, but his frank avowal to the Inspector that he had drawn commutation for his son under the conditions stated must be weighed in his favor as showing a lack of knowledge on his part that his claims were false or fraudulent."

Although a court-martial was now off the table, Helmick and others in the War Department thought that further action, in the way of a letter of reprimand, should be taken. That letter, dated December 14 and signed by the War Department assistant chief of staff, Brigadier General J. H. McRae, was delivered to Ike through the chief of infantry. Prepared by Helmick, the letter also received editing by McRae. The assistant chief of staff was a longtime friend of Conner and may have included him in preparing the final copy. The letter stated:

> With respect to the charges preferred against you for violation of the 94th and 98th Articles of War, in that you did draw commutation of quarters, heat, and light for a dependent son while your lawful wife was resident with you at Camp Meade, Md. and did, with you, during the period for which commutation was drawn for your son, actually occupy public quarters, heating, and lighting from public funds, the decision of the Secretary of War is that you not be brought to trial on these charges but be reprimanded instead. In arriving at this decision, due weight has been given to your voluntarily subjecting yourself to investigation nearly a year after the commutation was drawn by you. Your admitted ignorance of the law, however, is to your discredit, and your failure to take ordinary precautions to obtain from proper authority a decision as to the validity of your claims, is, in an officer of your grade, likewise to your discredit. Opinions of the Judge Advocate General and decisions of the Comptroller General are appropriately published for the guidance of all officers. A failure to conform to these opinions and decisions has, in the present case, led to these grave charges being properly preferred against you.

The letter ended nearly six months of worry and concern for Ike. Although Helmick directed a copy to be placed in his record, the actual letter had no further impact. Rather, it became just another hurdle and challenge that Ike had to overcome before he became the Eisenhower of history.

Considering Ike's character, previous performance, and voluntary self-reporting, little doubt exists that the commutation issue was an oversight and misunderstanding on his part rather than a deliberate effort to defraud the government, especially when one considers that he was married to a very wealthy woman and money was not a major issue for them. That the army spent so much time on such a small amount of improper funding illustrates more about the status of the military than about Eisenhower's integrity. For one thing, between the world wars the peacetime army was small and its subsistence austere. More important, however, was the ethics question. Commissioned officers were held to a higher standard than their civilian counterparts. The ethos from West Point that an officer "did not lie, cheat, or steal" pervaded. While Helmick might have been a bit overzealous, he was following the written and unwritten policies of the time.

Ike continued to coach the corps area football team during the investigation. The corps commander, Major General C. J. Bailey, formally recognized Ike's coaching abilities. Bailey wrote that he felt "great gratification and pleasure," as well as "appreciation and thanks," for Ike's performance as coach. He concluded, "The clean sportsmanship, endurance, and fighting-to-the-finish spirit displayed on the field by your men was most considerable."

Another indication of the importance Ike's commanders placed on the investigation was that they allowed him to remain in command while the process was ongoing, treating him as if nothing were out of the ordinary. Colonel Rockenbach hosted a departure party for the Eisenhowers, at which the unit presented Mamie with a silver vase inscribed, "To the Mascot of the Tanks Corps Football Team," in tribute to their son. The colonel also provided his personal automobile and driver to the couple in their final days at Fort Meade, when their own car had already been sent to New York for transport to Panama.

Although he was confident in Ike's honesty and personally liked his subordinate, Rockenbach did not rate him as "superior," rather judging him above average in most areas in his final Camp Meade efficiency report. In the characteristics of tact and judgment, the colonel rated him as only average.

Ike makes no mention of the investigation in *At Ease*, summarizing instead the six months by writing that "orders came out of the blue" to proceed to the Canal Zone. He concluded, "What had happened? Fox

Conner, a warm friend of General Pershing, now the Chief of Staff, had informed the Chief that he wanted me as his staff officer. The red tape was torn to pieces, orders were issued, and I was to arrive at the new station by January of 1922."

General Conner never explained why he selected Ike as his executive officer and thus ended the investigation and possible court-martial. While Ike certainly had impressed the general during their brief visit at the Patton home, many officers equally capable and even more experienced could have handled the position. Speculation is that his support for Ike may have stemmed from empathy, in that he himself had missed the chance to fight in his "first war" when he did not participate in the Spanish-American War. Conner had also been investigated by the inspector general—in his case, over an amount of $583.26 that was ultimately deducted from his salary. Perhaps Conner simply felt an obligation to mentor a junior officer as he himself had been mentored. It is also conceivable that the visionary and astute Conner saw in Ike a man who could in the future lead the largest army in the most extensive war in world history.

For all practical purposes, the Eisenhower investigation disappeared into the files of history, being replaced by the more pressing issues of the country preparing to fight another war. Early Eisenhower biographers do not mention the investigation, and it was only when his presidential library and museum opened in Abilene that his records were made available. Even then, some biographers skipped this part of Ike's life altogether. Apparently, none ever questioned him or sought his comments on the whole incident.

No doubt Ike was embarrassed and somewhat humiliated by the investigation, which cast an unearned shadow on his integrity and honor. Perhaps knowing he had not intended any fraudulent action helped him through the crisis. While such an ordeal would have embittered many against the profession, Ike never wavered in the way he loved the army, believed in rules and regulations, and felt confident about his vindication. Ike's dedication to being a soldier far outweighed the impact of the investigation. He ultimately found that the difficulties served a purpose, which influenced how he handled internal problems for the rest of his career.

The manner in which the investigation concluded was itself a major lesson for Ike—vividly illustrating for him the significance of having friends in high places and teaching him that mentors not only informed but also, importantly, looked after the interests of their subordinates.

The Eisenhowers must have been relieved to depart an assignment that had brought so much personal and professional heartache. When writing about their move from Camp Meade, Ike downplayed and brushed over the pain they had endured while living there. His only reference to the post was to note that they had "meager" resources. He did not suggest that this situation was partly due to the reduction of his pay for the unauthorized quarters commutation. Ike wrote, "We suddenly developed an appetite for low-cost meals and museums where no entrance fee was charged. Finally, the great day arrived and we started on our first foreign tour of military service."

CHAPTER 8

Panama and Fox Conner

ON JANUARY 16, 1922, THE EISENHOWERS SAILED ABOARD THE SS *ST. Mihiel* for Panama. Ike's recent difficulties had left him somewhat distracted from his usual attention to detail and, for the first time, uninterested in military history. The telltale sign was that he recorded the name of the ship as *San Miguel* in his notes rather than the vessel's actual name commemorating one of the most important battles of World War I. Another indicator of his state of mind was his lack of distress on discovering that his Ford Model T, which he had taken pride in maintaining, had been damaged by storms and robbed of parts while lashed to the deck during the trip to the Canal Zone.

Ike commanded the enlisted detachment aboard the ship and attempted to "make life easier for men who were convinced that neither they nor the ship would survive the voyage." He and Mamie were initially assigned luxurious quarters, but when two senior officers came aboard, the Eisenhowers were bumped to a cramped, austere cabin that Ike likened to a sardine can. Because the officers were on personal (rather than official) business, the incident reinforced Ike's dislike of officers abusing their position for their own comfort. Despite the poor quarters, Ike later wrote with pride that regardless of the rough seas, neither he nor Mamie ever missed a meal because of sea sickness. Ike's memory, however, was inaccurate, because Mamie, who was pregnant, claimed that she had the worst case of sea sickness she ever had.

After a brief port call in Puerto Rico, the *St. Mihiel* and the Eisenhowers landed at the Atlantic entrance to the canal, where General Fox

Conner's aide met and escorted them across the isthmus by rail. When they reached Camp Gaillard, located approximately in the middle of the zone, they had to walk the final few hundred yards in the tropical heat to the camp. Though Mamie had visited Panama with her parents on vacation several years earlier, she had stayed at the best hotels, and Ike noted, "For Mamie that walk was the worst possible avenue of entry to a foreign station."

Things did not improve when they reached their quarters. Built more than a quarter century earlier by the French during their unsuccessful efforts to construct the canal, the two-story house stood on stilts planted in unstable ground along the Culebra Cut, where mudslides occasionally occurred. (Years later, the entire hillside, with its houses, would in fact slide into the canal after a heavy rainstorm.) The house had not been occupied for several years, and the jungle was reclaiming the property with vines and other vegetation. Its porch was near collapse, and the interior was damp, rife with mildew and mold. Lizards, cockroaches, spiders, rats, and bed bugs scurried about, while bats swept through the house in pursuit of mosquitoes. Ike fought back with his ceremonial saber, sweeping through the air in pursuit of his quarry.

The Eisenhowers briefly stayed in a Panama City hotel while workers attempted to make their quarters habitable. However, conditions were still so bad when they moved in that they had to place the legs of their bed in cans of kerosene to keep the various bugs from sharing their covers. The one positive feature about the home was that it stood next to that of the Conners.

Virginia Conner, known to her family as "Bug," was the consummate hostess and welcomed the Eisenhowers into her home—complete with a swimming pool and tennis courts no less. More important, she befriended Mamie and became her advisor and confidant, for she knew the experience that the new arrival was facing. For more than twenty years, Virginia, the daughter of a wealthy father who made his fortune in patent medicine, had been either following her husband around the world or waiting at home when he served unaccompanied tours. Mamie obviously was not happy. Virginia later recalled, "She made no bones about how mad she was that they had been ordered to such a post." Mamie later admitted that Virginia thought she was a "namby-pamby."

The Eisenhower marriage suffered as a result of the adverse living conditions and the isolation of the area. Both still grieved the loss of their son, and as neither had fully adjusted to married life in the military, they sought solace in other sources. Ike dedicated himself even more to his work, while Mamie, like most army wives, attempted to adapt despite the boredom and lack of activities she preferred. Mostly, she felt that she had no life of her own. Ike wrote, "Although Mamie did a little horseback riding, she never has and never will consider outdoor sports a worthwhile way to spend her time. During our Canal Zone tour, there was little to find in the way of entertainment, except a dance on Friday night and a club bridge party on Wednesday."

Mamie did join other wives on shopping trips into Panama City, where she purchased items for their house—often buying them directly off arriving boats. She also helped establish a maternity hospital for the wives of the enlisted men and made plans to give birth there herself.

Virginia Conner recognized Mamie's malaise and the mounting difficulties in her marriage. According to Virginia, "The marriage was clearly in danger. They were two young people who were drifting apart. Ike was spending less and less time with Mamie, and there was no warmth between them. They seemed like two people moving in different directions."

Virginia attempted to spice up the marriage by encouraging Mamie to bob her hair, update her wardrobe, and "vamp" her husband. Mamie later noted that she did cut her hair, albeit not to follow the prevailing fashion or to impress her husband, but rather for comfort in the tropical heat.

As Mamie was making efforts to adjust, her parents visited Panama in May. Taken aback by the living conditions and tropical climate, they insisted Mamie accompany them back to Denver to give birth to the baby, which she did.

Ike secured leave and joined Mamie in Denver for the birth of their son, John Doud, on August 3, 1922. He wrote, "While his arrival did not, of course eliminate the grief we still felt—then and now—he was precious in his own right and he did much to take our minds off the tragedy. Living in the present with a healthy baby boy can take parents' minds off almost anything."

Mamie returned to Panama in November with John and a nurse, Kathrine Herrick—provided by her father—who would stay with the family for the next four years. Mamie, however, soon fell into a malaise, finding the Canal Zone no more to her liking than on her previous visit. She continued to disdain the tropical weather and lack of entertainment, but, more important, she resented the time Ike spent at work and with Fox Conner. In addition, she suffered digestive problems and insomnia, lost weight, and lived in fear of John contracting some tropical disease. Virginia again noted that the Eisenhowers seemed to be "drifting apart."

Against Ike's wishes, Mamie, with the baby and nurse, fled back to Denver after only a few months. She later recalled, "I was down to skin and bones and hollow-eyed; so ill I'd have to walk all night long. The porch was screened on three sides and I would walk all night listening to the mosquitoes buzz. I could hear the monkeys scream in the jungle and I felt like screaming too. I don't know what it was, but there was something about the tropics that got me. I just could not sleep—I would walk and walk. It was terrible. My health and vitality seemed to ebb away. I don't know how I existed."

This stay in Denver resulted in far more than a recovery of good health and resumption of social interactions, proving to be a turning point in Mamie's opinions and perspectives about Ike and the army. Her granddaughter Susan Eisenhower later wrote:

> Under the watchful eyes of her parents, Mamie's health improved and she started to see old friends and classmates again. She could not help but notice how her girlfriends were living: theirs were lives she could understand. These women had husbands who quit working at dinnertime and spent evenings with their families. They were bankers, lawyers, and doctors who led predictable lives in clean, safe places. But as Mamie began to feel better, she was able to take a harder look at the men themselves. As secure and stable as their lives seemed to be, Mamie realized she would not want to be married to any one of them—she missed Ike. And she had finally outgrown home.

Susan continued, "Mamie understood that to stay married to Ike she would have to complain less about circumstances and accommodate to her husband's career needs more. If that meant endless hours alone, she would have to adjust; there could be no other way. She would also have to make a greater effort to enter into whatever part of his life was open to her. She would have to learn to share at least some of his recreational interests, even if that meant a special effort to become sportier or more companionable."

Mamie returned to Panama with renewed dedication to Ike and their marriage. She later said, "I knew almost from the day I married Ike that he would be a great soldier. He was always dedicated, serious, and purposeful about his job. Nothing came before his duty. I was forced to match his spirit of personal sacrifice as best I could."

Virginia Conner noted, "I had the delight of seeing a rather callow young woman turn into a person to whom everyone turned. I have seen her, with her gay laugh and personality, smooth out Ike's occasional irritability."

In Ike's memoir, he made no mention of angst about his and Mamie's difficulties. Instead, he wrote, "My tour of duty was one of the most interesting and constructive of my life. The main reason was the presence of one man, General Fox Conner."

While Ike and Mamie stabilized their marriage to form a lasting team, Conner provided the influence and teachings that prepared Ike for the future. As the commander of the 20th Infantry Brigade, Conner was responsible for the defense of the Panama Canal—a facility critical to commercial shipping in peacetime and the movement of navies in time of war. Despite its importance, however, the poorly financed and manned army had limited assets to fulfill the mission.

Conner was convinced that the war to end all wars, the Great War, was anything but final. He foresaw another global conflict of far greater scope than the trench-bound World War I, and he wanted to prepare the small standing army of the United States as best possible.

Although his brigade was authorized three or four regiments, it had only one—a poorly trained and disciplined unit made up of Puerto Rican enlisted men with North American officers. Conner, with Ike at his side, immediately began a training program that emphasized marksmanship and maneuver. To combat the high rate of venereal disease among the troops, they initiated preventative measures and implemented severe penalties for those who continued to contract the malady. When not in the field with their soldiers, the two rode horseback up and down the canal to determine the best defensive positions and routes to move troops. They often remained in the jungle overnight discussing tactics over a campfire.

Ike noted in *At Ease*, "One change in my attitude he accomplished quickly—with profound and endless results." When Conner discovered Ike no longer had much interest in military history, he invited him into his extensive home library. He initially encouraged Ike to read several novels. When Ike returned the books, Conner asked whether he might be interested in the armies of the period. Ike responded in the affirmative, and his education began in a library he described as "magnificent."

Ike read the biographies of great military leaders as well as the works of Plato, Tacitus, Nietzsche, and Shakespeare. Conner insisted Ike reread Prussian general Carl von Clausewitz's masterful *On War*, first published in 1832, because he himself adhered to many of Clausewitz's theories and thought they provided an excellent basis for preparation for the next war. This knowledge was what he wanted to pass along to Ike.

Ike was ready to absorb the wisdom. In his writings, Clausewitz advocated viewing war and politics as one, maintaining that warfare must remain under the direction of the political leaders to achieve its objectives. He summarized this dictum: "War is the continuation of politics by other means." Ike was persuaded.

He also paid close attention to the readings when Clausewitz attempted to explain military operations as a science, emphasizing the concept of "friction," which he defined as the fatigue, minor errors, and luck or chance that cause good plans to yield failure instead of success. Ike also found value when the master of war added that, to achieve any gain, one must always base theory on fact and noted that seemingly easy objectives may very well prove difficult, if not impossible.

Ike found that throughout his writings, Clausewitz stressed that the primary mission of an army must be to engage and destroy the enemy's main force in a decisive battle. A general strategy should focus on the ultimate destruction of the opposing army.

Clausewitz recognized that for a general to win decisive battles and, in turn, achieve political objectives, subordinate commanders, as well as their soldiers, must believe in their cause and possess a high degree of morale. In *On War* he wrote, "A powerful emotion must stimulate the great ability of a military leader, whether it be ambition as in Caesar; hatred of the enemy, as in Hannibal; or the pride of glorious defeat, as in Frederick the Great. Open your heart to such emotion, determine to find a glorious end, and fate will crown your youthful brow with a shining glory, which is the ornament of princes, and engrave your image in the hearts of your last descendants." Ike found the instructions relevant to his own situation.

Ike also studied and was influenced by the writings of Dennis Hart Mahan, West Point Class of 1824 and later head of the Academy's engineering department, who had strong opinions on land warfare. Mahan advocated training of the state militias and using combined arms on the battlefield, believing that, rather than having the infantry fight battles with the support of artillery and cavalry, the three should function under a unified command. He rejected the concept of limited warfare. Once a country was at war, he believed, it should take maximum decisive action to achieve quick victory and an advantageous peace. Mahan's son, Alfred Thayer Mahan, became a navy admiral and the leading naval theorist of the nineteenth century.

To impress on Eisenhower his own lessons learned, Conner combined the teachings of Clausewitz with his observations on the Great War to form concise rules of warfare. He imparted to Ike three principles of war to achieve victory: "Never fight unless you have to, never fight alone, and never fight for long."

Ike noted in his memoirs that his mentor was an excellent teacher as well as "a natural leader and something of a philosopher." Conner also passed along two axioms that Ike said he later used "hundreds, if not thousands of times": "Always take your job seriously, never yourself" and "All generalities are false, including this one."

Although most of their interaction, especially early on, was teacher-student, the relationship advanced to one of colleagues who could disagree and seriously argue about different topics. Virginia Conner recognized their closeness and shared her thoughts at the time about the future, later writing, "I never saw two men more congenial than Ike and my husband. They spent hours discussing wars, past and future. Fox had always felt that the Versailles peace treaty had been the perfect breeder of a new war that would take place in about twenty years. Gradually Ike became convinced that Fox was right." Although Conner recognized that Ike wrote well, he demanded that he improve his skills by writing and issuing a daily field order for the brigade's operation.

Not all their time together was spent on work or study. They often went fishing, where Ike used angler skills learned in Kansas to bring home the catch. Conner, by contrast, was a master on the tennis court and attempted to teach Eisenhower the game, but this time the student never became anywhere near proficient. Because missed balls often brought out his temper, Ike soon hung up his racket and once again picked up a deck of cards. As an experienced poker player, Ike found bridge much more to his liking, his remarkable memory and calculation of chances allowing him to quickly master the game.

Conner also spent much time emphasizing to Eisenhower the importance of working with allies. Ike later remarked:

> He laid great stress to me on what he called "the art of persuasion." Since no foreigner could be given outright administrative command of troops of another nation, they would have to be coordinated very closely and needed persuasion. He would get out a book of applied psychology and we would talk it over. How do you get allies of different nations to march and think as a nation? There is no question about his molding my thinking on this from the time I was thirty-one. I would not say that his views had a specific influence on my conduct of SHAEF (Supreme Headquarters, Allied Expeditionary Force), but his forcing me to think about these things gave me preparation that was unusual in the army at that time.

Conner provided Eisenhower with not only theories but also practical advice. The general encouraged Ike to seek out the opportunity to serve with George Marshall, whom he described as "the ideal soldier" and "nothing short of genius." His highest praise for Ike was to say, "You handled that just the way Marshall would have done." Conner did not directly say so, but he clearly already saw the Marshall-Eisenhower duo as the leaders and victors of the next war.

When Marshall visited Conner in Panama, Ike was away on leave. Although both Eisenhower and Marshall denied being introduced until 1930, they were certainly aware of each other long before that time.

Ike later wrote, "General Fox Conner was a practical officer, down to earth, equally at home in the company of the most important people in the region and with any of the men in the regiment. He never put on airs of any kind, and he was as open and honest as any man I have ever known. . . . I served as his brigade exec for three years in Panama and never enjoyed any other three-year period as much. He has held a place in my affections for many years that no other, not even a relative could obtain."

Those last words are telling in many ways. Although Ike loved his father for taking care of his family and admired his work ethic, they were never close. Conner fulfilled the role of not only mentor but also father figure. Mamie later observed, "No man can make a successful career on his own. He needs help. And Ike was fortunate to have sponsors such as Fox Conner and later MacArthur and General Marshall who pushed him ahead."

Ike concluded, "It is clear now that life with General Conner was a sort of graduate school in military affairs and the humanities, leavened by the comments and discourses of a man who was experienced in his knowledge of men and their conduct. I can never adequately express my gratitude to this one gentleman, for it took years before I fully realized the value of what he had led me through. . . . [I]n a lifetime of association with good and great men, he is the one more or less invisible figure to whom I owe an incalculable debt."

Conner did more than just prepare Ike for the future. He saw, with the help of General John J. Pershing, that Ike's Distinguished Service

Medal recommendation for his service at Camp Colt during the war was finally approved. Conner personally pinned the medal on Ike before a parade by the 20th Infantry Regiment.

In his final efficiency report for Ike in 1924, Conner wrote that Eisenhower was "one of the most capable, efficient and loyal officers I have ever met." Many biographers and historians award Conner the title of "the man who made Eisenhower." Their evaluation is absolutely correct. Without the mentorship of Fox Conner, there is little doubt that Ike would not have become first General Eisenhower and then President Eisenhower.

Not everyone in the Canal Zone was as taken with Eisenhower's performance as Conner. Because many of the brigade's officers saw Panama as a backwater assignment where the largest challenges should be dealing with the tropical heat and insects, they resented Conner and Ike's passion for efficiency and demand that regulations be followed. They also understandably saw Ike as Conner's privileged protégé, even referring to him as a martinet and the general's pet.

An example of Ike's unrelenting demands for proficiency came when he overheard several officers speak disparagingly about the Browning automatic rifle (BAR). Ike immediately issued orders that every officer in the camp shoot and train with the BAR, requiring that they all qualify with the automatic weapon. While the staff complained, the BAR drilling was an example of Ike's understanding of the need to prepare for what might be coming their way. Although not officially adopted by the army until 1938, the BAR became admired and respected as an essential part of every infantry squad's weaponry during World War II and in the Korean conflict.

Conner and Ike were indeed harsh with their subordinates—neither caring about popularity and both believing they must train the officers and troops under their command for the inevitable next war.

Not surprisingly, the longest story in Ike's *At Ease* is about his time in Panama. Much of the account is about his selection, training, and adventures riding "a big, coal-black gelding a bit over sixteen hands" that he acquired for "transportation." Ike named the horse Blackie and concluded, "The tutoring by Fox Conner and the rewards of working with Blackie were important to me in Panama."

Along with Blackie came his Puerto Rican groom, Private Rafael "Lopez" Carattini, who worked closely with Ike in training and taking care of the horse. Lopez remained in the army after his time in Panama and, by the end of World War II, wore the stripes of a first sergeant. In May 1945, he wrote his old commander, reminding him of their time in Panama. On June 1, the then supreme Allied commander took the time to answer, writing respectfully, "I remember you as well as if our days in Panama were only a few months rather than twenty years behind us. I wish I could have Blackie with me now. Moreover, all the things you mentioned in your letter almost made me homesick for the days we were riding the jungle trails together. I am delighted that you have reached the grade of first sergeant."

Eisenhower found that training his horse influenced his understanding of the value of the process greatly: "In teaching skills, in developing self-confidence, the same sort of patience and kindness is needed with horses as with people." He continued, "In my experience with Blackie— and earlier with allegedly incompetent recruits at Camp Colt—is rooted my enduring conviction that far too often we write off a backward child as hopeless, a clumsy animal as worthless, a worn-out field as beyond restoration. This we do largely out of our own lack of willingness to take the time and spend the effort to prove ourselves wrong: to prove that a difficult boy can become a fine man, that an animal can respond to training, that the field can regain fertility." He concluded, "Long after Camp Colt and Panama, when I observed the young soldiers arriving in Europe, thousands of whom in appearance and attitude were evidently victims of heedless homes and a heedless society and were now expected to assault and destroy the Nazi elite, I determined that someday I would seek the opportunity to help correct this neglect."

In September 1924, Conner received orders to return to Washington, DC, where he would assume the duties of the army's chief of staff for supply. Ike was also due for assignment back in the States and requested that he attend the U.S. Army Infantry School at Fort Benning or, even better, skip that step and go directly to the Command and General Staff

School at Fort Leavenworth. Conner, who had also not attended his branch school, supported Ike's desire to go to Leavenworth and endorsed his efforts in his final efficiency report, writing that Eisenhower should attend "on account of his natural and professional abilities."

On August 13, 1924, Ike formally requested by letter to the army adjutant general (AG) that his next assignment be as a student in the Command and General Staff School. The AG turned down the request. Ike wrote, "I could dream about the orders until they arrived. Then I came back to earth with a thump. Back into the rut I had started to dig for myself a decade earlier. I was ordered back to Meade—to help coach a football team."

CHAPTER 9

Command and General Staff School

In September 1924, the Eisenhowers arrived at Fort Meade and settled into the same quarters they had renovated several years earlier. It must have been difficult for them, with every room, corner, and window bringing back memories of Icky. Reminders of the inspector general's investigation and possible court-martial also haunted the place. Even so, Ike's years in uniform and nearly as many as husband and wife had taught the couple to accept what nature dealt them and what the army demanded of them.

Ike never learned who had requested he join the football staff, describing it as a "cosmic top-secret wonder." The best he could determine was that some unidentified senior officer or officers at the War Department had tired of annually losing to the Quantico Marine Corps team. The solution was to transfer in the army's five superior coaches not only to achieve victory but also to improve the image of the army. Apparently that was as far as the planning of the ultimate army football team progressed, because no provisions existed to recruit players other than the troops stationed at Meade. Ike and his fellow coaches, all of whom he had known at West Point or during previous assignments, enjoyed having easy days with no duties other than coaching football.

In trying to rationalize himself into acceptance of once again being a coach, Ike journaled, "The War Department moves in mysterious ways its blunders to perform." Even more frustrating for him was that he was not the head coach but only an assistant in charge of the backfield. Acknowledging that he was "hardly a first-rate coach," he continued to rely on the system he had learned at West Point, with few innovations. He did try to find a "good passer" to open up the game.

Although well coached, the army team did poorly. "The players tried hard. We seldom won," wrote Ike. Against a half dozen small area colleges, the army eleven achieved victory only once. In the season finale, they fell to the Marine Corps team 20–0. The players returned to their units, and the coaches reported to new assignments.

Ike's efficiency report for his coaching duties rated him as merely average. His only reward was the dubious opportunity to remain at Meade and command the same battalion of tanks he had led on his previous tour. Not wanting to take another step backward, he went to see the chief of infantry in Washington, DC, to request assignment to the Command and General Staff School. Ike, aware that he was not in good standing with the infantry because of his previous criticisms and his numerous desk assignments, noted, "I should have known better; he refused even to listen to my arguments."

Mamie and Ike journeyed to Denver, with a brief stop in Abilene, on official leave to await further orders. Whenever stationed within the States, Ike visited Abilene at least once a year. While in Kansas, he did not just visit family and friends and eat his mother's cooking. Using the same skills he had employed to renovate their quarters at Fort Meade, he made improvements to the Eisenhower family home. On one visit, he built a rose arbor for the backyard, and then, over the ensuing years, he painted the barn, poured the foundation for a porch, and added a sidewalk.

Shortly after their arrival in Denver, a cryptic telegram arrived from Fox Conner, stating, "No matter what orders you receive from the War Department, make no protest. Accept them without question."

"For several days I was in a quandary until orders arrived," Ike recalled. "Normally, they would have been so difficult to accept that it was well I had advance warning." The orders relieved Ike from the infantry and assigned him to recruiting duty. He continued, "To be assigned to the recruiting service in those days, unless it was to meet an immediate and temporary personal requirement of an officer, was felt by most of us to be a rebuke a little less devastating than a reprimand."

Disappointed and somewhat confused, Ike nevertheless had faith in Conner and accepted the orders without protest. The only factor that made the assignment palatable was that it called for Ike's recruitment duty to be performed a mere eight miles from downtown Denver at Camp Logan.

Ike and Mamie spent much of their off-duty time with the Douds in the home where they had married and held the funeral service for their son. Youthful and very social, the Douds included the Eisenhowers in their entertainment events and activities. Mamie enjoyed the assignment, especially the close proximity to her family and the free time that Ike had. Whenever possible, the Eisenhowers also joined the Douds in their somber Sunday ritual before church, which was to visit the cemetery and place flowers on the graves of the two daughters they had lost and on that of little Icky.

Because recruiting duty was not taxing, Ike had time to contemplate the issues related to getting into the Command and General Staff School. The problem was not his performance or qualifications, for ratings from his superior were "average" and "superior" with comments declaring him "a splendid officer" and "exceptionally efficient." Finally, a letter arrived from Conner that explained his behind-the-scenes maneuvering on Ike's behalf. Because an infantry officer could not get assigned to Fort Benning or to the Command and General Staff School without the approval of the branch chief—an officer who did not hold Ike in high esteem—Conner had arranged Ike's temporary transfer from the infantry to the Adjutant General's Corps because the chief there, who controlled recruiting, was Conner's West Point classmate. Ike had initially felt disappointed in himself for deserting his branch, but with his solid belief in Fox Conner, he kept his displeasure in check. He later recalled, "Under this arrangement, a final order came to me which said that I had been selected by the Adjutant General as one of his quota of officers to go to the Command and General Staff School at Fort Leavenworth. I was to arrive there in August 1925."

Ike wrote, "I was ready to fly—and needed no airplane." Along with feeling jubilant, he thoroughly understood the circumstances of his success:

To the cynic, all this may seem proof of "It's not *what* you know, it's *who* you know." There is just enough truth in that phrase to assure its survival so long as humans must save face or nurse an ego. Certainly, had I been denied the good fortune of knowing Fox Conner, the course of my career might have been radically different. Because I *did* know him, I did go to Leavenworth. And I must confess that the school there, a watershed in my life, might not have been half so professionally profitable to me had I gone there years later on the schedule the Chief of Infantry thought suitable.

He added, "But on this business of who you know, a one-minute lecture to any young person who may read these words: Always try to associate yourself closely with and learn as much as you can from those who know more than you, who do better than you, who see more clearly than you. Don't be afraid to reach upward. Apart from the rewards of friendship, the association might pay off at some unforeseen time—that is only an accidental by-product. The important thing is that the learning will make you a better person."

When exhilaration from his selection for Leavenworth calmed, Ike began to have concerns, if not doubts, about his actual qualifications. He had not attended the preparatory instruction at the Infantry School, and he feared his going to Command and General Staff School without first attending branch instruction would be like going to college without attending high school. Further undermining his confidence was a letter he received from an aide in the Office of the Chief of Infantry, reminding him of his shortcomings and declaring, "You will probably fail."

Ike wrote to Conner about his growing anxiety. His mentor replied, "You may not know it, but because of your three-years' work in Panama, you are far better trained and ready for Leavenworth than anybody I know. You will recall that during your entire service [with me] I required that you write a field order for the operation of the post every day for the years you were there. You became so well acquainted with the technics and routine of preparing plans and orders for operations that included their logistics, that they will be second nature to you. You will feel no sense of inferiority."

Somewhat reassured, Ike continued his preparations prior to reporting to Leavenworth. He wrote to George Patton, asking for his notes from the previous year when he had graduated number 25 out of a class of 248 officers.

The Eisenhowers arrived at Fort Leavenworth in August 1925 for the eleven-month course. Because Ike was senior in rank to most of his classmates, they were assigned a spacious four-bedroom apartment in a brick building on Otis Avenue rather than the smaller quarters called the Beehive occupied by his classmates.

Established in 1881 by General William Tecumseh Sherman as a training vehicle for infantry and cavalry officers, the Command and General Staff School had evolved over the years to include all branches and become a critical step to choice assignments and quicker promotions. Even though no one fails and everyone graduates, the course is extremely competitive because every student knows his final class standing will influence his assignments for the remainder of his career. More important, the school offers an opportunity for officers, particularly those of support branches, to compete directly with their combat arms contemporaries.

Ike wrote, "I found the school itself to be exhilarating. There were no examinations as such, no tests of memory. There was a period of instruction covering medical, ordnance, quartermaster, signal services, as well as operations of the fighting arms. Then we began to get problems—instructed under which is now known as the 'case method.'"

Leavenworth was the first postgraduate school to employ the "case method" of instruction and evaluation, generally defined as the creation of problem situations that raise issues in sufficient detail for students to analyze and suggest their own solutions. At Leavenworth, Eisenhower and his fellow students were given problems centered on units in both offensive and defensive modes. They then had to determine the correct positioning or maneuvering of those units from a command level and to procure supply services to support their actions. Their results were subsequently compared to and graded against the "school solution."

Many of the projects included "ride-alongs," exercises in which the students mounted horses to ride the Kansas countryside to determine lines of defense, routes of attacks, and supply lines. Other case studies involved using maps and terrain boards. Ike found case studies based on the Battle of Gettysburg particularly easy because he had walked or ridden over every acre of the battlefield while stationed at Camp Colt.

Ike described the methodology thusly: "A pamphlet outlined a supposition force, located in a particular spot, with indications of the enemy's strength and the mission of the Blue Force, which the student always commanded. The first step was to decide what actions should be taken. Second, after your decision was turned in, the correct decision was given to the student, and he was then asked to give the proper plans and disposition to support it. Fox Conner had been correct. We had done this kind of 'war gaming' in Panama."

Proper use of time, Ike realized, was critical to successful study and stress reduction: "I established a routine that limited my night study to two hours and a half; from seven to nine-thirty. Mamie was charged with the duty of seeing that I got to bed by that time. This went on five nights a week. There were no classes on Saturday and on Friday nights and Saturday nights we unwound completely at parties at the Officers Club or in friends' quarters. Sunday night we began studying for the next day's lessons."

Most of the students studied in work groups of four to eight members. Ike thought that such arrangements involved too much conversation, discussion, and argument to be productive. Instead, he determined that teaming with only one man would be the ideal solution. His choice was Leonard Townsend "Gee" Gerow, who had served with Ike in the 19th Infantry in San Antonio, where the two had developed a mutual professional respect and a personal friendship that would now pay dividends at Leavenworth. Gerow, a 1911 graduate of the Virginia Military Institute, brought to the study sessions his experiences of having served in the occupation of Veracruz and fought in Europe on the western front. The two set up a "command post" on the third floor of Ike's apartment and covered the walls with maps and shelves of reference materials. "We learned more in quiet concentration than in the lecture room," Ike recalled. Ike's son, John, later said that the room was strictly off limits during study time. On one occasion he did wander in to find his father and Gerow huddled over a map. They welcomed the boy but in less than half a minute ushered him out the door.

An added benefit to the study pairing was that Mamie and Gerow's wife, Kathryn, a former army nurse whom she called Katie, were already good friends from their time in Texas.

Ike excelled both in the classroom and in the field exercises. Pressures of the course seemed not to bother him, and he developed good relationships with his fellow students. He excelled in his ability to see the big picture without getting bogged down in details and his talent for absorbing vast amounts of information to produce simple, logical solutions and orders.

Leavenworth certainly was not "all work and no play" for Ike. In addition to the weekend parties, he took up the game of golf on the post's recently built course. Unlike the tennis he had attempted to master while in Panama, golf provided both the challenge and the relaxation that Ike sought in an off-duty pastime. His initial experiences on the links, however, were not that positive. He later said, "If my progress in academics had been no greater than in golf I would have never gotten through the course."

Like everything else Ike pursued, he took his golf seriously. After each round, he would go back to whichever hole had given him the most difficulty and practice his shots until he had mastered that green. Still, golf provided a mental escape from the army, and later from politics, as Ike allowed no discussion of those subjects while on the links.

Ike's progress in the classroom exceeded his improvement in golf, and by the end of the course in May, Ike stood at the top of his class of 245 fellow students. Some biographies have reported that Gerow finished second, but he actually came in a very respectable number eleven. Ike modestly minimized his standing as first in class in *At Ease*, writing that his study method with Gerow had been successful, as "we both graduated with high marks."

Finally, Ike was being recognized for his excellence in performance. A memo from the school secretary on June 18, 1926, documented his final ranking at the top of the class with an overall score of 93.08 percent. His efficiency report for the period rated him "superior," stating that he was "considered especially qualified" for any position on a division or corps staff and "proficient in theoretical training for high command."

Congratulations arrived from his classmates, Conner, Patton, and other friends and associates. Patton wrote to him, "Congratulations, you are kind to think my notes helped you, though I feel sure that you would have done as well without them. If a man thinks about war long enough it is bound to affect him in a good way."

Many years later, in 1968, the West Point alumni magazine, *Assembly*, noted, "If a point is reached in anyone's career when it turns upward, then possibly ranking first in his class at Leavenworth was this point in Eisenhower's career." Ike simply referred to Leavenworth as "the watershed in my life."

Shortly after his departure from Leavenworth, Ike prepared an essay titled "On the Command and General Staff School" for the school's commandant, with a copy going to the army adjutant general. The *Infantry Journal* published the article under the title "The Leavenworth Course" in its June 1927 issue. Ike signed the essay as "A Young Graduate" and took no personal credit. He never explained this action, but it was likely his modesty once again showing through. Also, he was aware that his superiors would know the identity of the author. Like everything else in his life, Ike had approached Leavenworth as a challenge that could be met by appropriately focusing his time and abilities. In the essay, he advised, "Don't worry about things which belong in the past; the water over the dam no longer turns the wheel." He also reminded future students to keep their sense of humor.

The eight-thousand-plus-word treatise began with an informal, disconnected collection of observations and facts. Its purpose, he wrote, "is to place before you as a prospective student at Leavenworth a reasonably accurate conception of the place, in order that you will not be compelled to undergo a more or less complete mental readjustment after taking up your studies there." He continued:

> The belief is rather prevalent among officers who have never attended the school that the course can be mastered only through unnatural and strained exertions, that the instructors are tricky and mysterious, and

that in fact the whole year is one of worry, fretting, and nervous tension. Such erroneous ideas, especially when firmly fixed in mind, are bound to operate adversely against the student, particularly at the beginning of the school year. If they are not eradicated early in the course their effects may well be so serious as to actually spoil a year which should, and can be, one of the most enjoyable and in many ways finest of an officer's peacetime service.

Ike then followed this section with paragraphs on preparing for Leavenworth. He included details such as mental attitude, personal habits, methods of study, and problem solving. He concluded his essay by stating, "Everyone graduates. . . . So have no hesitancy about going, nor doubts concerning your ability to absorb the instruction. Do your work, but do not slave, understand the teachings, but do not try to 'speck' the course. If you'll maintain this attitude throughout the year, Leavenworth, both while you are there and in retrospect, will in many ways be one of the brightest spots of your military career."

Although humble in his writings, Ike did not limit the celebration of his achievements. He borrowed $150 (about $2,500 in today's money) from his brother Arthur, a successful banker in Kansas City, to rent a party room at the city's historic downtown Muehlbach Hotel, which had hosted every U.S. president since its opening in 1915.

Despite Prohibition, Ike's brother Arthur secured sufficient bootleg gin and whiskey, and the hotel provided an excellent food spread. The well-fed and lubricated guests partied until dawn. Ike led sing-alongs of his favorite songs, including "Casey Jones," "Steamboat Bill," and "Abdul the Bulbul," with his booming voice. Following the party and a day of recuperation, Ike and Mamie set off for their next assignment in another reward they had given themselves—a new Buick.

Wedding portrait of David and Ida Eisenhower, 1885. (National Archives, Eisenhower Presidential Library, Abilene, Kansas)

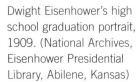

Dwight Eisenhower's high school graduation portrait, 1909. (National Archives, Eisenhower Presidential Library, Abilene, Kansas)

Cadet Eisenhower, West Point, 1915. (National Archives, Eisenhower Presidential Library, Abilene, Kansas)

Mamie Doud, Denver, Colorado, 1916. (National Archives, Eisenhower Presidential Library, Abilene, Kansas)

Dwight and Mamie Eisenhower on their wedding day, July 1, 1916. (National Archives, Eisenhower Presidential Library, Abilene, Kansas)

Eisenhowers, San Antonio, 1917. (National Archives, Eisenhower Presidential Library, Abilene, Kansas)

Eisenhower with tank at Camp Colt, Pennsylvania, 1918. (National Archives, Eisenhower Presidential Library, Abilene, Kansas)

Eisenhower during a brief stop in Boone, Iowa, during the 1919 Transcontinental Motor Convoy, July 1919. (National Archives, Eisenhower Presidential Library, Abilene, Kansas)

Eisenhower coaches the Tank Corps football team at Camp Meade, Maryland, 1921. (National Archives, Eisenhower Presidential Library, Abilene, Kansas)

Eisenhower visits his family in Abilene while attending Command and General Staff School, Fort Leavenworth, in 1926. *L to R:* Roy, Arthur, Earl, Edgar, David, Dwight, Milton, and Ida. (National Archives, Eisenhower Presidential Library, Abilene, Kansas)

Departure luncheon given in honor of Eisenhower by Philippine president Manuel Quezon. *L to R:* General Douglas MacArthur, Mamie Eisenhower, Manuel Quezon, and Dwight D. Eisenhower, Manila, Philippines, 1939. (National Archives, Eisenhower Presidential Library, Abilene, Kansas)

L to R: Captain T. J. Davis (MacArthur's aide), General Douglas MacArthur, and Major Dwight D. Eisenhower in formal dress at Malacañan Palace in Manila, the Philippines, 1935. (National Archives, Eisenhower Presidential Library, Abilene, Kansas)

Eisenhower and officers who participated in the Louisiana Maneuvers, September 1941. (National Archives, Eisenhower Presidential Library, Abilene, Kansas)

Fox Conner. (U.S. Army)

Charles F.
Thompson.
(U.S. Army)

Ike, 1943. (National
Archives, Eisenhower
Presidential Library,
Abilene, Kansas)

Eisenhower observes D-Day landings from a ship off the French coast on June 7, 1944. (National Archives, Eisenhower Presidential Library, Abilene, Kansas)

Eisenhower and General Walter Krueger at Fort Sam Houston in San Antonio, Texas, 1941. (National Archives, Eisenhower Presidential Library, Abilene, Kansas)

George Moseley.
(U.S. Army)

Ike and George Marshall. (U.S. Army)

CHAPTER 10

Fort Benning, Washington, and the American Battle Monuments Commission

NEAR THE END OF HIS YEAR AT THE COMMAND AND GENERAL STAFF School, Ike began receiving offers for his next assignment. Unlike in previous transfers, this time it appeared he would have a choice—or at least be able express his preferences. The chief of infantry wanted Ike to transfer to Fort Benning to command the 2nd Battalion of the 24th Infantry Regiment. A better offer (at least financially) came from the War Department for him to be a Reserve Officer Training Corps instructor at a northwestern university. Ike did not mention the name of the school, but he noted that the job came with the extra duty of being football coach, which would add a stipend of $3,500 per year (more than $60,000 today). Either of these would have significantly added to Ike's meager salary. A third offer came from the commandant of the Command and General Staff School, who wanted him to remain at Leavenworth as an instructor.

Ike found all three offers attractive, but he knew that officers, even those graduating first in class at Leavenworth, advanced in command based on their performance with troop units rather than as instructors or football coaches. He wrote, "I don't think it's possible for a man to meet the requirements of two rather exacting jobs. If I have to coach football all the time, I might as well resign and try to concentrate on the sport."

In the end, the decision to accept the Fort Benning assignment was easy.

Before heading for Georgia, Ike joined his brothers for a reunion in Abilene. It was the first—and last—gathering of all six Eisenhower sons since they had begun leaving home some fifteen years earlier. Ike later explained that getting all the brothers back from their far-flung residences was more difficult than planning the D-Day invasion of Europe.

During their three-day gathering, the brothers spent an afternoon on the local golf course. One afternoon they crossed the railroad tracks arm in arm and marched through downtown. They jokingly claimed to be looking for Chief of Police Henry Engle to revenge minor brushes with him in their youth. Their real purpose, other than good fun, was to flaunt the Eisenhower pride and to show their success. People on the streets and businessmen exited their offices to shake hands and offer their greetings and admiration for the brothers. The incident remained in the minds of the citizens of Abilene, who later referred to the march as the Big Parade of 1926.

The people of the small town recognized that the "Eisenhower boys" were doing well. An article about their visit appeared in the *Daily-Reflector* and the *Topeka Daily Capital*. Ike, however, made no mention of the reunion in *At Ease*.

Before their departure, the Eisenhower sons posed for a local photographer, Paul "Bud" Jeffcoat, who had established his studio five years earlier. He first placed the group on the east side of the family house in front of the bay window and then moved them to the porch for another shot with his big box camera. This latter picture, in which the family appears somber—except for smiling Ike, dressed in full uniform complete with shined boots—would be reprinted in newspapers, magazines, and books in the coming years as representative of the Eisenhower family. Interestingly, Jeffcoat and his family continued their photography until 2007, when they converted their office into a museum that exhibits copies of the Eisenhower photographs as well as those of Abilene's people and events over the years.

Brother Roy died in 1942, preventing another reunion of the six brothers from ever occurring.

Ike looked forward to the fall and spring months at Fort Benning, "when the air is balmy and the weather refreshing," as he described the seasonal weather, but he did not like the summer heat, which was fast approaching. He stated, "But if Georgia temperatures declined, mine didn't. A week after I reached Benning, I was told that I would have to coach the soldier football team. With an enormous effort of will, I said quietly that I just turned down $3,500 a year additional to do the same thing. I asked the executive officer of the post if I could decline the responsibility of head coach. I would take charge of the backfield and the offensive tactics but I didn't want to carry the administration or training or lining up other coaches."

Eisenhower's being the number one graduate in his Leavenworth class did not diminish the army's appreciation of his coaching abilities over his troop leadership skills, though he did receive approval to act only as an assistant coach. Ike wrote, "The material at hand was willing but raw and the season was not one to divert attention from Notre Dame, Wisconsin, West Point, and others. Fortunately, I didn't have to face another. In mid-December the War Department ordered me to report to Washington, D.C. for duty in the office of General [John J.] Pershing."

In *At Ease*, Ike summarized his five-month tour at Benning in three paragraphs, making no mention of the family's excellent quarters or that Mamie developed a serious gastrointestinal condition. He did write about his frustration at once again being called on to coach football.

Neither Ike nor most of his biographers make mention of his command of the 2nd Battalion of the 24th Infantry Regiment. The ones who do so fail to note that the unit was composed of African American enlisted men reporting to white officers. Although General Pershing, who earned his nickname "Black Jack" for leading black troops, and several other senior officers—including Ranald S. MacKenzie, Abner S. Doubleday, and Zenas R. Bliss—had likewise served with African American units, such duty did not generally lead to higher rank and command positions. A study by the Department of the Army Center of Military History stated that the black soldiers of the 24th considered it the "penal" regiment for officers who had "screwed up." Perhaps infantry was still punishing Ike for his published writings, or maybe Ike's assignment was merely the luck of the draw.

Formed in 1869 by merging several other black units, the 24th prided itself on its mixed history, which included serving in Texas, the Indian Territory, New Mexico, and Utah during the wars with Native Americans. In the late nineteenth century, the regiment protected mining properties and monitored civil disputes, among them the anti-Chinese riots of 1885 and the labor disputes among miners in Idaho and Montana in the 1890s. The black troops, known as buffalo soldiers, fought their way up San Juan Hill in Cuba in 1898 and then served three years in the Philippines, where they returned from 1906 to 1908 and then again from 1912 to 1915.

Overall, the regiment enjoyed a good reputation. Its men were the first African Americans to serve in the eastern United States when they were stationed at Madison Barracks in New York between 1908 and 1911. Its soldiers also served honorably on the border during the Mexican Punitive Expedition.

In the summer of 1917, part of the 24th was stationed at Camp Logan in Houston, Texas, where local discrimination and Jim Crow laws so infuriated the black soldiers that a group of them rioted and marched into downtown Houston, killing seventeen people, including five policemen. Ultimately, 118 black soldiers were court-martialed, with 110 found guilty; 19 were hanged, and another 63 were sentenced to life in prison.

Up until this point, Eisenhower had had limited experience with different races except for the mixed-race Puerto Rican soldiers he had led in Panama. Few blacks lived in Abilene when he was growing up, and the Corps of Cadets at West Point was strictly segregated. If nothing else, during his Fort Benning tour, he learned that black soldiers were tough, dedicated troops. Later, at the height of the move toward Germany from the Normandy beachhead, Eisenhower formed the six-thousand-truck unit known as the Red Ball Express, which provided the logistics for the continued offensive; 75 percent of the unit was African American. Near the end of 1944, with many units depleted from losses in the Battle of the Bulge, Ike authorized the first (albeit limited) integration of blacks into white units.

Eisenhower had never had problems with the black soldiers themselves. His irritation at Fort Benning was not that they were colored but that the army was wasting resources with the way it employed them. Instead of undergoing marksmanship training and performing field exercises, the black soldiers were assigned as bricklayers to construct the barracks and headquarters buildings that still dominate Fort Benning today. Black soldiers were further misused by being assigned to "housekeeping duties" on the post.

Although Ike did not quarrel with his orders to the 24th, he made short his Benning stint by wrangling to get his assignment there reduced to a mere five months. Undoubtedly, Fox Conner had come to his aid once again. Ike's only comment was a single sentence in *At Ease* at the end of his three-paragraph report on Fort Benning: "In mid-December the War Department ordered me to report to Washington, D. C. for duty in the office of General Pershing."

On his departure, his commander rated him "superior" as a football coach but only "above average" as a battalion commander. This was hardly the evaluation that Ike expected; he would have preferred the two reversed.

The Eisenhowers arrived in Washington on January 15, 1927, and moved into a two-bedroom—and then a three-bedroom—apartment in the historic six-story Wyoming Building just off Connecticut Avenue near Dupont Circle. Known for its elegant Corinthian columns and marble hallways, the building's occupants included Gee and Katie Gerow, old friends from Leavenworth, as well as a U.S. senator, several members of Congress, the U.S. surgeon general, and more than a dozen field-grade and general officers. Three members of the Supreme Court also lived in the neighborhood.

Military officers mostly did not wear uniforms in Washington between the wars, so Ike had to expand to his civilian wardrobe. Rent for the apartment required about a third of his total salary, but Mamie still received a monthly check from her father that helped cover expenses. She loved the apartment, where she and Ike would live off and on for the next nine years. Membership in the Army-Navy Club provided social activities, as well as a golf course for Ike to continue his developing dedication to the game. They added to their Oriental rug collection to provide a bit of color and elegance to the quarters, and once again Club Eisenhower opened to visitors.

On January 21, Ike reported to the State-War-Navy Building. He penned:

> Whatever the wishes of the War Department to have me stationed at Fort Benning, General Pershing, the famed "Black Jack" and leader of our [American Expeditionary Force (AEF)] in World War I, outranked everyone else in the Infantry or the Department who had designs on me. The new agency he headed, the Battle Monuments Commission, was not only building and beautifying the cemeteries where our war dead were gathered abroad but it was also preparing a battlefield guide, a sort of Baedeker to the actions of Americans in the war. The guide-book writing was assigned to me.

Pershing had returned from Europe to assume the duties of army chief of staff in 1921. In 1924, he reached the age of sixty-four and, by regulation, had to retire from active duty. He then became the chairman of the American Battle Monuments Commission, established by the U.S. Congress the previous year. Congress directed the commission "to commemorate the service of U.S. Armed Forces where they have served since April 6, 1917; establish suitable War memorials; designing, constructing, operating, and maintaining permanent U.S. military burial grounds in foreign countries; control the design and construction of U.S. military monuments and markers in foreign countries by other U.S. citizens and organizations both public and private; encourage the maintenance of such monuments and markers by their sponsors."

Pershing added to these responsibilities the publication of a guide-book that would provide information on the battles of the AEF, as well as a guide to memorials and cemeteries. Fox Conner had suggested that Ike's writing skills would be essential to the book's completion and success, and Pershing quickly added him to his staff. Once again, Ike's pen was considered more important than his sword.

Ike faced a daunting task. Massive stacks of reports, essays, photographs, maps, and charts awaited him, but no particular outline or format for the guidebook had been established. Furthermore, Pershing wanted the final product to appeal to veterans of the war as well as the casual tourist, and he demanded it be published for the tenth anniversary of the U.S. entry into the Great War, allowing Ike only six months to complete the project.

After a review of the source material, Ike determined that Fox Conner's 1919 after-action report on the war could serve as a working outline and that a detailed description of each battle that led to a memorial should be included. Pershing gave Ike great leeway in preparing the book, while he himself not only came to the office late but also stayed late and expected his subordinates to do the same. In addition, Pershing expected Eisenhower to act as his personal aide, a duty that Ike neither appreciated nor felt was his responsibility.

Ike completed the guide, containing 282 pages of text and numerous photographs, and had it ready for publication, at a proposed price to the public of seventy-five cents a copy, within the allotted time. Pershing had it rushed to the publishers so they could make it available to the large number of servicemen and their families planning visits to Europe in the fall of 1927 for the tenth anniversary of the U.S. entry into the war. While the volume did not bear Ike's name as its writer—or give him any credit—everyone, especially Pershing, knew that the "bald-headed major" deserved full credit for its contents and on-time delivery.

Ike made no comment about the guide in his later writings; he only modestly referred to this period, stating, "I had been in the job hardly long enough to do any damage when the word was sent that I had been selected as a student for the War College." Once again, this development was likely to have been the result of Fox Conner's connections.

Ike's efficiency reports for the period all rated him "superior." Although Eisenhower and Pershing did not develop a close personal relationship, the general did recognize the talents of the young major. He wrote to the chief of infantry on August 15, 1927, stating:

> As the detail of Major Dwight D. Eisenhower with the American Battle Monuments Commission expires today, I wish to take this occasion to express my appreciation of the splendid service which he has rendered since being with us. In the discharge of his duties, which were

most difficult by reason of the short time available for their completion, he has shown superior ability not only in visualizing his work as a whole but in executing its many details in an efficient and timely matter. What he has done was accomplished only by the exercise of unusual intelligence and constant devotion to duty.

The letter pleased Ike immensely; it made him aware that not only did he have the confidence of Fox Conner, but he also now had the support of the army's former senior officer. He pasted the letter inside a copy of the battlefield guidebook with the inscription "To my mother and father . . . with love and devotion" and mailed it to his parents.

Ike was joyful about his selection for the War College. Where Leavenworth had been the pathway to staff and command at the battalion and regimental levels, the War College prepared colonels and generals for division and larger-unit positions. Not everyone, however, was enthusiastic about Ike attending the course. Pershing's executive officer, Major Xenophon Price, who had graduated from West Point a year before Ike and served in World War I in the Engineer Corps, wanted him to remain with the commission. He said, "Every officer attached to the Commission is going to be known as a man of special merit."

Ike responded that for once he had been given a choice in his assignment of either remaining with the commission or attending the War College and that he preferred the latter. Price was not pleased; the consequences of Ike's decision would later resurface.

In September 1927, Ike—along with his eighty-nine classmates— reported to the War College, established in 1901, at what is now known as Fort McNair. Located on the Potomac River at Greenleaf Point (now Buzzard Point) near downtown Washington, DC, the post—one of the army's most beautiful—boasted neoclassical buildings; broad, grassy parade grounds; and its own golf course. Given that the school had neither tests nor grades, students often referred to it as "the country club of the army."

Major General William D. Conner (no relation to Fox Conner), West Point Class of 1897, welcomed the class, saying, "In a very large measure the period of your self-development begins right now for in this institution there are no marks applied to your daily work and there are no periodic tests or final examinations that you must undergo to show the faculty what progress you have made or what advantages you have accumulated during the year's work. From now on you become, more than ever before, subject to the critical judgement of your fellow officers."

The environment described by Conner was perfect for Ike. His likeability and professionalism easily gained him the respect and friendship of his classmates—many of whom would go on to be senior leaders in World War II. Ike made friends, not enemies—even among competitors.

In 2019, Dr. Thomas Bruscino, a member of the War College faculty, analyzed the influence of the college on Eisenhower. In *Developing Strategists: Dwight D. Eisenhower and the Interwar Army War College*, he wrote:

> This study finds that the Army War College had a thorough and rigorous curriculum, organized around war planning and the functions of the War Department General Staff. The first two-thirds of the college program emphasized study, and then stressed detailed practice by having students produce a complete and workable war plan in the final part of the year. Although the students received lectures from experts inside and out of the school and the military, the majority of the instruction was student-centered in that the faculty broke the students into committees that researched and presented on all manner of topics. By the end, they had studied personnel, military intelligence, operations, logistics, mobilization, and war planning from a wide variety of functional, regional, historical, theoretical, civilian, allied, and joint perspectives.

Bruscino concluded, "As a result, the Army War College contributed to the development of Eisenhower and the overwhelming majority of the senior leaders who would guide the United States through World War II. More specifically to Eisenhower, his War College year would yield lessons and experiences that carried on throughout his careers inside and outside of the military. To a remarkable degree, Eisenhower would apply his Army War College education to his roles as strategic advisor, theater commander, service chief, and even President of the United States."

An important part of each student's study at the War College was the preparation of a research paper then called a "staff memorandum." According to college directions, the result should be "broad enough to require General Staff action in that it is of interest to the Army or Navy," and it "should contribute something of value to the betterment of national defense."

In determining the topic for his staff memorandum, Ike thought back to his discussions with Fox Conner in Panama about the importance of reserve forces to the procurement of manpower in time of war. Although a rather dull subject, Ike realized that the maintenance of a trained, experienced reserve would be key to expanding the current small standing army. He stated his objective: "To determine the advisability of establishing an enlisted reserve for the Regular Army, and a practical method of procuring and organizing such a reserve."

Aware that existing laws restricted the size of the regular army and reserves, Ike added, "In the effort to make the conclusions practicable and reasonable, and applicable to present conditions, the subject is limited to a consideration of the effects on our military position that would be produced through the accumulation of an enlisted reserve for the Regular Army, and of economical and acceptable methods of securing it."

Ike's basic premise was, he wrote, that "experience has shown that the cost of maintaining a soldier in the reserve is only a small fraction of that necessary to maintain him in the active force." The seventeen-page memorandum included charts, graphs, tables, and endnotes, but Ike followed the War College's guidance principles of "brevity, lucidity, and practicality" as he outlined procedures for the size, organization, duties, and payment of such a force. He concluded with his recommendation: "That efforts be made to secure authorization from Congress for a reserve created under the general system."

General William Conner made notes in the margin of Ike's memorandum before returning it at the end of the course. An important point he made, and one that Ike certainly took to heart, was the importance of accommodating the political desires of Congress in adopting a reserve with "few frills."

William Conner and Fox Conner shared more than just a surname as far as Ike was concerned. Both men earned his respect and appreciation as teacher and mentor. As with Fox Conner, Ike and William Conner were a mutual admiration society. This commander rated Ike "superior" in his efficiency report and wrote, "The evaluation of your staff memorandum shows it to be of exceptional merit." In a letter to him from North Africa on March 22, 1943, Ike wrote, "There is not any doubt about the extent of the influence that you are still exerting on operations in this war." He continued, "I remember you said: 'Attack with whatever you've got at any point where you get it up, and attack and keep attacking until this invader realizes that he has got to stop and reorganize, and thus give us the chance to deliver a finishing blow.'"

In *At Ease*, Ike included only a single paragraph about his attendance at the War College, though not because it was a year spent solely concentrating on academics and writing a memorandum. It was not. Golf and bridge remained his pastimes, and Club Eisenhower continued to be the center of his and Mamie's social circle—enhanced by Ike's improvements in making his bathtub gin. Parlor games and tricks accompanied libations and conversations. Ike's contribution to the party tricks was to demonstrate his ability to totally focus on a single action. Standing rigidly at attention with his arms at his sides, he would fall forward without bending his knees. Then as his nose was about to be the first body part to hit the floor, he would fling out his arms to break his fall.

Ike's time in Washington also allowed him the opportunity to reunite with his younger brother, Milton, who, after graduating from Kansas State, went to work for the federal government. The age difference of nine years meant they had not been close growing up, but while in the nation's capital, they developed a personal and professional relationship that endured for the rest of their lives. Milton became Ike's advisor and confidant. By the time Ike joined him in Washington, his brother had advanced to assume the position of director of information for William H. Jardine, head of the Department of Agriculture and a fellow Kansan.

The younger Eisenhower and his fiancée, Helen Eakin, were frequent visitors to the Wyoming Building apartment. Helen closely resembled Mamie in her vivaciousness, social abilities, and background. Her father owned the largest department store in Manhattan, Kansas, and served as director of the town's major bank. He also dabbled in real estate and oil exploration. The Eakins had recently moved to Washington, where her father purchased a large plot of what was then farmland, just across the Potomac River from the Lincoln Memorial.

Ike hosted Milton's bachelor party at the Wyoming. The only record of the event in Ike's musings is an acknowledgment of rather severe hangovers the following day. Milton and Helen married on October 12, 1927, in Washington's Mayflower Hotel. Ike wore his full dress uniform complete with scabbard and sword. Helen used his blade to cut the wedding cake.

Milton had the "Eisenhower charm," which earned him many friends both inside and outside the government. He frequently took Ike along to social functions and introduced him to many high-ranking officials, to whom he became known as "Milton's brother." In one instance, Milton encouraged a news reporter not to leave a party before meeting his brother, who was "a major in the army and going places." The reporter took one look at the nearly forty-year-old, balding officer and replied, "If he's going far, he had better start soon."

Milton and Helen were also frequent visitors to the White House, where they socialized with President Calvin Coolidge. Ike was not included in those invitations and later said the closest he got to the president during this time was when he took his son, John, to an Easter egg hunt on the White House lawn.

Milton's social circle proved fortuitous for Ike because one of his acquaintances, Harry C. Butcher, would become a major figure, both professionally and personally, in his future. At the time, however, Butcher was just another associate of his brother's who became one of many frequent visitors to the Eisenhower apartment. Charming, quick witted, and gregarious, Butcher was a bit of a gossip, which perfectly suited his being editor of the *Fertilizer Review*, a magazine published by the National Fertilizer Association.

An Iowa native born in 1901, Butcher shared Ike's background of growing up in a small town and helping the family stave off poverty. Butcher had begun doing odd jobs after his father's death when he was not yet in his teens. He then worked his way through Iowa State University to become an agricultural journalist. Soon after he and his wife, Ruth, befriended the Eisenhowers, Butcher became the director of the CBS Radio Network office in Washington. He later would originate the term "fireside chat" for President Franklin Roosevelt's radio speeches to the American public.

Through his military connections, Ike arranged for Butcher to receive direct commission in the U.S. Navy in 1939; Ike made him his naval aide in 1942. In reality, Butcher had no responsibility for naval matters, serving instead basically as Ike's unofficial press and political advisor as well as his bridge partner for the next three years. On Ike's orders, Butcher kept a diary, later published as *My Three Years with Eisenhower*, which continues to offer the best insights into the intimate working of the command headquarters. In another contribution Butcher made to the war's history, it was he who secured and kept the press release that Ike prepared prior to D-Day—for use in case the operation failed.

CHAPTER 11

Paris and General Pershing

MOST OF THE WAR COLLEGE STUDENTS RECEIVED ORDERS TO THE WAR Department staff when they graduated. Ike, however, was given a choice. He could either follow suit or return to the American Battle Monuments Commission, which General John J. Pershing had relocated to Paris, to expand and revise the battlefield guide he had previously written. He believed that a position in the War Department would be more likely to advance his career, but—even knowing that—he found the idea of a tour in the City of Lights certainly had its appeal. His only concern was that the army, which at least no longer seemed to be emphasizing his coaching talent over his soldiering abilities, would begin to look upon him more as a talented writer than as a field soldier.

While Mamie usually made no attempt to influence Ike's assignment choices, this time she stepped forward in favor of Paris. She later recalled, "I said, Honey, let's go to Europe. Let's take this assignment. This gives us the opportunity to see the Old World and travel."

Ike, of course, ultimately made the decision, but the two remembered the deliberation process quite differently. Ike recalled in *At Ease*, "When I learned that to complete the work of revising the guidebook written earlier I would have to go to France to study [the battlefields] firsthand, my choice was easy." Mamie, probably more accurately, described the decision to go to Paris as having been reached only after much argument and remembered that "very much against his will we went." Likely Ike felt he owed Mamie a choice after all the support she had given him, and, after all, Paris was Paris.

While waiting for his sailing orders, Ike reported to the commission's remaining office in Washington, DC, on July 1. There he spent his time recruiting and vetting several officers for the commission, keeping Major Xenophon Price, now in the Paris office, apprised of their status. He also met with U.S. Navy representatives about revising and expanding the guidebook's entries on naval operations in the war.

Ike and Mamie had been quite happy at the Wyoming, so they arranged to sublet the apartment in anticipation of returning after their tour in France. For the crossing, they invited the Douds to join them, and, on July 31, they all sailed from New York aboard the 1905 Irish-built SS *America*, a formerly German-owned luxury cruise liner that had become property of the United States as reparation under the provisions of the Treaty of Versailles.

The family enjoyed the nine-day voyage only to find no one to meet their ship at Cherbourg or at the train station when they arrived in Paris in the early morning hours of August 9. Ike was furious. He managed to secure a taxi that took them to an adequate hotel, but he believed that an escort should have been provided. He held Price responsible for this breach of protocol, straining an already tense relationship between the two men because of Price's resentment about Ike's departure from the commission for the War College. Ike used this incident to make sure future arrivals to the commission were met at the port and given every assistance. If no one was available for the escort duty, Ike himself met the boat.

After a few days in the hotel, and with Ike already at work, Mamie—with the assistance of several other wives of commission officers—found an apartment at 110, rue d'Auteuil, on the Right Bank of the Seine River. Located about a mile and a half downstream from the Eiffel Tower, the roomy three-bedroom apartment was only a short walk to Ike's office at 20, rue Molitor, allowing him to frequently eat lunch at home. It had adequate space for entertaining and a stone courtyard that served as a playground for John. Once the Eisenhowers were settled, Mamie put her parents on a train bound for a visit with Mrs. Doud's extended family in Sweden before sailing for home.

Ike appreciated the assistance provided by the Douds, and although he did not have much in common with his father-in-law, he respected John Doud for his success. Ike believed that success bred success and that it was to his advantage to surround himself with those of great accomplishment, whatever their field of endeavor.

The apartment was pricy by French standards, but the very favorable postwar exchange rate for dollars had increased more than fivefold by the time the Eisenhowers arrived. The economic advantage to the couple was described by Ernest Hemingway in the *Toronto Star* when he wrote about this period, saying, "Paris in winter is rainy, cold, beautiful, and cheap. It is also noisy, jostling, crowded, and cheap. It is anything you want—and cheap."

"Cheap" meant the Eisenhowers could hire a cook as well as a housekeeper, with ample funds left over to reopen Club Eisenhower. Ike noted, "The apartment became a sort of informal, junior-size American Express for Army friends who were visiting Paris." Mamie browsed the many designer shops to enhance her wardrobe and scoured flea markets to complete their apartment's decor.

Postwar Paris was a mecca for writers, artists, and bohemians from across Europe and from America for its creative environment as much as its reasonable cost of living. No place in the world "roared" like Paris in the 1920s. The Eisenhowers, however—like most American officer families—kept mostly to themselves and did not mingle with those outside the military.

Nevertheless, Ike and Mamie immersed themselves in learning the local language. Mamie, however, soon tired of the lessons and used a pocket dictionary to communicate for the rest of the tour. Ike quickly became proficient in reading and writing French but, to his frustration, never mastered the spoken word.

Ike's duties for the commission offered great insights into the land and people he would encounter nearly two decades later under markedly different circumstances. He wrote, "This was my first chance to get to know a European country. . . . I saw Paris for the first time. The job now took on new interest. It involved travel, all the way from the Vosges in southeast France to the English Channel, following the lines of trench warfare that had stabilized almost rigidly between late 1914 and the weeks preceding the Armistice in 1918."

The snobby, elitest Parisians did not impress Ike, but he liked the people he met in the countryside: "I came to see the small towns of France and to meet the sound and friendly people working in the fields and along the roads." He found that "they were unlike some of the city people, warm and jolly and courteous."

Ike often joined the locals along the road or in the inns for lunch. With his rudimentary French and through his interpreter, he furthered his knowledge of rural France and its inhabitants. He frequently spent days away from Paris as he walked the battlefields, taking notes and drawing maps on land that was again returning to farms and meadows. Occasionally, his son, John, accompanied him and later recalled that unexploded ordnance still made for dangerous exploration.

One of the sites that had the most profound impact on Ike was the Trench of Bayonets on the Verdun battlefield. In 1916, a French battalion had occupied forward trenches under German fire, and its soldiers had propped their bayonet-fitted rifles against the side of the trench in preparation for "going over the top." Now, years later, Ike stood and surveyed the ground the French had defended only to die before they could advance when an unusually heavy artillery barrage ruptured the ground around the trench and completely covered over and killed the soldiers, leaving only their bayonets exposed above ground. To Ike, the Trench of Bayonets must have come to represent the horrors of war and the sacrifices made by ordinary infantrymen. By the time he finished his inspection of the battlefields, Ike was likely the most knowledgeable American officer on the overall conduct of World War I.

The Paris assignment also provided Ike with additional time with General Pershing. Ike's overall response to the general was respectful but somewhat tepid: "To all the veterans of World War I he is the single hero and they remember him with respect and admiration, even if not affection. He had the reputation of being something of a martinet, but at the same time he was knowledgeable and fair. I liked him, and we all owed him respect and admiration for the way he had carried responsibility in that war."

Ike also noted that Pershing continued to keep odd hours at work and complained that the general had "one deplorable habit: he was always late—up to an hour or more—for every engagement." Occasionally Ike acted as the general's aide and found it "always difficult, indeed embarrassing to try and explain to the host why we were so late. The general seemed to be oblivious to the passage of time and he made no excuses for the long hours of waiting he imposed."

As for Pershing and the written word, Ike found his style "cautious and slow. Several times he asked me to draft speeches and in no case was I successful in producing anything he wanted." Ike had more success in preparing correspondence, but Pershing "always edited carefully and with a precise regard for the exact definition of words. If I had used the word 'exhaustively' I would find it changed to 'thoroughly'; if I should use 'speedily' he would change it to 'rapidly.'"

Ike, priding himself on his own writing prowess and appreciating that his competency with written communications had advanced his career, must have been disappointed with his inability to please the general. This frustration increased when Pershing asked for assistance with his ongoing effort to prepare his memoirs based on his wartime diaries. Ike found the daily format "destroyed the continuity of any major episode, of course. A battle could not have a beginning and a body and an end for the simple reason that it had to be told in the form of General Pershing's daily experiences, along with a score of other affairs coincident with it."

Pershing, like most writers, was more likely looking for praise rather than criticism, constructive or not. However, he did ask Ike for assistance, saying, "I'm unhappy about this description of Saint-Mihiel in the first part of September 1918—and also about the Argonne. Read the parts of the book that cover these two periods and let me know what you think."

Ike reviewed the diary format in the manuscript and recommended that Pershing instead "tell the story of each battle as seen from his position as the commander of the American Expeditionary Force." Ike wrote, "He listened and seemed to be enthused." Afterward, "he told me to take the two chapters and draft them as I thought they should be."

After what he said was "considerable effort," Ike submitted the rewritten chapters to Pershing. The general seemed "happy with them" but said he would like to get the opinion of Colonel George Marshall—a fellow World War I veteran and the officer with whom Fox Conner had recommended Ike develop a relationship.

Marshall met with Pershing a short time later, but Ike was not included. Ike later recalled, "When his conference with the General was done, he came out through my office. For the first time in my life, I met George Marshall. He did not sit down but remarked that he had read over my chapters. 'I think they're interesting. Nevertheless, I've advised General Pershing to stick with his original idea. I think to break up the format right at the climax of the war would be a mistake.'"

The two debated for a while, with Ike standing by his idea that the two battles should be covered in a single narrative. Marshall, while admitting that Ike's idea had merit, was not swayed from his recommendation that Pershing maintain his original concept. He continued to stand, and in his infamous fashion Marshall did not smile or show any emotion whatsoever during the conversation. While Marshall must have been familiar with Eisenhower's reputation through Fox Conner, he never commented on or wrote what he thought of Ike in their initial meeting.

When finally published in 1932, the memoir received mixed reviews, with some critics declaring the book all but unreadable. Despite the negative comments, the book received a Pulitzer Prize.

In the meantime, Ike's interaction with Pershing also provided his first look into the working of politics and lobbying. Various groups came to the office to encourage the war hero to run for president in the upcoming 1928 election. Ike, who, like most professional military officers, lacked interest in politics and never voted, knew that public office held no allure for Pershing and "that the White House was not his choice of residence."

Although he admired neither Pershing's work habits nor his writing abilities, Ike benefited from the general's letter of appreciation and his formal introduction to Marshall. Also, once again, Ike was looking out for his future success by surrounding himself with those who had already proven themselves to be great achievers.

Years later, Ike visited General Pershing in his rooms at Walter Reed General Hospital in Washington. Ike wrote that, although ailing, Pershing spoke from his hospital bed "as a senior commander. I had the impression that he was standing stiffly erect, Sam Browne belt and all." Then, in 1948, General Eisenhower attended Pershing's funeral. During the long march from the Capitol to Arlington Cemetery, a cold rain began falling. Automobiles rushed forward to pick up the procession, which consisted of many mourners advanced in years, but Ike refused to get into any of the cars. He wrote later that it would be a bad example and that he would not accept transport on such an auspicious occasion—"not in the last walk for General Pershing of the AEF."

Despite Ike and Mamie's busy schedule of work and entertaining, they had sufficient time to enjoy other aspects of living in Paris. Ike discovered the Musée Grévin, a waxworks similar to London's famous Madame Tussaud's. He wrote, "This place—I suppose I was still an unsophisticated Kansan at heart—stayed in my memory as a unique Paris attraction." Ike often recommended the museum to visitors, though many must have wondered why, with all of Paris and its history around him, he would favor the display.

The Eisenhowers also had ample time for travel, which they used for both entertainment and historical appreciation. In April 1929, Ike, Mamie, and John motored to Belgium to visit the cathedrals and art galleries of Ghent. Along the way, they toured the British cemeteries of World War I. In a letter home, Mamie noted, "You can't imagine the number of British cemeteries. . . . It was terrible. . . . Ypres had 65,000 names of British unknowns. . . . You can't imagine such loss." The following June, the family took another automobile trip to the French Rivera and San Remo, Italy.

In September, with Ike's assignment near an end, he applied for another leave for a more extended tour of Europe. For companionship and to share the expenses, the Eisenhowers joined fellow American officer Major William R. Gruber and his wife, Helen, for a seventeen-day tour through France. Gruber, an artillery officer who had been one of Ike's instructors at Leavenworth and who had shared duties with him at the Monuments Commission, provided in-depth insights into the battlefields where he had fought during the war.

At the beginning of the party's departure from Paris on August 28, Ike began a journal with the primary purpose of recording all their expenses so they could be shared equally. Along with entries for gasoline, food, lodging, and incidentals, Ike included observations of the land and its people. About halfway through the trip, Gruber took over the journal, resulting in its eventual label as the "Gruber-Eisenhower Diary."

Ike began the diary, "The principal idea the four of us have upon starting this trip is to see something of France, Belgium, Germany, and Switzerland, and possibly Italy or Austria. Due to the fact Mamie and I must sail on *Leviathan*, Sept. 17, we are somewhat limited in our choice of itineraries, and cannot tarry long in any one place if we are to complete the trip contemplated. On the other hand, we have determined not to overdo—we have no intention of making the tour a disagreeable task."

The Eisenhowers and Grubers marveled at the beauty of the Grand Place in Brussels and stood on the huge pyramid of earth that marked the Battle of Waterloo. They noted that some roads were "very beautiful and picturesque," while others were "poor and everything dusty and dirty."

On August 30, the couples crossed into Germany, about which Ike wrote, "We seemed to experience a very definite exhilaration upon leaving Belgium and entering the Fatherland. Maybe it's because both Bill and I have our family roots in this country, as our names testify." Ike admired the countryside and appreciated the friendliness and helpfulness of the people. He also enjoyed the German food, which was much more basic and "Kansas like" than the rich sauce-covered fare offered by his French cook in Paris. When they departed Germany, they concluded in the diary, "We like Germany!"

After two and a half weeks on the road, including a harrowing drive over the Alps and a visit to Switzerland, the couples had covered eighteen hundred miles before returning to Paris. Mamie later said that the trip was "magnificent" and one to "never be forgotten by any of us."

On September 17, 1929, the Eisenhowers sailed for home aboard the SS *Leviathan*, another ship that had been seized from the Germans after World War I. They moved back into their Wyoming Building apartment, reopened Club Eisenhower, and resumed a busy life. Milton and his wife were frequent visitors, and he continued to introduce Ike to Washington leaders. Dinners at the finest hotels included Ike's military bosses as well as national dignitaries, such as Secretary of War Patrick J. Hurley. Since George Patton was also stationed in Washington, the two renewed their friendship, with the Eisenhowers frequently visiting the Pattons in their spacious six-bedroom home in the northwest part of the city. Although his leisure time was limited, Ike played golf as often as possible.

In the final weeks before his reassignment to the War Department, Ike reported to the commission's office, where he wrote a series of letters to Major Xenophon Price in Paris. They began with a complaint that their shipboard quarters were cramped and that, considering the price of passage, the commission should ensure better accommodations for its officers.

Over the next few months, Ike continued his letters to Price with candid observations about the deficiencies of the commission and criticism of how it was carrying out its mission in France. His recommendations for improvements, which apparently did not please Price, cost Ike on his efficiency report ratings. Previously Price had ranked Ike as "superior" but now, in his final report, rated him as only "satisfactory." Price noted that Ike was "an excellent officer of great natural ability" and that he possessed a "fine command of the English language" but added that he was "not especially versatile in adjusting to changing conditions" and that he "had difficulty in adjusting to Paris."

Not requiring any evidence as to the veracity of Price's claims, the report—the lowest evaluation Ike had received—went into Ike's permanent file. Ike rarely wrote negatively about his superiors and, in typical Eisenhower style, downplayed his adversarial relationship with Price. When recalling his Paris tour, he noted, "The year was very interesting to me, in spite of the old maidish attitude of my immediate superior [Price]. I was not so successful as I should have been in concealing my impatience with some of his impossible ideas and methods of operating. However, we are good friends—in spite of the fact that from the standpoint of piling up a perfect record in the W.D. I was not sufficiently suave and flattering." Ike never mentioned the fact that, when the commission's revised guidebook was finally published in 1938, it gave no credit to him for all his research and writing.

Many a military career has been diverted or even destroyed by personality conflicts. However, the report did neither and apparently had no impact on Eisenhower's future.

Fortunately for Price, Ike was not one to hold grudges. According to a letter written by his son, John, when Ike returned to Washington in 1946, as the army chief of staff, and inquired about Price, it was reported that he was still on active duty as a lieutenant colonel in the Corps of Engineers. When Ike asked why Price was still a lieutenant colonel, the answer he received in response was "bad judgement." Ike replied, "Hell, he's not that bad," and ordered Price's promotion to full colonel.

CHAPTER 12

War Department and General MacArthur

BY THE LATE FALL OF 1929, THE ARMY—AS WELL AS THE COUNTRY AS a whole—was much different from the one Ike had left when he sailed for France a year earlier. The October stock market crash had plunged the country into a depression. While Ike's and his fellow officers' jobs were secure, no pay raises would be forthcoming for more than a decade. Funds for the training of the armed forces or for increasing troop numbers were limited or nonexistent. Austerity dominated. In addition to contending with scarce resources, the United States faced the rise of the Nazis in Germany and the expansionist desires of Japan.

When he completed his work for the American Battle Monuments Commission, Ike requested reassignment to a troop unit. The transfer was approved; the troop assignment was not. Instead of commanding soldiers, Ike would be handling administrative matters and employing his writing abilities—once more, his secondary skills overshadowed his career priorities. After a month's leave, he reported to the War Department on November 9 as the assistant to General George Van Horn Moseley, the assistant secretary of war, whose duty it was to study the ways American industry could mobilize in the event of another conflict. Ike wrote, "I now undertook work that was intriguing and frustrating but gave me an early look at the military-industrial complex of whose pressures I would later warn."

Most of Ike's inner thoughts about his job and superiors, such as the ones noted above, come from his book *At Ease*, written more than two decades after the conclusion of World War II. In his new job at the

War Department, Ike began making irregular entries in what he titled his "Chief of Staff Diary," entries that revealed his current thoughts and evaluations. Ike occasionally indicated expletives in these notes, but still he never completely spelled out the curse words.

In his first entry on November 9, 1929, Ike wrote:

> I reported for duty in the Office of the Assistant Secretary of War yesterday. I am to be a direct assistant to General Van Horn Moseley, and will spend my time principally on studies connected with "Industrial Mobilization." Except for the fact I do not like to live in a city I am particularly pleased with this detail. The general is alert and energetic and currently enjoys a fine reputation for accomplishment in the Army. I am looking forward to the opportunity of learning something about the economic and industrial conditions that will probably prevail in this country in the event of a major war.

Eisenhower would indeed learn much from his association with Moseley, an Illinois native and 1899 graduate of West Point, who had served in the Philippines and as the chief logistics officer for General John J. Pershing in the American Expeditionary Force. He was a man admired by George Marshall, who occasionally sought his advice and considered him one of his few close contemporaries. No surprise, Moseley and Fox Conner were old friends, and Ike's new boss assumed Conner's role as mentor. Eisenhower and Moseley immediately formed a bond of mutual respect and admiration.

Ike later penned, "General George Moseley was dynamic. He always delved into new ideas, and he was an inspiration to the rest of us. He was always quick with his praise and was ready to take responsibility for any little error or criticism that came our way from outside."

Moseley returned the accolades, as he often referred to Ike as his "brainy assistant" and "one of the coming men of the army." He rated Ike in his efficiency report as "superior" and noted, "No limit should be placed on this officer. . . . He represents the best type of Regular Army officer." Eisenhower welcomed the praise, but it did not change his status. The austerity of the army's budget dictated that the policy of promotions based on seniority rather than talent be continued. Thus, Ike would remain a major.

Despite Eisenhower's respect for Moseley, he knew the general's significant flaws. Like many of his generation—both in and outside the army—Moseley was a racist, an anti-Semite, and an opponent of immigration. Unlike his more circumspect peers, however, Moseley was vocal about his beliefs, writing, "We pay great attention to the breeding of our hogs, our dogs, our horses, and our cattle, but we are just beginning to realize the . . . effects of absorbing objectionable blood in our breed of human beings. The pages of history give us the tragic stories of one-time leading nations which . . . imported manpower of an inferior kind and then . . . intermarried with this inferior stock. . . . Those nations have either passed out of separate existence entirely or have remained as decadent entities without influence in world affairs."

Moseley viewed immigrants as a significant problem: "With all the troubles we have at the present moment in the United States why should we allow these aliens, who are now unlawfully within our gates, to work against us? It seems to me all such aliens should be gathered up and either returned to Russia or segregated and held segregated within the United States." Later, he recommended that the Jews fleeing Adolf Hitler's Europe be admitted into the United States only "with the understanding that they be sterilized before being permitted to embark. Only that way can we properly protect our future."

Ike had a unique ability to recognize and take advantage of the "good" while ignoring the "bad" in people. In his usual way of avoiding derogatory comments about those he liked, he wrote, "Years later, his outspoken reaction to public questions, often political, got him bad press. Many who did not know the man himself may have thought him a reactionary or a militarist. The impression he created was a distortion, I am sure; he was a patriotic American unafraid to disagree with a consensus."

One of Ike's first major challenges was dealing with a topic that could be taken from today's news stories as easily as from those of the 1930s. Illegal activities related to Prohibition, as well as the pressures from the Depression, had greatly increased the number of crimes committed with handguns. Public outrage over easy access to such weapons had prompted the Massachusetts legislature to propose laws that would close handgun manufacturers in the state. This development was particularly troubling to the War Department, as four of the major U.S. gun factories were located there.

Ike composed a letter to the Smith & Wesson Company for Secretary of War Patrick J. Hurley's signature. The letter, expressing the secretary's appreciation for the gunsmiths, addressed the bill, stating, "Since in any future emergency, the Nation would be absolutely dependent on private industry for 90% of the pistols and revolvers necessary to munition our forces, it is essential, in the interests of national defense, that existing establishments of the manufacture of these weapons remain in being."

In a display of his diplomatic abilities, Ike added, "On the other hand, the War Department is in entire accord with the efforts being made to prevent the acquisition of firearms by our criminal classes, but trusts that the various legislative bodies will find a way to accomplish this without lessening the ability of the country properly to arm its citizens in case we are forced into a war."

Writing under the signature of Moseley, Ike then drafted a letter to the army chief of ordnance explaining the situation and including a copy of the secretary of war's letter to Smith & Wesson. It continued, "It occurred to this office that the Ordnance Department's representative in the Boston Procurement District might be able to assist the Committee holding the hearing to appreciate the importance of munitions production to national defense."

Apparently, the letters were successful. The legislation failed.

Moseley and Eisenhower realized that while some war munitions and fighting equipment could easily be manufactured in the United States, some necessary items would be more difficult to procure. With the modernization of the army that replaced horses and mules with trucks and other wheeled vehicles, the demand for rubber was insatiable. In the event of war, the East Indies source would likely be cut off by naval activities. The secondary rubber source in Latin American might also be restricted.

The men determined that they must find a more stable alternative. They first looked to officials of the Intercontinental Rubber Company of

New York, which, early in the twentieth century, had discovered that the guayule plant growing in the northern desert of Mexico produced a sap that could be manufactured into a rubber substitute. Because the Mexican Revolution in 1911 had forced the investors to leave the country, the company had established guayule plantations in Salinas, California, and Laredo, Texas. Officials were eager to evaluate their product's use for the U.S. Army.

Ike, accompanied by Major Gilbert Van B. Wilkes—a graduate of the West Point Class of 1909 and a member of the Corps of Engineers—departed Washington on April 8. On May 8, Ike recorded in his Chief of Staff Diary, "Returned today from a month's trip which I made, in company with Major Wilkes (C.E.) through California, Mexico, and Texas. The object of the trip was to gather first-hand information concerning the guayule industry that had been under development in Mexico and the southwest United States for some years. The points at which we spent the most time were Salinas, California, Torreon, Los Cedros, and Etacion Catorce, in Old Mexico, and Dilley, Texas."

In his lengthy final report, dated June 6 and titled "Report of Inspection of Guayule Rubber Industry," Ike summarized the history of the experiment, its current production status in Mexico, and its possible replication in the United States. He noted that the plant did indeed contain a large amount of a rubberlike substance that could be extracted mechanically through a crushing, rolling, and washing process. He estimated that the product could be produced at a cost of about twelve cents per pound. He concluded that the operation could provide an emergency supply of rubber, but the industry would not flourish without government assistance.

Before the guayule industry could get on its feet, however, the process was overtaken by technology. Around the same time that Ike was conducting his inspection trip, scientists developed a petroleum-based synthetic rubber. With abundant oil reserves, the United States could and did solve its rubber supply issue.

Usually accompanied by Wilkes, Ike visited other industrial firms as well. The officers questioned manufacturers about their plans to convert their factories to produce ammunition, vehicles, uniforms, and other items in the event of mobilization. The results were discouraging, as the industry leaders believed the hype that the "war to end all wars" was behind them. They were not contemplating another large conflict.

Because Ike had learned to seek advice from the most experienced, he approached Bernard Baruch, head of the War Industries Board during that previous war. Baruch, born into a Jewish family in South Carolina in 1870, had graduated from the City College of New York before amassing a huge fortune by speculating in the Hawaiian sugar market. He then added to his wealth as one of the New York Stock Exchange's most successful traders. Anticipating the crash of 1929, he sold or shorted his stocks to maintain and even increase his wealth during the looming Depression.

President Woodrow Wilson had appointed Baruch to head the War Industries Board to mobilize the country for the Great War. His efforts had been so impressive throughout the war that Wilson asked him to serve as a staff member at the Paris Peace Conference at the end of the conflict. For his accomplishments, Baruch received the army's Distinguished Service Medal with a citation reading:

> For exceptional meritorious and distinguished services to the Government of the United States, in a duty of great responsibility during World War I, in the organization and administration of the War Industries Board and in the coordination of allied purchases in the United States. By establishing a broad and comprehensive policy for the supervision and control of raw materials, manufacturing facilities, and distribution of the products of industry, he stimulated the production of war supplies, coordinated the needs of the military service and civilian population, and contributed alike to the completeness and speed of mobilization and equipment of the military forces and the continuity of their supply.

Ike found another role model, as well as long-term friend, in Baruch, writing, "He was a man who was not only cooperative; he was anxious that the American public, as well as the armed services, understand the complexities of conversion to war. He was ready to talk to me at any time."

Ike quickly adopted Baruch's ideas on mobilization:

> Mr. Baruch believed that immediately upon the outbreak of war, preferably in advance, if the emergency could be foreseen, prices, wages, and costs of materials and services should be frozen. None of these could be changed except on decision of a special agency. In this way he hoped to avoid the inflation that had accompanied every one of our prior wars. At the same time, he advocated measures for eliminating black marketing. He convinced me of the soundness of his basic views, and I made them part of the plans that I was charged with drawing up.

Ike and Baruch did not find much support in business boardrooms or among military ranks. Businessmen wanted to protect potential profits, while military officers wanted to retain negotiating powers for the army and navy. Ike wrote, "Our antagonist persisted. Whenever we accomplished an industrial mobilization it was done on our own and in a rather isolated atmosphere."

In an effort to generate support, Ike composed an article for publication in *Army Ordnance* with the byline of Assistant Secretary of War Frederick Payne. Titled "Fundamentals of Industrial Mobilization," Ike wrote for Payne, "The plan concerns itself with the fundamental relationships that should exist in war between the Government and industry, and with the methods whereby military forces will secure necessary munitions from industrial establishments." The piece continued, "Our purpose is simple—to see to it that every individual and every material thing shall contribute, in the manner demanded by inherent characteristics, their full share to the winning of any war in which we may become involved. Simplicity and practicability are the foundation stones of the plan through which it is proposed that this result shall be attained."

Support for the industrial call to arms came in late 1930 from both internal and external sources. In June, the U.S. Congress passed a joint resolution calling for a War Policies Commission "to study and consider amending the Constitution, so that, should there be a war, its burden would fall equally on everyone and it would be profitable for no one."

A major problem in establishing a proficient industrial rally was that many in uniform looked on those in the technical service, particularly supply and production, as inferior to combat arms officers. The army had established the Industrial College in 1924, in an attempt to gain more prestige for those in these specialties, but the school was poorly attended and occupied, Ike noted, "a little section of one room in the old Munitions Building."

Ike, with Moseley's support, took measures to increase the size of the college in both physical space and enrollment. They also ensured that its graduates were given credit toward their eventual promotions. Ike would later attend the course himself and return on occasion as a guest lecturer.

At this point in Ike's efforts to assess and promote America's readiness for another war, General Douglas MacArthur replaced General Charles Summerall as the army chief of staff on November 21, 1930. MacArthur, Ike noted, "was receptive to the ideas we had been advocating."

Douglas MacArthur, born in 1880 to a father who had received the Medal of Honor in the Civil War, graduated number one in the West Point Class of 1903. In World War I, he rose to the rank of brigadier general and earned the Distinguished Service Cross twice and the Silver Star seven times. He served as the superintendent of the U.S. Military Academy from 1919 to 1922 and became the army's youngest major general in 1925.

As part of his restructuring of the army into his vision of what he believed it should be, MacArthur replaced all principal general staff officers and promoted Moseley to deputy chief of staff. Ike, accompanying Moseley to his new position, prepared documents and held hearings for a newly formed War Policies Commission; he later described his position as "sort of a working secretary but with no official title or authority." Preparation of the mobilization plan fell to him when the commission—chaired by the secretary of war and composed of four cabinet members, four senators, and four representatives—charged the War Department with the plan's development.

Ultimately, MacArthur delivered the finished proposal to the congressional committee on May 13, 1931. In his diary, Ike noted, "I worked for ten days (and nights) getting it ready." He further explained in *At*

Ease, "The Commission called in witnesses and finally asked the War Department to propose a plan. We had been anticipating this and I was selected to draft the plan, working with Colonel Wilkes. The Chief of Staff presented it on behalf of the entire War Department. The plan was far from being a masterpiece, but it did make an impression."

The "impression" was not only on the committee but also on MacArthur. In a letter of commendation, which Mamie had framed and posted on the wall of their quarters, MacArthur wrote on November 4, 1931:

My Dear Major,

I desire to place on official record this special commendation for excellent work of a highly important nature which you have just completed under my personal direction. You not only accepted this assignment willingly—an assignment which involved much hard work—performing it in addition to your regular duties in the office of The Assistant Secretary of War, but you gave me a most acceptable solution within the minimum of time.

This is not the first occasion when you have been called upon to perform a special task of this nature. In each case you have registered successful accomplishments in the highest degree.

I write you this special commendation so that you may fully realize that your outstanding talents and your ability to perform these highly important missions are fully appreciated.

SINCERELY YOURS,
DOUGLAS MACARTHUR
GENERAL
CHIEF OF STAFF

Ike's efficiency report for this period mirrored MacArthur's praise. Secretary Frederick Payne wrote, "I know Major Eisenhower very well. In the preparation of studies and articles for my use, he has been superb." Another superior praised Ike's "extraordinary literary ability," while another said, "Here is a man I should always like to have with me," while still another noted that Ike "has no superior to his age and grade."

Ike continued to work with the commission until it made its final report to President Herbert Hoover the following March. During that time, he again prepared speeches, letters, and other documents for Secretary Payne, Moseley, and MacArthur, further enhancing his reputation as an accomplished staff officer. His recognition as a writer spread outside the military as well. Newspaper magnate William Randolph Hearst, anticipating the forthcoming conflicts in Europe and the Far East, asked Ike to resign his commission and become his military correspondent. Hearst's offer of an income three times Ike's present one must have been tempting. He, however, turned down the offer for two reasons. First, his salary supplemented by the monthly stipend from the Douds provided a sufficiently comfortable lifestyle. Second, and more important, Ike liked being a soldier, and despite his earlier doubts about Fox Conner's warning about a second major war, he now believed another conflict was on the horizon. Ike had no intention of missing out on the war this time.

With the approach of 1932, Ike was nearing three years at the War Department, meaning he was due for a new assignment the following summer. He strongly desired to get back to a troop assignment for his own personal and professional development, as he remained acutely aware that promotions went to field (not staff) officers. Mamie, for her part, wanted them to return to the 19th Infantry in San Antonio. Ike, while acknowledging that he hated the Texas heat, noted in his journal, "Family so insistent thought it the best thing to do. Mamie is concerned chiefly with getting a post where servants are good—cheap—plentiful. I'd like a place that offers some interesting outdoor work. . . . So I asked for it."

While Ike pursued reassignment to San Antonio, others were seeking his talents. General William Conner, leaving the War College to become the superintendent of the U.S. Military Academy, invited Ike to be the West Point athletic director. The commander of Leavenworth asked Ike to join the Command and General Staff School faculty while also commanding the post's infantry battalion.

Ike did not consider either offer favorably, as each seemed a step backward rather than forward. Of course, he need not have fretted because he had never been in control of his next assignment, as neither Moseley nor MacArthur wanted Ike to leave the War Department. Ike wrote that MacArthur called him into his office "for a short conference relative to my prospective transfer." MacArthur said he wanted him to remain for a fourth year, and then he would then see to it that Ike got an infantry command at nearby Fort Washington. Ike agreed, writing, "Gen MacA. was very nice to me—and after all I know of no greater compliment the bosses can give you than I want you hanging around."

During the following months, Ike not only continued to work for Moseley but also expanded his workload to include drafting more letters and memos for MacArthur. He focused on wartime mobilization while also assisting with the army's oversight of the Civilian Conservation Corps and the Public Works Administration.

Then came the "Bonus March" in July 1932, over which Eisenhower and MacArthur disagreed. Ike later wrote, "An event occurred which brought the General a measure of lasting unfavorable publicity."

During the first half of the year, about forty-three thousand veterans of World War I, their families, and affiliated supporters gathered in Washington to demand immediate payment of their service bonus certificates, which had been authorized by Congress in 1924. Although the certificates were not due to be paid until 1945, most of the veterans, like many Americans, were out of work and desperate for money.

Ike explained, "We were in the depths of a depression. Men were out of work. The government had to alleviate distress and minimize hardships. Despite the fact that this was a national calamity affecting almost all citizens, some veterans seemed to feel that they should be regarded as a special class entitled to special privileges. They marched to Washington to get the promised money."

Some of the marchers occupied abandoned buildings near the Capitol, while the majority established a shanty town just across the Anacostia River, where they cooked on outdoor fires. Ike described the situation as follows: "To a number of citizens, they were a nuisance whose picketing and placards disturbed the quiet of Washington. To others, they were the menace of Bolshevism attacking the government at its very Capitol."

Washinton, DC, police had instructions to demolish the unauthorized ghetto from buildings near the Capitol. Despite firing on and killing two marchers, they were unsuccessful in displacing the veterans in July. President Hoover then ordered the army to clear the area.

Ike was opposed to the removal of the Bonus Marchers from Washington by members of the U.S. Army, but scant evidence exists to show that he made any effort to stop or limit the actions of his boss. Regardless of their increased personal and professional relationship, a major has little influence on the actions of a general and army chief of staff.

MacArthur gathered a thousand infantrymen and cavalrymen and six light tanks. With Major George Patton leading the horse soldiers, the troops quickly pushed the squatters out of the downtown buildings and drove them across the Anacostia. Despite instructions from the secretary of war that the soldiers were not to follow the fleeing protestors across the river, MacArthur ordered the troops to continue the pursuit, which they did in a cloud of tear gas. The shanty village caught fire—whether set by accident or by the squatters themselves—and burned to the ground. The demonstrators left Washington without their bonuses—which were finally paid in 1936 when Congress overrode a presidential veto.

MacArthur and the army were condemned by the press, as was President Hoover. The incident likely played a role in Hoover's loss to Franklin Roosevelt in the following November election. Ike's only comment at the time was an entry in his diary: "As Gen. MacA's aide took part in Bonus Incident of July 28, a lot of furor had been stirred up but mostly to make political capital. I wrote the General's report, which is as accurate as I could make it."

Ike might have been more correct to report that he made the account "as accurate as a subordinate can when writing in his bosses' name." In the lengthy assessment, he wrote that the army's "allotted tasks were performed rapidly and efficiently, but with the maximum consideration for members of the riotous groups consistent with their compulsory eviction. The results speak for themselves. Within a few hours a riot rapidly assuming alarming proportions was completely quelled, and from the time troops arrived at the scene of the disorder no soldier or civilian received a permanent or dangerous injury. Thus, a most disagreeable task was performed in such a way as to leave behind it a minimum of unpleasant aftermath and legitimate resentment."

Ike described his objections to the use of the army and, in particular, to the participation of MacArthur when he wrote, "I told him that the matter could easily become a riot and I thought it highly inappropriate for the Chief of Staff of the Army to be involved in anything like a local or street-corner embroilment. General MacArthur disagreed, saying that it was a question of Federal authority in the District of Columbia, and because of his belief that there was 'incipient revolution in the air' as he called it, he paid no attention to my dissent."

More than two decades passed before Ike recorded his actual feelings about MacArthur and the Bonus March. On December 12, 1954, he wrote in his diary, "I just can't understand how such a damn fool could have gotten to be a general." In an interview a short time later, he reportedly added, "I told the dumb son-of-a-bitch he had no business going down there. I told him it was no place for the chief of staff."

At the time, however, MacArthur approved and signed Ike's report on the Bonus Marchers, becoming more and more dependent on his assistance. Ike wrote, "General MacArthur, it developed, had need for a personal military assistant other than his aides, a man who could be an amanuensis to draft statements, reports, and letters for his signature. He asked me to take the job. I moved over to General MacArthur's office about the first of January 1933, and established a working relationship with him that was not to end until December 1939."

Ike's very use of the obscure word "amanuensis" in his later writing illuminates his real feelings. Merriam-Webster defines it as "one employed to write from dictation or to copy manuscript." In Latin, the phrase is more revealing. *Servus a manu* translates loosely as "slave with secretarial duties." In the seventeenth century, the second part of this phrase entered the English language to become amanuensis, a word for a person who is employed (willingly) to do the important but sometimes menial work of transcribing the words of another. Ike more clearly wrote of his "bondage" in Washington, stating, "I always resented the years I spent as a slave in the War Department."

General Moseley also continued to call on Ike to prepare important papers, which pleased him because it told him that Moseley recognized

his talents. After Ike's transfer to MacArthur's office, Moseley summarized the keys to Eisenhower's success, writing in a letter:

> You possess one of those exceptional minds which enables you to assem-
> ble and to analyze a set of facts, always drawing sound conclusions and,
> equally important, you have the ability to express those conclusions in
> clear and convincing form. Many officers can take the first two steps of
> a problem, but few have your ability of expression. The subjects that
> you have worked upon have covered a very wide field. . . . My earnest
> hope is that you will guard your strength and talents carefully and that
> promotion may be given you in order that your government may use
> your talents in positions of great responsibility.

Assistant Secretary Payne, just prior to his departure from the War
Department, sent correspondence to Major General James F. McKinley,
adjutant general of the army, on March 4, echoing Moseley's praise. He
wrote for inclusion in Ike's personnel file, "Major Eisenhower has been
of great personal help to me. . . . He excels, he has a remarkable power of
expression, a rare balance of judgement, and a special aptitude for quickly
picking out the critical points in any subject assigned to him for study."

Ike enjoyed the prestige of working for the chief of staff and being at
the center of army decision making, but he knew that he remained little
more than a glorified clerk. Staff officers might receive accolades, but
promotions and advancement went to field commanders.

In reality, Ike was an indispensable man in a dispensable job—a
position that had no authorized title. His officer efficiency report listed
his official status as "on duty in the Office of the Chief of Staff." Despite
his misgivings, his position as MacArthur's assistant provided unique
insights into the internal operations of the army as well as the challenges
of mobilizing peacetime armed forces into wartime fighting units.

On June 14, 1932, Ike began to log in his diary his observations
about those with whom he served: "Occurred to me I might jot down
from time to time impressions of people with whom I came in contact. Sometime in the future it will be fun to review these to determine
whether my impression was a permanent one."

Ike added, "There are no 'great men' as we understood that expression when we were shavers. The man whose brain is all-embracing in its grasp of events, so infallible in its logic, and so swift in formulation of perfect decisions, is only a figment of the imagination. Yet as kids we were taught to believe in the shibboleth of the 'superman'—possibly because it is easier to exaggerate than not."

In his entry about MacArthur, Ike addressed his boss's tendency to promote older and more senior officers and MacArthur's disdain for age-based forced retirement. Specifically, he wrote, "In this one thing even those who have known him longest seem to consider him reactionary and almost bigoted." He continued, calling MacArthur "essentially a romantic figure. . . . Very appreciative of good work, positive in his convictions—a genius at giving concise and clear instructions. . . . Magnetic and extremely likable. Placed a letter of commendation on my record—and has assured me that as long as he stays in the Army I am one of the people earmarked for his 'gang.' . . . He is impulsive— able, even brilliant—quick—tenacious of his views and extremely self-confident."

Thirty-five years later, Ike expanded on his opinion of the general. In *At Ease*, he elaborated:

Douglas MacArthur was a forceful—some thought overpowering— individual, blessed with a fast and facile mind, interested in both the military and political side of our government. From the beginning, I found that he was well acquainted with most of the people in the government in almost every department. Working with him brought an additional dimension to my experience. . . . He was decisive, personable, and he had one habit that never ceased to startle me. In reminiscing or in telling stories of the current scene, he talked of himself in the third person. Although I had heard of this idiosyncrasy, the sensation was unusual. In time I got used to it and saw it not as objectionable, just odd. On any subject he chose to discuss, his knowledge, always amazingly comprehensive, and largely accurate, poured out in a torrent of words. "Discuss" is hardly the correct word; discussion suggests dialogue and the General's conversations were usually monologues.

Ike noted that MacArthur "was a rewarding man to work for." He did not care what hours Ike kept if he accomplished his work. This task usually required late shifts, but Ike noted that the general never objected to him taking a few days' or a week's leave.

Although his superior was publicly lauded for the same characteristics Ike noted, MacArthur was privately criticized for behavior that was considered narcissistic, egotistic, bombastic, and overpowering. Ike mused that his boss "could never see another sun in the heavens."

"My office was next to his; only a slatted door separated us," Ike remembered. "He called me into his office by raising his voice." What Ike did not write was that his "office" was so small that it barely held his desk and chair and was badly in need of a fresh coat of paint.

By this time, MacArthur had been a general, with all its privileges, for fourteen years—about the same tenure Ike had had as a major. Despite their difference in rank, MacArthur seemed to genuinely like his subordinate.

While MacArthur usually totally dominated all other conversations he was involved in, with Ike there was a mutual interchange of thoughts and ideas. These exchanges usually occurred in a fog of cigarette smoke, both being chain smokers. In addition to their concern for official matters, both were zealous followers of the West Point football team—particularly in its annual contest with the Naval Academy. Mamie and Ike also joined MacArthur at parties and dinners.

Regardless of their closeness, the older man's ego and thoughtlessness were at times more than unpleasant. One example in particular—perhaps intended to reinforce to Ike their senior-subordinate relationship—seemed small at the time but remained with Ike over the decades. As the chief of staff, MacArthur had a chauffeured limousine to transport him around Washington. Ike, who frequently had to visit Capitol Hill or other offices in the city, was forced to take streetcars or taxis to his destinations. On his return each time, he had to file a travel voucher for reimbursement. MacArthur never once offered Ike the use of his automobile, regardless of the importance of the major's errand. The treatment still rankled Ike years later when he told a reporter, "No matter what happens later you never forget something like that."

MacArthur also expected his aide to do his "dirty work." After dispatching the Bonus Marchers, for example, two Hearst journalists—Robert Allen and Drew Pearson—began a series of articles critical of the general. When MacArthur filed a $1.75 million lawsuit against the two, they threatened to expose the fact that the general had had a Eurasian mistress whom he had maintained in a luxurious apartment on 16th Street, only ten blocks from the White House. Although the relationship had ended, MacArthur—apparently fearing his mother's reaction, as well as the public condemnation should the relationship become known—dispatched Ike to find the woman and learn what it would take to dissuade her from testifying. When Eisenhower failed to locate her, MacArthur dropped the lawsuit.

Ike, like most military officers, did not vote in the presidential election of 1932; however, he found himself becoming more interested in politics as he worked with Washington's elected and appointed officials. His awareness of the continuing national depression caused Ike to contemplate subjects outside the army. Three weeks after the election, he admitted in his diary that while he had no "definite leanings toward any political party," he believed that "it is a good thing the Democrats won." Ike trusted in Roosevelt's New Deal and thought that it would take an empowered president to lift the country out of the Depression. He did not, however, think highly of Roosevelt himself. He later said, "I think Mr. Roosevelt is a mediocre man who has a pleasant sounding voice on the radio."

Ike's partisan ideas were developing. His brother Milton was a Republican holdover in the Department of Agriculture, and the brothers met frequently to talk politics.

On October 29, 1933, Ike recorded in his journal, "I believe that unity of action is essential to success in the current struggle. I believe that individual rights must be subordinated to public good, and that the public good can be served only by unanimous adherence to an authoritative plan. We must conform to the President's program regardless of the consequences. Otherwise, dissention, confusion, and partisan politics will ruin us."

Ike's continued service under MacArthur reinforced his reputation as "a master of the pen." He had a unique skill in writing in the voice of the person who was to sign the final document.

The most important paper Ike prepared for MacArthur was his annual report. On October 24, he logged in his Chief of Staff Diary, "Sent Gen. MacA's 1933 annual report to the Public Printer. I am curious to find out what comment it will inspire, as it is a frank presentation of our situation with respect to military preparedness."

The document began, "Time and again national leaders have likened existing conditions to those of war," and stated that the government was in a "powerful offensive against the forces of depression." It noted that establishing and providing health, welfare, and maintenance for the three-hundred-thousand-man Civilian Conservation Corps in small camps across the country had allowed for "valuable training in mobilization processes and leadership."

The report then noted that the army's austere budget and the shortage of matériel and officers limited its ability to satisfactorily perform basic defense duties. The report outlined future trends in organizing, equipping, and training the army and noted that, while weapons, tactics, and organization of the military might change, "the only unchanging element in armies is man himself."

Proposals for necessary changes followed, including a recommendation that the infantry should replace the current bolt-action rifles with semiautomatic shoulder weapons and light machine guns. As for the cavalry, the report read, "the time has arrived when the Cavalry arm must either replace or assist the horse as a means of transportation." The recommendation was for the adaptation of mechanized and motorized vehicles for both the cavalry and artillery. The Air Corps, according to the report, had benefited from sacrifices in other programs to make it the best prepared of the services.

The report concluded:

The inevitable trend in warfare is toward greater speed of strategic maneuver through maximum utilization of relatively fast machines for transportation; increased fire-power on the battlefield through employment of weapons of much greater efficiency, with a resultant wider dispersion in tactical formations; more power in the attack through utilization of combat vehicles invulnerable to small-arms fire and capable of cross-country travel; growing dependency upon air forces for information, for assistance in defense of the coast line, for attacks against hostile ground forces, and for bombardment of sensitive points in the enemy's supply organization.

On December 9, Ike recorded in his diary, "Publication of Gen. MacA's annual report elicited a volume of press comment throughout the country. In general this publicity was sympathetic and favorable, although a half dozen editorials were distinctly hostile [primarily due to the cost of modernization]. I think that the C. of S. is, on the whole, much pleased with the reception his report experienced."

Even in his personal notes, Ike took no credit for his writing or the reception of the report, giving full credit to his boss. Military officers, as well as civilian officials, understood, however, that Ike spoke for the general. They often approached him for his opinions and recommendations, knowing that they would be the same as MacArthur's.

Because Ike was very much aware that mentors—such as Fox Conner—had been positive influences not only in his development as a soldier but also in his assignments, he did his best to follow their example. While at the War Department, he frequently received communications from classmates and friends inquiring about their assignment status or requesting assistance in attending the Command and General Staff School and the War College. Ike did his best to help and, along the way, built loyalties among many officers—several of whom would hold senior commands in World War II.

MacArthur completed his four-year tour as the chief of staff in the fall of 1934. President Roosevelt did not like MacArthur personally and feared that he might be a political opponent in the next election. He also had no desire to elevate the next in line for the job, General Moseley, because of his radical beliefs. Further, General Pershing, although retired, still advised the president and recommended a one-year extension for MacArthur. Roosevelt, adhering to the axiom of keeping your friends close and your enemies even closer, reluctantly agreed.

Ike summarized in *At Ease*, writing, "Ordinarily, General MacArthur would have been relieved as Chief of Staff in the fall of 1934. However, reorganization in the War Department was going on and it is possible that the President had not yet chosen a man he wanted to appoint as the next Chief. General MacArthur's tour was extended by one year."

MacArthur's additional commitment meant another year for Ike as well. Given no choice, Ike reapplied himself to writing for the chief, including another annual report. The year was made the more trying by the death of Katie Gerow—the wife of Ike's good friend Gee Gerow—who had been hospitalized shortly after their transfer from the Philippines to Washington. Her death on June 17 was attributed by some to a mysterious disease contracted in the Philippines, but the more likely cause was cancer.

The Eisenhowers hosted the extended Gerow family for dinner after Katie's funeral and continued to comfort Gee over the summer. Although neither Ike nor Mamie mentioned it in their writings, Katie's death no doubt brought back memories of losing Icky.

During MacArthur and Ike's final year in the War Department, the U.S. Congress passed the Tydings-McDuffie Act granting the Philippines—a group of 7,641 islands in Southeast Asia that the United States had controlled since the end of the Spanish-American War in 1898—the status of commonwealth for ten years before gaining independence.

MacArthur's father had fought against Filipino guerrillas and served as the first U.S. military governor of the islands. Son Douglas MacArthur had served two tours in the Philippines, finding both the country and its inhabitants quite to his liking. During his second tour in 1925, MacArthur began a friendship with Manuel Quezon, who would become the first president of the Philippines in 1935.

Among Quezon's vast challenges in preparing his country for independence was the formation of a defense force. Quezon approached Roosevelt and asked that MacArthur be appointed military advisor to the Philippines to assist in the formation of its armed forces. Roosevelt, more than happy to have MacArthur thousands of miles and an ocean away from Washington, readily agreed. The general, not wanting to be subordinate to a new chief of staff and welcoming the opportunity to return to the Philippines, enthusiastically accepted the appointment with instructions from the president "to survey the military needs of the Philippine commonwealth, in anticipation of the commonwealth's independence in 1946."

MacArthur told Ike that, since they worked well together and he did not want to train anyone new, he wanted Ike to accompany him to the Philippines. Aware that MacArthur's star was fading and that remaining with the general would not advance his career, Ike asked instead for a transfer to an infantry battalion because had not had a troop assignment since 1924.

At least two of Ike's bosses—MacArthur and his friend George Patton, in particular—believed they were destined for greatness. Another trait that they shared was their displeasure at anyone disagreeing with them, which is where Ike found himself when he suggested that he would rather have a troop assignment than a tour in the Philippines. He dared broach the topic with his temperamental boss only because he knew that troop command was so critical to his own career path.

Ike later described MacArthur's reaction, writing that the general "lowered the boom" on him, ending the conversation. He admitted, "I was in no position to argue with the Chief of Staff."

MacArthur did make two concessions. First, he informed Ike that he could select one regular army officer to accompany them to the island chain. Ike chose Major James "Jimmy" B. Ord, a West Point classmate and old friend who had walked punishment tours with him at the Academy. The short and rather rotund Ord—often described as looking like a midwestern banker—did not strike an impressive figure, but he had a brilliant mind for planning mobilization and operations. He also had a background to support his selection, having himself served with Pershing in the Mexican Punitive Expedition and having a grandfather who had commanded a corps under Ulysses S. Grant in the Civil War. Ike wrote that Ord was "a man whom I wanted with us not only because of his quickness of mind and ability as a staff officer but because he was as much at home in Spanish—the principal language of the Philippines after Tagalog—as he was in English. Jimmy Ord was eager to go."

The second concession MacArthur made involved another letter of appreciation, which he penned on September 30, 1935:

My dear Major Eisenhower,

Upon relinquishing the position of Chief of Staff, I want to leave a written record of my appreciation of certain important considerations connected with your work which have not been easy to describe in normal reports.

You were retained by the Secretary of War, and later by myself, on critical duties in the Department long past the duration of ordinary staff tours, solely because of your success in performing difficult tasks whose accomplishments required a comprehensive grasp of the military profession in all its principal phases, as well as analytical thought and forceful expression. Through all these years I have been impressed by the cheerful and efficient devotion of your best efforts to confining, difficult, and often strenuous duties, in spite of the fact that your own personal desires involved a return to troop command and other physically active phases of Army life, for which your characteristics so well qualify you. In this connection I should like to point out to you that your unusual experience in the Department will be of no less future value to you as a commander than as a staff officer, since all problems presented to you were nevertheless solved from the viewpoint of the High Command. Then too, I have noted with satisfaction that you have never sought to employ staff authority in lieu of a proper application of leadership methods, but to the contrary, have invariably demonstrated an ability to organize complicated tasks quickly and efficiently, to secure cheerful cooperation from all concerned, and to carry group efforts to successful conclusion. The number of personal requests for your services brought to me by the heads of many of the Army's principal activities during the past few years furnish convincing proof of the reputation you have established as an outstanding soldier. I can say no more than that this reputation coincides exactly with my own judgement.

With personal regard,
Sincerely,
Douglas MacArthur

Despite being disappointed about not going to a troop assignment, Ike did look forward to serving in the Philippines—not only had it been his first choice of postings when he graduated from West Point, but the Philippine government also agreed to supplement the pay of the military advisors. This stipend would double Ike's regular salary. In *At Ease*, Ike joked that the reason he had never previously been assigned to the islands was that "there was no Filipino football teams to coach."

Neither the pay increase nor the assurance of luxurious quarters inspired Mamie to share her husband's enthusiasm. She did not want to leave the comfort of their Wyoming Building apartment and the Washington social scene, and she would not be enticed by the low cost of living her friend Katie Gerow had described before she became ill and died—Katie had written that everything in the Philippines was so cheap that "all you had to do was breath[e]." Mainly, however, Mamie feared that either she or John might come down with whatever disease she believed had killed her friend.

Persuading Mamie to move to the Philippines was further complicated by the fact that MacArthur did not promise Ike a transfer after a year, instead leaving his tour length indefinite. After much conversation—some of it heated—the couple agreed that Mamie would remain in Washington at least until the end of John's school year.

Chapter 13

Philippines and General MacArthur

General Douglas MacArthur and his staff departed Washington on October 1, 1935, by train for a cross-country journey to San Francisco, where they would board the SS *President Harding* for a three-week voyage to Manila. Eisenhower, who had been on leave in Abilene and Denver, planned to join the entourage at a scheduled stop in Cheyenne, Wyoming. Little did he suspect that he would be boarding just in time to witness one of MacArthur's greatest calamities.

The general believed he had Franklin Roosevelt's permission to officially remain chief of staff and to retain his rank of four-star general until December 15, thus enabling him to arrive in Manila wearing the army's highest rank. That was his vision until two days into the train ride, when the train stopped in Cheyenne.

Not only did Ike come aboard, but so did a telegram for MacArthur from Acting Secretary of War Harry H. Woodring, stating, "The President has just informed me that he has appointed Malin Craig Chief of Staff, effective this date."

Roosevelt had outsmarted MacArthur. In the military world, where an officer's word is his bond, the general was unprepared for the falsehoods, doublespeak, and out-and-out lies of politics. By appointing a rival and thus reverting MacArthur to two-star rank, the president had demonstrated his desire to end the "MacArthur era" in the War Department.

According to Ike, the telegram caused MacArthur "to express himself freely. It was an explosive denunciation of politics, bad manners, bad judgement, broken promises, arrogance, unconstitutionality, insensitivity, and the way the world had gone to hell."

MacArthur, however, was not one to burn bridges. Once his anger had subsided, he sent a telegram to Craig, writing, "The entire Army will look forward with keen anticipation to what cannot fail to be a successful tenure of office." As for responding to the president, he wrote that Craig's appointment was "not only admirable but timely." The incident was another "lesson learned" for Ike in that it provided insights into the nature of politics at the Washington level. It also revealed a lack of concern and support from the White House and Capitol for arming the Philippines.

The American Military Mission made port in Manila on October 26, 1935. General MacArthur and his mother took up quarters in the Manila Hotel—known as one of the "jewels of the Orient" and still ranked as a five-star destination today. Ike occupied a smaller suite in the same facility, where neither he nor MacArthur had to pay for the luxury accommodations. Meanwhile, the mission headquarters set up offices at 1 Calle Victoria in a large building that stood inside Manila's fortified seventeenth-century wall. Ike later had an office in the Malacañan Palace, which housed the Philippine government.

While Ike and Jimmy Ord immediately began to finalize their plans for the formation of the Philippines' armed forces, which they had begun before leaving Washington, MacArthur provided little guidance or support. Eisenhower, as usual, made excuses for his boss as well as rationalizing his mother's influence, writing that she was "imbued with assurance that her son was destined for greatness; she lived for him and his success." He further noted, "Despite his own immense talents, the General relied heavily on her when the going was tough; he shared with her as a partner the joys of achievement. Shortly after we boarded the *President Harding*, she became ill. Not long after our arrival in Manila, she was dead. Her departure from his side, and from his counsels, affected the General's spirit for many months."

The disheartened MacArthur left the day-to-day operations of the mission to Eisenhower and Ord, providing them with only guidelines while expecting them to come up with details and execution. The general conducted most of his business from his hotel suite, usually visiting head-quarters for only an hour or so during the afternoon. This routine caused some members of the mission to speculate that MacArthur appeared to be enjoying semi-retirement more than executing his assigned duties as direct commander.

To keep a record of their unusual assignment in the Philippines—and perhaps to provide a venue for letting off a bit of steam—Ike again kept a journal. He made his first entry on December 27, 1935, writing, "The Military Mission, headed by General MacArthur, landed in Manila two months ago, on October 26. It has been my intention from the start to keep a brief narrative record of the principal recommendations and activities of the mission. Due to unsettled conditions, there has been, up to this time, no opportunity to make a methodical record of events." He then wrote that this initial entry would summarize the first two months of the mission, while subsequent entries would "represent a daily running account of the Mission's activities."

On May 29, 1936, Ike recorded his continued difficulties in getting his boss's direct involvement in working with the Philippine govern-ment: "We've tried also, time and time again, to get the general to stay in closer contact with Q [Manuel Quezon]. Things happen, and we know nothing of them. We're constantly wondering whether the president will approve or disapprove. We ought to know. We could if the general would take the trouble to see Q weekly—but he apparently thinks it would not be in keeping with his rank and position for him to do so."

There were also problems with MacArthur's concept of the Philip-pine military and its defense of the islands. The general, understanding that a country comprising more than seven thousand islands spread over a vast ocean could not be totally defended, called for a plan to defend only the major islands. A shortcoming of this strategy was that the nation's navy did not exist, nor was its token-only air force able to defend its skies. The U.S. naval and air forces could hardly reinforce that which was nonexistent.

Other challenges also faced the mission. Since the 1898 victory, a sizable U.S. Army contingent known as the Philippine Department had been stationed in the islands. Its commander, Major General Frank

Parker, instructed by the War Department to support MacArthur, did little to cooperate, as Parker and his subordinates resented the intrusion into what they considered a very easy and comfortable assignment. A lieutenant colonel, writing in 1910 about duties in the Philippines, had said, "The post is like a big country club. A little work in the morning. Golf, polo, tennis, riding in the hills in the afternoon. The Club at sunset. Dinner in the evening. A lazy man's paradise."

Frank Murphy, appointed by President Roosevelt as the high commissioner of the Philippines, also opposed the mission. Not only was he a pacifist, but he also believed the islands were indefensible.

Many Americans had concluded that a viable Filipino army was impossible. Speculation was that if one were formed, it might rebel against its own government. In general, the Americans held the native population in low regard, often declaring, "What do you expect? They're Filipinos." In essence, the Americans and Filipinos were entangled in a cultural conflict to which neither seemed able or willing to seek solutions.

Ike did not share these racist views. The nearest he came to criticizing the Filipinos was in his diary, where he recorded, "We—at least Jimmy and myself—have learned to expect from the Filipinos with whom we deal a minimum of performance from a maximum of promise. Among individuals there is no lack of intelligence, but to us they seem with few exceptions, unaccustomed to the requirements of administrative and executive procedure."

Beyond these difficulties loomed an even greater problem. The Philippines had extremely limited funds for the formation of a military force, and, as Ike noted, the United States allocated money based more on an entity's ability to influence the November elections than on meeting the actual needs of the military. Every projection he and Ord submitted required that they go back and reduce numbers and expenditures.

Ike realized that the mission faced an impossible task but nevertheless continued to strive to make it viable. A draft of all eligible Filipinos was initiated, and ninety training camps were established across the islands. With limited transportation available, it was more economical to send small training cadres to remote sites than to bring recruits to a central training center. Once trained, the recruits remained on their home island as a part of its defense force. A military academy, based on the West Point model, was established to produce officers. Obsolete U.S. weapons—mostly World War I Enfield rifles—and equipment were to be either purchased or donated.

There were other needs as well. Ike wrote, "We soon saw that it was necessary to have a small 'air force' even if for nothing else than to get to training stations. The road net of the Philippine archipelago, comprising something over seven thousand islands, was still primitive except in Luzon. Light planes that could land and take off from short strips would make every training site accessible. So, aiming at two birds with one stone, we bought a few primary trainers of the type used at Randolph Field and borrowed two instructors from the Army Air Corps."

Once the sites were established and running well, Ike began to take flying lessons, an activity he had wanted to pursue since his first assignment in San Antonio but had not because of Mamie's fear of the early airplanes' vulnerabilities. Now planes were much improved, and Mamie was still across the Pacific in Washington. Without getting her permission or even informing her, he took to the air. Ike noted that, at the age of forty-six, he had slower reflexes than the younger men. Nevertheless, his instructors reported that he was "a natural pilot."

Thereafter, Ike continued to take lessons from the Air Corps instructors, usually arriving at the airfield at 6:30 a.m., flying for an hour or so, and then arriving at his office by the time others reported for work. By the summer of 1939, he had accumulated 350 flight hours and, on July 5, received his private pilot's license.

Ike continued to fly until 1947. He wrote, "After World War II, I had ceased to fly altogether, except that once in a while, on a long trip, to relieve my boredom (and demolish the pilot's), I would move into the co-pilot's seat and take over the controls. But when the jet age arrived, I realized that I had come out of a horse-and-buggy background, recognized my limitations, and kept to a seat in the back."

Flying served a much more significant role in Eisenhower's life than just amusement and relief from boredom. The knowledge of aviation that he accrued through his piloting exploits would later aid greatly in his understanding and deployment of the U.S. Army Air Corps assets—which became the Army Air Forces in 1941 and the U.S. Air Force in 1947. Because of his flying experiences, he could more clearly visualize the aerial combat in North Africa and the bombing campaigns against Germany. Although Eisenhower never wore aviator insignia, the American airmen and commanders who served under him were aware that their boss shared in all that came with the symbolic wings.

In September 1936, General William Conner, who had become the superintendent at West Point, requested that MacArthur release Ike from his command in order for him to become the commandant of cadets. MacArthur refused, responding that Eisenhower was engaged in "duties of gravest importance. He could not adequately be replaced." Ike was not consulted but would have turned down the option because, as he wrote, he wanted "no part of that." In his view, the commandant was only in charge of disciplining the cadets, and he "had no ambition to get into that kind of business."

Ike continued working his way into the inner circles of senior military and civilian leaders. The more he interacted with President Quezon, the stronger their relationship became. Ike wrote, "He had prepared a private office for me in his Malacanan Palace because of the amount of work I had to do between his office and ours as liaison agent."

The two also developed a social relationship. Ike had resumed playing poker, and the Philippine president invited him to sit in on his regular games. Quezon also enjoyed bridge and included Ike at his table. On weekends, Quezon hosted Ike on his presidential yacht for card games that frequently lasted late into the night.

July 1, 1936, was a notable date for Eisenhower because it was the day—after having served as a major for sixteen years—that the army promoted him to lieutenant colonel. The day also marked his twentieth wedding anniversary. The advancement to a silver oak leaf made little difference other than a small pay increase. His duties, already far above the responsibilities of most majors or lieutenant colonels, did not change.

As for the second occasion, Mamie understood from the fewer and fewer letters she received from her husband that if she wished for the marriage to continue, she must join him in the Philippines. She and

John arrived in Manila aboard the army transport *President Grant* on November 3, 1936.

Try as she might, however, Mamie could not adapt to her new circumstances: She dreaded living in the tropics again. She was less than enamored of Ike's shaved head when he met her at the dock, having removed what little hair remained for the cooling benefit in the hot climate. She was not happy with their un-air-conditioned suite at the Manila Hotel, where she suffered claustrophobia and couldn't sleep under the mosquito netting over their bed.

Even more challenges awaited Mamie as she strove to assimilate to life in the Pacific. For one thing, she resented the paternalistic culture of the islands, which she found, according to their granddaughter's book, to be a "man's country" where "the 'master' is the whole cheese." Another irritant for Mamie was Marian Huff, Ike's frequent golf partner and wife of naval officer Sidney Huff. Although Sidney did not seem the least concerned about the relationship—and there is no evidence of anything other than friendship between Ike and Marian—Mamie viewed Marian as a threat.

According to her granddaughter Susan Eisenhower in *Mrs. Ike: Mamie Eisenhower*, "It didn't seem to occur to her that she had been escorted around Washington by a number of male friends during her year alone. But jealousy knows no logic nor does it respect reciprocity, and proud Mamie fought with conflicting emotions of embarrassment and possibly humiliation."

Tensions between the Eisenhowers did not ease until an emergency caused Mamie to reevaluate their relationship. During a two-hour trip to Baguio, where John was at boarding school, a blood vessel in her stomach ruptured, and she began vomiting blood. Rushed to the hospital, she was in a coma for several days. Ike was at her bedside when she awoke. Mamie stayed in the hospital for a month while she recovered and evaluated the relationship with her husband. Her granddaughter wrote, "The disagreements with Ike that had surfaced after her arrival began to disappear, and any unpleasantness that may have revolved around Mrs. Huff all but vanished."

On recovery, Mamie joined the island's extensive American social scene of shopping, dining, and partying. She befriended Jean Faircloth, the wealthy Tennessee native whom MacArthur had married in New York City on April 30, 1937, while back in the States to bury his mother. After laying his mother to rest beside her late husband in Arlington National Cemetery, MacArthur—ever focused on his priorities—went to the Pentagon in search of funds for raising the Philippine army.

A move to a suite in the newly air-conditioned wing of their Manila hotel also lifted Mamie's spirits and helped her accept life on the island. Although never happy in the outdoors, she took up golf to be Ike's partner on the links, replacing Mrs. Huff. Ike's increase in salary as a lieutenant colonel and his bonus from the Philippine government helped as well. In a letter to her parents on February 8, Mamie wrote, "We've been financially on easy street for the first time in our married life. We're having pretty near anything we wish."

In early April 1938, Mamie again wrote to her parents, this time letting them know that she had finally come to terms with being an army wife to her husband. She wrote, "I told him the other day that it has taken me 22 years to find out that the only way I can get along with him is to give him his own way constantly." A week later, she wrote them once more, this time confessing, "I made a terrible mistake in not coming out here with Ike. It's up to me to rectify lots of things."

Even as Ike and Mamie's relationship grew stronger, his relationship with General MacArthur deteriorated. MacArthur gave broad orders to Eisenhower and Ord and then did little to pave the way for his subordinates to carry them out. The general had minimal respect for President Quezon but played the role of happy partner in public. In private, Ike once heard the general refer to the president as a "conceited little monkey."

Personalities aside, the primary problem for both countries remained a lack of funds. The Philippines had few resources, and the U.S. government remained reluctant to allocate money for the defense of the island nation. The American armed forces also suffered a lack of men and equipment because of their own limited budget caused by the lengthy Depression.

MacArthur continued to demand the training of Philippine soldiers and units in numbers that could not be attained. Ike—the only MacArthur subordinate in the Philippines or elsewhere who stood up to the general and survived to tell about it—disagreed and proposed a lower number. Although MacArthur frequently yelled at Ike in bursts of anger, he never fired him, recognizing his subordinate's talents and unwilling to send him back to the States.

Ike encouraged MacArthur to return to Washington to lobby for additional finances and equipment. Instead, according to Ike's diary, MacArthur refused and directed him to prepare a paper for the War Department to explain the "efficiency and soundness of the Philippine Defense Plan, and the idea that the American War Department should cooperate efficiently toward its development."

The treatise had little impact on the provision of support for the islands. It was not until the spring of 1937 that MacArthur returned to the States seeking additional assistance. Meanwhile, his main concern became his promotion to field marshal of the Philippine army by President Quezon.

Only years later would Ike learn that the promotion was MacArthur's idea and not Quezon's. The Philippine president went along with the proposal and suggested that he also commission Eisenhower, Ord, and Thomas Jefferson David (MacArthur's aide) and promote them to senior positions in his army and award them higher salaries. Ike convinced his colleagues that the promotions would not only hinder the mission's efforts but also raise ethical questions. They agreed; MacArthur did not.

Ike confronted his boss, saying, "General you have been a four-star general. . . . This is a proud thing. Why in the hell do you want a banana republic giving you a field-marshalship?" Ike wrote that his boss "just gave [him] hell."

Quezon, with great ceremony, promoted MacArthur to field marshal of the Philippine army on August 24, 1936. The promotion stroked MacArthur's ego and allowed him to strut around in a sharkskin uniform consisting of black pants and a white tunic loaded with ribbons and medals that he had personally designed.

Situations other than military matters also brought on MacArthur's wrath. In his diary on September 26, 1936, Ike wrote, "I came in for a terrible bawling out over a most ridiculous affair. The Gen. has been following the *Literary Digest* poll, and has convinced himself that [Republican Alf] Landon is to be elected, probably by a landslide." Friends back home, as well as his brother in Washington, had written Ike that their fellow Kansan had no chance in his 1936 challenge against President Roosevelt. Ike later explained MacArthur's outrage, writing, "We couldn't understand the reason for his almost hysterical condemnation of our STUPIDITY until he suddenly let drop that he had gone out and urged Q. to shape his plans for going to U.S. on the theory Landon will be elected." When Roosevelt soundly defeated Landon in November, Ike again took to the pages of his journal: "Boy did the General back pedal rapidly. I hear he went out to Q. on the first or second and 'took back' what he had said at first. Accused the *Literary Digest* of 'crookedness' when he heard Wall Street odds had gone up to 4–1 on Roosevelt against Landon. . . . But he never expressed to . . . me any regret of his awful bawling out a couple of months ago."

With the increased aggression of Japan across Asia, MacArthur and Quezon continued to demand the training of more and more Philippine divisions. When Eisenhower and Ord reported that there was no money to do so, MacArthur ranted that his staff were "arguing technicalities" to thwart his grand concepts.

Ike's facts about insufficient funds did not sway MacArthur. Yet the general's stubborn insistence on getting his way provided another object lesson for Ike. On October 8, 1937, Ike wrote in his diary about the incident:

> For some months, I've remained on this job, not because of the General, but in spite of him. I've got interested in this riddle of whether or not we can develop a W.D. [Philippine War Department] and an army capable of running itself, and I prefer to dig away at it to being on a "mark time" basis somewhere else. But now I am at the cross road. If the Marshal is to persist in his arbitrary methods, and is going to make things as unpleasant, if not impossible, as today's homily indicated, then

I'm for home. We should be able to get a better line on the situation in a few days! Right now I am disgusted and in something of a temper, a bad state of mind in which to make any decisions.

MacArthur must have sensed that he had seriously offended his right-hand man, for he took measures to mediate their conflict. On October 12, the general officially made Ike his chief of staff. The position did not really change Ike's responsibilities but did give him more control over other members of the mission.

Into the midst of all the relationship turmoil between Ike and MacArthur and the difficulties in establishing the Filipino army came directions from the War Department that the general, having completed his tour of duty there, was to return to the States as a major general. Having served as army chief of staff in a four-star position, the egotistical MacArthur had no desire to assume a subordinate position that carried only two stars.

MacArthur took out his frustrations on his subordinates. Ike noted in his diary, "Every time one of these tempest in a teapot sweeps the office, I find myself, sooner or later, bearing the brunt of the General's displeasure, *which always manifests itself against anyone who fails in toto with his theories and hypotheses* [Eisenhower's emphasis], no matter how astounding they may be. These comic opera wars never center around any problem incident to the job we are on. They invariably involve something personal to the Gen.; I could be the fair-haired boy if I'd only yes, yes, yes!! That would be so easy, too!!"

MacArthur reacted by retiring from the U.S. Army on December 31 and, at the request of Quezon, remaining in the Philippines as the field marshal of its armed forces. The general's wife, among others, found the situation amusing, saying that her husband had gone from the highest rank in the U.S. Army to the highest rank in a nonexistent army. Ike and the rest of the mission remained under MacArthur's command.

The greatest break in the Eisenhower–McArthur relationship came in January 1938. Although disappointing, the incident reinforced for Ike the requisite for a commander to take responsibility for his actions rather than laying the blame for failures on his subordinates. Ike explained in *At Ease*:

> There was an incident that chilled the warm relationship that Jimmy Ord and I had with General MacArthur. The General had an idea that the morale of the whole population would be enhanced if the people could see something of their emerging army in the capital city, Manila. He suggested a large demonstration of strength, bringing units from all over the Islands to a field near the city, and camping them there for three or four days. The city's population could visit them and it would all end with a big parade.
>
> Jimmy and I estimated the cost. We told the General that it was impossible to do the thing within our budget. Carrying out this demonstration would take money that was desperately needed for more important purposes. But following the General's orders, we began to do the necessary staff work.
>
> Among other details, we had to arrange with island shipping firms to bring in the troops. It wasn't long until the news of this reached the Philippine government. President Quezon called me in from the little office in Malacanan, said he had heard about the planned troop movement, and asked me what it was all about.
>
> I was astonished. We had assumed that the project had first been agreed on between the President and General MacArthur. When I discovered that this was not the case, I told Quezon that I thought we should discuss it no further until I could see General MacArthur. But Quezon was disturbed and said he was going to telephone the General. I said I would withdraw to my office and when he wanted me again, he could reach me there.
>
> He didn't call and I returned to my other office in the Walled City within the hour. General MacArthur was exceedingly unhappy with his entire staff. By the time I saw him, he was visibly upset. He said he had never meant for us to proceed with preparations for the parade. He had only wanted us to investigate it quietly. Now the matter had come to the ears of the President who was horrified to think that we were ready for a costly national parade. Because General MacArthur denied he had given us an order—which was certainly news to us—there was nothing to do except stop the proceedings. This misunderstanding

caused considerable resentment—and never again were we on the same warm and cordial terms.

Ike was disappointed to the point of anger that MacArthur failed to support his staff. He believed that his boss had, in effect, made him look like a liar to the Philippine president. To MacArthur, he exclaimed, "General, all you're saying is that I'm a liar, and I am not a liar and so I'd like to go back to the States right away."

MacArthur, who never admitted a fault or apologized for anything— but who also did not want to lose his talented subordinate—laid on all his charm and warmly placed his arm around Ike. He then parried, "Ike, it's just fun to see that damn Dutch temper. . . . It's just a misunderstanding, and let it go at that." Ike "let it go at that" and went back to work because he had no other choice if he wanted to continue his career.

Shortly thereafter, events would make this incident seem far less important and remind Ike that being a soldier in peacetime could also be dangerous. On January 30, Jimmy Ord, with a Filipino pilot at the controls, took off from Manila to inspect training at Baguio. Their plane crashed on the approach to the airfield, killing Ord. President Quezon awarded the Distinguished Service Star to Ord; the citation read:

As one of the principal assistants of the Military Adviser, Colonel Ord continuously, from the inauguration of the Commonwealth to the moment of his untimely death, devoted his exceptional talents to the development of adequate security forces for the Philippines. Through his professional attainments, his breadth of understanding, his zeal and his magnetic leadership he was directly responsible for notable progress in the Philippine Army. Through his outstanding achievements, in the service of the Philippine Government, to which service he gave his life, he increased the brilliance of his already enviable military reputation, became an inspiration to the officers and enlisted men of the Army, and earned the gratitude and affection of the Philippine Government and of the Filipino people.

Ike wrote in his diary about his friend's death: "Many people have lost a close companion and an intimate friend. I've lost this, also my right hand,

and my partner on a tough job, who furnished most of the inspiration needed to keep me plugging away. With him gone much of the zest has departed from a job that we always tackled as a team, never as two individuals." To a friend, Ike penned, "As a companion and comrade, no one could fill the void left by Jimmy's death."

Eisenhower noticed a change following the tragedy. In their discussions about budget and troop strengths, MacArthur listened more thoughtfully to Ike's opinions and recommendations. Their relationship again became so close that Ike wrote in his diary on June 18 that the general had told him, "In all respects you represent a special case, and it is my hope to keep you here a long time." Ike noted, "The atmosphere has cleared to such an extent that this job, at long last, has become personally agreeable to me as well as professionally interesting."

Ike's three-year tour in the Philippines was due to conclude in October, but MacArthur and Quezon convinced him to extend it for another year. Flattered by his bosses' and the president's encouragement, Ike, with the support of Mamie, agreed to the extension. It would not be long before he regretted that decision.

In the meantime, as a means of pacifying his subordinate with a leave and—more important—seeking additional funding for the Philippine military, MacArthur dispatched Ike to the States. On June 28, Ike, Mamie, and John boarded the *President Coolidge*. Mamie later recalled, "It was a grand send-off, such gorgeous flowers—presents and liqueurs. . . . The nice things friends and things done for us is what makes me sorry to leave, but I didn't shed a tear at leaving Manila, and never even stayed on deck to see us out of the breakwater."

Back in the States, the Eisenhowers visited the Douds in Denver and his parents in Abilene; this was the year when he poured the concrete patio for his parents' home before going to Washington. With war clouds rising in both the Pacific and Europe, Ike found the War Department somewhat more favorably inclined now to the idea of providing arms and equipment to the Philippines.

In a letter written as much as to stroke MacArthur's ego as to inform him of progress, Ike wrote on September 30, 1938, "I feel that my Washington trips were very successful. . . . All people I talked to in the War

Department feel that you are making much more progress than they originally believed possible. They have become convinced that you are doing a worthwhile job, in a fine way."

In *At Ease*, Ike stated, "There wasn't much the Army could do for the Philippines without cutting the ground out from under U.S. preparedness. The War Department put us in touch with manufacturers who were ready to do business at the right price, and the Army provided obsolete but useful equipment—such as World War I Enfield rifles." He continued, "After begging or borrowing everything I could from Signal, Quartermaster, Ordnance, and Medical groups, I went to Wichita, bought several planes, then to Winchester Arms Company in Connecticut. With what I had 'liberated' and bought, I went back to Manila."

The Eisenhowers boarded the *Empress of Japan*, a Canadian Pacific liner, on October 14 for their return to the islands. On his arrival, Ike found significant changes. During his absence, MacArthur had learned that Filipino legislators were considering a bill that would abolish his position and leave Ike in charge. Although there was no evidence that Eisenhower had anything to do with the proposal, which never made it to a vote, MacArthur held him responsible, withdrawing his confidence in and affection for his subordinate.

The general eliminated Ike's position as chief of staff and transferred many of his responsibilities to Lieutenant Colonel Richard K. Sutherland, who had arrived from the 15th Infantry in China as Jimmy Ord's replacement. Ike wrote in his diary about Sutherland, "He is an excellent officer and I expect him to take a huge burden off my shoulders."

Sutherland did lessen Ike's workload, but he also strove to erode Eisenhower's favor with MacArthur. In a diary entry, Ike called Sutherland a "bootlicker." Later entries about Sutherland were not so diplomatic, with Ike referring to him as "ruthless," "abrasive," "dour," "humorless," and "autocratic," as a "martinet" and a "hatchman."

Through it all, Ike held his temper and soldiered on. In his journal entry dated November 10, 1938, he lamented that the reorganization was designed to keep him at his desk and "to rob [him] of any influence in the Army or Malacanan." He continued, "Why the man [MacArthur] should so patently exhibit a jealousy of a subordinate is beyond me." He concluded, "On the surface all is lovely, I will not give him the satisfaction of showing my resentment. But my usefulness is so curtailed as to rob the job of much of its interest, so I'm going at the earliest possible moment. If the d____ fool had only sent me this plan while I was in the States I would not have returned." Ike summarized, "But I must say it is incomprehensible that after 8 years of working for him, writing every word he publishes, keeping his secrets . . . he should suddenly turn on me as he has all others who have ever been around him. He'd like to occupy a throne room surrounded by experts in flattery."

Regardless of his personality and leadership style—or perhaps because of them—Sutherland fit well into MacArthur's "throne room" and remained MacArthur's chief of staff throughout World War II.

While eager to depart the Philippines, Ike had no desire to resign from the army and pursue other opportunities, though several presented themselves. For example, in the fall of 1938, Alexander Frieder, president of the Jewish Relief Committee of Manila, and other influential Jews in the Philippines approached Ike with what he deemed "an unusual offer." Ike recorded the meeting, writing, "I was asked to take a job in China, Southeast Asia, Indonesia, and every country where they might be accepted, a haven for Jewish refugees from Nazi Germany."

Ike, having Jewish friends in the Philippines, protected them from the anti-Semitic jokes told by his contemporaries. Years later, he would say, "I grew up believing that the Jews were the chosen people, that they gave us the high ethical and moral principles of our civilization." The Zionist population of Manila had recognized Ike's attitudes toward them and offered him an exceptionally generous salary and expense account. Ike found the proposal "appealing." He turned down the offer, however, explaining, "I had become so committed to my profession that I declined."

Ike began a letter campaign, through official channels and to old friends, seeking reassignment to a troop unit in the States. Meanwhile, despite Sutherland's successful efforts to reduce Eisenhower's responsibilities and undermine his relationship with MacArthur, Ike's closeness with President Quezon endured. The two continued their professional discussions and card games.

On March 24, 1939, Ike gave a speech to a graduating class of the Philippine Reserve Officers' Training Corps. Some of his comments were attributable to his interactions with MacArthur, but, on the whole, they mostly highlighted Eisenhower's principles learned over the past quarter century in uniform. He emphasized the importance of physical preparedness and the study of military tactics and field exercises. Ike admonished the graduates to be loyal to subordinates, as well as superiors, and to be fair and honest; he said that each cadet "must learn to make firm decisions and to accept responsibility for them without seeking to shift it either to superior or subordinate." He continued, "Military discussions need not, in these days, be prefaced with long and exhaustive arguments to prove a nation's need for defensive strength. World events, daily reported in our newspapers, continue to hammer home the deplorable fact that life, liberty, and property are not safe in a defenseless nation when coveted by a more powerful neighbor. Indeed, this is not a newly discovered truth— two thousand years ago the greatest of all men said, 'When a strong man armed keepeth his palace, his goods are in peace.'"

Ike, disgusted by Sutherland and MacArthur's treatment of him, persisted in his efforts at reassignment. During his home leave, he laid the foundation for transfer to a troop assignment at Fort Lewis, Washington, but continued to contact friends there and in Washington, DC, about his desire to command soldiers.

On May 24, 1939, the War Department finally heeded Ike's pleas and issued orders for his assignment to the 15th Infantry Regiment at Fort Lewis. Ike was elated. During the past eighteen years, he had served a mere six months with troops. Not only would the undertaking be fulfilling, but it could also open a path for his promotion. In his letters and diary, he still wrote of hopes of advancement to full colonel when he became eligible in 1950. Ike, unknown outside the military and the small population of Abilene, Kansas, continued to have no hint of his destiny.

Ike's fellow staff officers in the Philippines did not share his enthusiasm about the departure orders—except, that is, for Sutherland, who gleefully recorded that they finally had "gotten rid of Eisenhower." Conversely, both President Quezon and General MacArthur would have preferred that Ike stay even though his relationship with the latter had deteriorated appreciably. In *At Ease*, Ike wrote, "MacArthur said that I was making a mistake. The work I as doing in the Philippines was far more important than any I could do as a mere lieutenant colonel."

Ike recorded that he responded by bringing up the fighting in Europe, saying, "General, in my opinion the United States cannot remain out of this war for long. I want to go home as soon as possible. I want to participate in the preparatory work that I'm sure is going to be intense." Eisenhower then reminded MacArthur that he had missed combat in World War I and "was now determined to do everything [he] could to make sure [he] would not miss this crisis of our country."

President Quezon made an even greater effort to keep him in the Philippines. Ike recalled, "He handed me a blank contract for my services and said, 'We'll tear up the old contract. I've already signed this one and it is filled in—except what you want as your emoluments for remaining. You will write that in.'"

"Mr. President," Ike replied, "your offer is flattering. But no amount of money can make me change my mind. My entire life has been given to this one thing, my country and profession. I want to be there if what I fear is going to come about actually happens."

Once it was settled that the Eisenhowers were leaving the Philippines, both the Filipinos and the Americans honored them with send-offs. President Quezon hosted a farewell luncheon in the Malacañan Palace, where he awarded the U.S. lieutenant colonel the Philippine Distinguished Service Star. Despite the glowing praise attached to the award for all that Eisenhower had accomplished, both leaders realized that they had failed to field a sufficient armed force for the islands' defense. Lack of local funds and limited budgets from the United States, as well as the absence of support on the part of MacArthur, left the islands vulnerable to attack.

Although MacArthur wrote that he deeply regretted Eisenhower's departure, praised his performance, and even went to the docks to see the Eisenhowers off for home, he harbored resentments against his subordinate that would grow over the coming years with each of Ike's successes.

Ike's personal final evaluation of his situation was briefer: "I got out clean—and that's that."

During the following years, Ike made several mentions in his diary about MacArthur's continuing failures in the Philippines and his doubts about the general's leadership in the Pacific once World War II had begun. In turn, as the war progressed, MacArthur criticized Eisenhower, saying, "He let his generals in the field fight the war for him. They were good and covered up for him. He drank tea with kings and queens. Just up Eisenhower's alley." When he learned that Canada had named a mountain in Ike's honor, MacArthur, showing that he could be petty, sneered, "You know, it's a very small peak, considering the Canadian terrain." In another instance, MacArthur made his infamous evaluation of Ike when he said the junior officer "was the best clerk I ever had."

Ike took his own shots at his former boss on occasion as well. When asked by a female acquaintance whether he knew MacArthur, Ike responded, "Not only have I met him, Madam, but I studied dramatics under him for three years in Washington and four in the Philippines."

Sources for the "best clerk" and "studied dramatics" quips have never been identified. However, both comments appeared in biographies of the two men as early as 1952, and neither Eisenhower nor MacArthur made any effort to deny the quotes.

Rivalry between the two continued during and after World War II. It was not until the 1960s that their animosity mellowed, and they again became cordial. Eisenhower put their differences behind him, saying, "Hostility between us has been exaggerated. After all, there must be a strong tie for two men to work so closely for seven years."

During those intervening years, Eisenhower assessed techniques for separating the good from the bad by analyzing the actions of General MacArthur and his leadership—or lack thereof—in the Philippines. His superior's performance reinforced for Ike the absolute necessity for a commander to own his actions. Ike later recorded that the administrative skills learned under MacArthur helped prepare him for "the great responsibilities of the war period."

The Philippines also gave Eisenhower the opportunity to experience how to man, supply, and train an army from the ground up. His responsibilities far exceeded those routine for his rank, allowing him to learn the problems and interstices of a large army. His relations with President

Quezon and other Filipino officials provided insights into the highest levels of political actions. Ike may have written that he "got away clean," but in reality, when he left the Philippines, he got away with a vast knowledge about military and political issues that would serve him well in the future.

CHAPTER 14

San Francisco, Fort Lewis, and San Antonio

THE EISENHOWERS DEPARTED MANILA FOR THE FINAL TIME ABOARD the SS *President Cleveland* on December 13, 1939, bound for San Francisco via Hong Kong, Shanghai, Kobe, Yokohama, and Honolulu. In his writings, Ike made no comments about the Japanese military per se but did note that the guides for his several shopping trips while enroute, in all likelihood, were Japanese intelligence agents. The long transoceanic voyage was made interminable by turbulent seas and even more so by the lack of competitive bridge partners.

Ike spent much of the time on board discussing with son John his recent decision to seek an appointment to West Point. He used his own career as an example to highlight the disadvantages of the many moves and frequently frustrating assignments—as well as the low pay of a career army officer—that John would face. Ike wrote, "I thought it wise, before his desire became decision, to ask him to consider, objectively, the possible advantages of a civilian educational institution." Despite an offer from Ike's brother Edgar to pay John's way through law school and then employ him at his practice, John stood firm in his desire to attend the U.S. Military Academy. Ike again began a letter-writing campaign, this time to secure an appointment for his son.

Some of the entries in Ike's journal for this period differ from what he recorded in *At Ease*. In San Francisco on January 25, 1940, for example, he noted in his journal, "Twelve hours before landing at this port I received a radio [message] directing me to report to Fourth Army Hdqrs, located here, for temporary duty." In later interviews, he recalled the temporary duty orders being delivered by a sergeant after they landed.

Whichever story of the notification is accurate, the effect was the same. In his diary, Ike wrote, "I thought it was the old, old story, and once more I was to start a tour of 'staff' duty instead of getting to troops."

At the Presidio, Eisenhower learned from Lieutenant General John L. DeWitt, commander of the IX Corps, that his duties would be to develop a plan for transporting National Guard and regular army units to California for one of the first large-scale training exercises of the expanding army. DeWitt, who was aware of Eisenhower's talents from his time as commander of the Philippine Department from 1937 to 1938, promised him that the planning should take only a month, and he would then be released to report to Fort Lewis.

The task was not an easy one, as the IX Corps included units from throughout the West from the Mississippi River to the Pacific Ocean. Ike quickly ascertained that the War Department order for the corps to unite at a single location was not possible in the available time frame. With the limited period authorized for the National Guard units to be on active duty, some would no sooner arrive in California than they would be reboarding trains for home.

Ike determined that two, instead of one, mobilization stations would be required to have all the units arrive in time for training. He faced some opposition from DeWitt's staff, who believed the War Department's orders should be followed verbatim. Once DeWitt was briefed, however, the general approved Eisenhower's "two-stop" mobilization plan and released him to report to Fort Lewis.

Before his departure, Eisenhower had his second encounter with General George Marshall, who was in California to observe the mobilization exercise. Marshall, having recently become the army chief of staff, had previously served in the Philippines, where even junior officers could afford domestic help. Marshall asked Ike, "Have you learned to tie your own shoes again since coming back, Eisenhower?" Somewhat taken aback by Marshall's rare effort at humor, Eisenhower responded with a grin, "Yes, sir, I am capable of that chore anyhow."

That the no-nonsense Marshall, having been selected by President Franklin Roosevelt over thirty-three more senior generals for his current position, remembered meeting Eisenhower was nothing short of amazing to the junior officer. Marshall was, after all, in the midst of reorganizing the army, procuring new weapons and equipment, and discharging officers who had gained their positions by tenure rather than talent.

Some historians claim that after this encounter, Marshall added Eisenhower to his "little black book" of names of those he intended to place in high positions if the army continued to expand for war. While it is a good story—almost too good to check—like many tales that have become woven into history as fact, it simply is not true. Marshall never kept a "black book." He had no need to do so, having the brilliant memory that he did. In all likelihood, the chief already had other upcoming positions in mind for Eisenhower.

At Fort Lewis on February 5, 1940, Ike joined the 15th Infantry Regiment of the 3rd Infantry Division, a regiment that had recently returned to the States from China as part of the U.S. effort to avoid becoming involved with the Sino-Japanese conflict. Assignment to this prodigious outfit was considered a top duty because of its glorified history. In China, the unit had experienced combat during the Boxer Rebellion; in France, it had stopped a major German offensive during World War I, earning its motto "Rock of the Marne."

Ike assumed the role of regimental executive officer of the 15th Infantry, the same position Marshall had held in the mid-1920s. He soon took command of the regiment's 1st Battalion. On July 1, Ike wrote to his West Point classmate Omar Bradley, expressing satisfaction with his new assignment. Along with updating details on his job, he revealed a bit of ambition: "I've been with this regiment about five months, and am having the time of my life. Like everyone else in the Army, we're up to our necks in work, but this work is fun. I could not conceive of a better job; except having one's own regiment, which is out of question because of rank."

Shortly after accepting battalion command, Ike led his unit through what he called "a thorough job of combat training over some of the most difficult terrain in the country, the 'cut over' land of Washington State." He concluded, "Through the day, like everyone else on maneuvers,

I sweated and accumulated a grime of caked dust. At night, we froze. Never in any one stretch did I have more than two hours' sleep. At times, I was really fagged out. But all of us learned lessons that would pay off in combat. The experience fortified my convictions that I belonged with troops; with them I was always happy."

Ike was popular with his men, who found him fair and humane as well as tough and demanding. He earned the respect of his battalion's cooks when, on visits to the mess halls, he snacked on uncooked hamburger and raw onion. His troops appreciated his sense of humor, especially when he did things like resolve a feud between two soldiers by having them face each other as they cleaned opposite sides of barracks windows.

Junior officers, however, often found themselves the target of Ike's wrath when they performed below par. When he discovered that marksmanship scores were not being properly recorded on the rifle range, Eisenhower held the platoon leader, Lieutenant Burton Barr, responsible. Barr later recalled, "I've heard about being eaten out and I've seen it, but this was unique. This wasn't being eaten out. This was Eisenhower having a buffet supper, and I was the complete meal."

Later that the same day, Ike again approached Barr and said, "I'm going to tell you something, lieutenant, and you'd better listen carefully. This morning you did something wrong, and I bawled you out for it. That was the end. We don't carry grudges around here."

Ike understood the importance of morale as well as discipline. In *At Ease*, he elaborated on his understanding of troops and military history:

There is at least one striking difference between the American soldier and numerous other soldiers in history. The Army, however, as far back as the days of Von Steuben, learned that Americans either will not or cannot fight at maximum efficiency unless they understand the why and wherefore of their orders. To Von Steuben, after his professional career in Europe, where troops were only pawns to be moved about the board of war without consideration of them as individual human beings, this was a wonder. To meet it, changing his own practice and attitude completely, he worked to develop in Washington's army an understanding by the individual—down to the last private—of his place in the scheme of battle and of the training drudgery necessary for him to maintain that place honorably.

Ike also valued the lighter side of morale. He adopted the Czech song "Beer Barrel Polka" as his battalion's marching music.

While the training was intense as news arrived daily about Japan's march across Asia and Germany's blitzkrieg through Europe, a considerable number of military officials still did not think the United States would become involved in the expanding war. Ike, based on his own observations in the Philippines and his memory of Fox Conner's prediction about a second world war, warned his contemporaries of the probabilities. So vocal were his warnings that he earned the nickname "Alarmist Ike."

Meanwhile, at the family quarters, the Eisenhowers' household goods and personal items had arrived from Manila in poor condition. Dishes and furniture were broken or missing; clothes were lost. The situation, though, was hardly a surprise to any military family, as moving shipment contracts go to the lowest bidder. Ike wrote of his ire about the expense of buying new uniforms, saying, "It grinds my soul to put out money I have to spend—but there's no way out unless I retire. Guess I'm hardly ready to do that." He had a one-word conclusion: "Ouch!!"

The impact of the damaged goods and uniform expenses were lessened by the Eisenhowers' assignment to a two-story, four-bedroom brick home on the east side of the fort's parade field offering a view of the majestic Mount Rainier. John enrolled in a preparatory academy in nearby Tacoma and soon received an appointment to West Point. Ike and Mamie settled in, reopened Club Eisenhower, and planted a garden.

Although it had been more than a decade since Mamie had lived on an army post, she adapted quickly. She joined the Women's Club, served on the committee to redecorate the Officers' Club, and volunteered with the Red Cross. Fort Lewis, like other military installations, provided all the goods and services of a small town. And like a small town, the post offered wives a sense of community. At the same time, however, being essentially cordoned off from civilians, with only military families for companionship, created disadvantages as well. With rank came privileges, such as better quarters, assigned drivers, and ample domestic help—all based solely on the husband's rank. It was inevitable that some wives would be tempted to "wear" their husband's rank and lord over wives of more junior officers.

Mamie bridled against this artificial caste system. While she displayed proper respect to the wives of Ike's superiors, she remained on a first name basis with those of his subordinates. Susan Eisenhower wrote that her grandmother "never made anyone conscious of rank." She quoted Mamie as saying, "You know, you don't have any rank, it is your husband [who does]. You're only in the army [because of] your husband." The spouse of one of Ike's former subordinates recalled, "Mamie never made me feel she was high ranking. [She and Ike] were just down-to-earth people."

In the early fall of 1940, Ike received a letter from George Patton advising him that he expected to be given command of one of the armored divisions that would soon be organized for what he anticipated would be "a long and bloody war." Patton wrote that he wanted Ike as one of his regimental commanders. Eisenhower immediately picked up his pen to begin campaigning with old friends in Washington to help him secure orders to join Patton when the time came.

On September 17, he answered Patton, saying, "I'm at long last doing my 'command duty.' It's not only that, like yourself, I like to work with soldiers, but I'm weary of desk duty. I suppose it's too much to hope that I could have a regiment in your division, because I'm still almost three years away from my colonelcy. But *I think* I could do a damn good job of commanding a regiment."

Ike's emphasis of "I think" and his spelling out "damn" indicate his confidence that he was ready for higher command. They also served as a reminder to his old friend that he desired leadership duty rather than a staff position.

Ike's satisfaction with his battalion duties and hopes for serving under Patton were both short lived. After only eight months in command, Eisenhower was blindsided by the consequences of his own stellar reputation. In his diary, he wrote, "The roof fell in on me shortly after the middle of November when the signal officer at Fort Lewis passed to me a telegram from Leonard 'Gee' Gerow, my classmate and associate at Leavenworth in the two-man command post we conducted in the attic of my quarters there fifteen years earlier. Now a brigadier general and chief of the War Plans Division in the War Department, he wired, 'I need you in war plans division. Do you seriously object to being detailed on the War Dept. general staff and assigned here? Please reply immediately.'"

Ike responded the same day, opening his letter with the revelation that Gerow's telegram had sent him "into a tailspin." The ever-diplomatic Ike then acquiesced on the point that he would leave the decision about his transfer to Gerow but asked him to first read all of the enclosed narrative.

"In the first place," Ike wrote, "I want to make clear that I am, and have always been, very serious in my belief that the individual's preferences and desires should have little, if any, weight in determining his assignment, when superior authority is making a decision in the matter."

Ike dedicated three pages to the reasons why he should be permitted to remain with troops. He began by acknowledging that his opening paragraph was a "somewhat pompous-sounding preamble" and stated how "flattered" he was that Gerow had used the word "need" in asking for his service. The following paragraphs outlined how much Ike wanted to stay at Fort Lewis and how strongly he felt that he deserved to do so rather than be relegated to additional staff time. "In the body of the letter," he later wrote, "I tried to present, as factually as I could, my record and my wishes." He added that the 3rd Division commander, Major General Charles F. Thompson—a native South Dakotan and 1904 graduate of West Point—was asking for Ike to be reassigned as his chief of staff.

Evidently, Thompson's desire for Ike to join his staff held sway in Washington. Gerow responded, "After careful consideration of contents of your letter and the wishes of General Thompson . . . I have withdrawn my request for your detail to War Plans Divn. . . . Regret our service together must be postponed."

Ike responded immediately with a letter expressing his thanks for the decision to keep him on "troop duty." He continued, "In trying to explain to you a situation that has been tossed in my teeth more than once [my lack of extended troop duty in recent years], all I accomplished was to pass up something I *wanted* to do, in favor of something I thought I *ought* to do, and then . . . find myself not even doing the latter."

Two weeks later, "the wishes of General Thompson" were fulfilled. Ike later wrote, "On the last day of November, with Pearl Harbor twelve months and one week off, my active service with troops came to an end. Orders arrived that day detailing me to the General Staff Corps, assigned to duty as Chief of Staff, 3rd Division, Fort Lewis, effective immediately. I was back on staff—but at least with the designation 'General Staff with Troops.' I had escaped Washington and, to that extent, felt lucky."

Once again, Ike acquiesced to the wishes and experience of his superior. Thompson, an infantry veteran of tours in the Philippines and along the Texas–Mexico border, had been an American Expeditionary Force intelligence officer in World War I. This was Ike's first opportunity to serve with a senior officer with experience in the intelligence field. Ike and Thompson also shared interest in reserve units, as the general had been the army's first head of reserve affairs in 1923.

Ike liked and respected Thompson, but he was not happy with being removed from direct command of troops. He wrote to a friend, "I'd been ducking Staff positions for some time but finally the War Department failed to listen to my sob story. So again I'm looking down a pen instead of a gun." To another friend, he wrote, "I'm weary of these eternal staff details. I'd like to get a command of my own, even if just a squad."

Ike joined the 3rd Infantry Division staff at a busy time. With war clouds gathering in both Europe and Asia, National Guard and reserve units were being called to active duty, and the Selective Service was inducting fifty thousand drafted men a month. The army of fewer than 200,000 when Ike had returned from the Philippines numbered nearly 1.5 million by mid-1941. To accommodate this expansion of troops, General Marshall had finally received authorization to promote officers on merit rather than seniority, and he was in the process of replacing marginal senior officers with talented younger men whom he had collected in his mental black book.

Fort Lewis was one of the major induction and training centers for the exploding army. Ike's time as Thompson's chief of staff was short, as it concluded after only three months. Again his job changed, but he remained at Fort Lewis. When the IX Corps relocated from San Francisco to Fort Lewis, its commander, General Kenyon A. Joyce, requested Eisenhower as his chief of staff. The War Department not only approved the assignment but also, in line with Marshall's new authority to promote on merit rather than time in service, promoted Ike to full colonel.

In his diary on March 12, 1941, Ike wrote, "Read radio from W.D. appointing me a temp. Colonel in Army of U.S. from March 6." Ike's comments about the promotion were nearly as brief and just as modest in *At Ease*. He expanded on his elevated position, writing, "A few days after the transfer, I was promoted to temporary colonel. I was too busy to meditate on the fact that I had now reached the rank that for a good many peacetime years had stood as the certain terminus of my career."

Ike's journal entry about the promotion did not reflect the joy and satisfaction he actually felt about earning his set of eagles a full decade earlier than he had anticipated—or even dared hope. Nor did it reveal the inkling that the next rank—one-star or brigadier general—was now not out of the question. To his son, he protested, "Damn it, as soon as you get a promotion, they start talking about another one. Why can't they let a guy be happy with what he has? They take all the joy out of it."

Despite his complaint, Ike had no desire to "be happy with" what he had and continued to learn as much as possible to accomplish his current missions and to prepare for the future. Even though his new duties kept him at Fort Lewis, they greatly expanded his geographical area of responsibility. He wrote, "The Corps was made up of all posts, camps, and stations in the northwestern part of the country."

Eisenhower found Joyce a masterful teacher, role model, and mentor. He admired how General Joyce—born in Brooklyn and reared in Chicago—had enlisted as a private during the Spanish-American War and had earned his commission as a second lieutenant in 1901. Having fought in the Philippines and in World War I, where he was seriously wounded by a trench mortar explosion that left him without the use of one hand, Joyce inspired Ike's admiration. The general, despite his disability, had steadily advanced in rank to command the 3rd Cavalry Regiment at Fort Myer, Virginia—where George Patton was his executive officer—and to lead the 1st Cavalry Division before going on to take charge of the IX Corps.

Another trait Eisenhower respected was Joyce's ability to continuously assess situations and make needed adjustments. Although Joyce had earned a reputation as the consummate cavalry commander, he had been instrumental in converting the horse-and-mule army into a mechanized and wheeled force. He also was a brilliant trainer, formulating much of the basic curriculum that enabled the huge influx of draftees to become efficient soldiers. Where Fox Conner had drilled Ike in administration procedures, instilling in him the importance for studying history and writing well, Joyce demonstrated how to command troops and execute battlefield tactics. After only a month as Joyce's chief of staff, Eisenhower wrote in his diary, "I am finding this job most intriguing and interesting. General Joyce is a swell commander and a fine person to work for."

Some months later, when Ike departed IX Corps for Fort Sam Houston, he left a memorandum for his replacement. The memo not only provided useful day-to-day operational information for the new arrival but also contained important insights Ike had gained from this role model: "The commanding general's method of operation is to announce policies and major decisions in definite terms and then to require his Chief of Staff to see to their execution. Daily you will find that the General spends long periods with the troops. General Joyce does not read long directives, regulations, or circulars. He expects his Chief of Staff to absorb the essentials and to keep him informed."

The letter also noted that Joyce emphasized properly wearing uniforms, saluting, and conducting oneself professionally. Ike wrote, "These subjects are important to him as outward signs of real discipline, and he insists that our big job is to inculcate in all ranks a conception and practice of fundamental discipline."

By the summer of 1941, no one used the moniker "Alarmist Ike" for Eisenhower. The Japanese offensive to occupy all of Asia and the German invasion of the Soviet Union convinced even the most skeptical that the United States would soon be forced to enter the war.

Still, Eisenhower's talents and reputation as a staff officer overshadowed his command potential, as became apparent when Lieutenant

General Walter Krueger, having recently assumed command of the 270,000-man Third Army headquartered in San Antonio, sought Ike as his chief of staff. To get the officer he wanted to help him prepare his units—which stretched from New Mexico to Florida—Krueger bypassed the chief of infantry and appealed directly to his old friend General Marshall, requesting a man "possessing broad vision, progressive ideas, a thorough grasp of the magnitude of the problems involved in handling an army, and lots of initiative and resourcefulness. Lieutenant Colonel [Krueger was not aware of Eisenhower's recent promotion] Dwight D. Eisenhower, Infantry, is such a man and I urgently request that he be detailed."

Marshall approved the transfer. Eisenhower later wrote that he was on a hillside observing training at the Hunter-Liggett, California, military reservation with Joyce when a messenger arrived instructing the general to call the War Department. Joyce made the call, turned to his subordinate, and said, "Start packing. Go back to Fort Lewis for orders, which will direct you to go to San Antonio as chief of staff, Third Army."

Ike and Mamie arrived at Fort Sam Houston on July 1, 1941—their twenty-fifth wedding anniversary. Instead of the two-room quarters they had occupied when first married, they moved into one of the stately five-bedroom houses that lined Artillery Row. On that same day, their son, John, joined the Long Gray Line as a plebe at West Point.

In his role as chief of staff, Ike was authorized to have an executive assistant and an orderly. Ike inherited Lieutenant Ernest R. "Tex" Lee as his assistant and, after several intense interviews, decided to retain him on his personal staff despite the fact that the forty-year-old looked more like the automobile salesman and insurance agent—which he had been before being called to active duty from his reserve unit—than a military officer. A San Antonio native, Lee was jovial and unflappable, but he was also an excellent organizer and office manager. More important, he never attempted to "wear his boss's rank," and his loyalty was beyond reproach.

For the orderly position, the Eisenhowers selected Private First Class Michael J. McKeogh, a Long Island native and the son of Irish immigrants who, before receiving his draft notice, had worked for seven years as a bellhop at New York's Plaza Hotel. As the household striker,

McKeogh acted as chauffeur, bartender, and cook. He also assisted Mamie in keeping a neat, orderly house—a challenge with Ike's casual disposal of newspapers and cigarette butts.

Lee and McKeogh proved so valuable that Ike took them along to his next assignment and then on to Europe, where they formed the nucleus of Ike's personal staff for the duration of World War II. Their relationship with Ike was the exception to the French axiom "No one is a hero to his valet." Both during and after the war, the two had nothing but accolades for their boss.

McKeogh later said that he liked Eisenhower "straight off" because "you absolutely knew exactly where you stood with him." He appreciated Ike's lack of "master-servant" attitude and found Mamie to be "a very gracious lady." Later, during the North Africa campaign, McKeogh arrived with Ike at an airfield at the front, though Ike had told him that it was unnecessary for him to make the flight. The orderly responded, "Sir, my mother wrote me that my job in this war was to take care of you and that if General Eisenhower doesn't come back from this war, don't you dare come back."

For Lee, Ike's command presence and character were displayed by the way he answered telephone calls. Instead of saying, "This is General Eisenhower," he merely answered, "This is Eisenhower." Lee believed that Ike was a "right guy."

Meanwhile, Eisenhower adjusted to his position as General Krueger's chief of staff, finding his new boss the perfect role model because he combined the administrative talent and professional development of Fox Conner with the tactical genius of Kenyon Joyce. Officers and enlisted men alike referred to Krueger as a "soldier's soldier."

Born in the Prussia area of Germany, Krueger had immigrated to the United States at age eight with his widowed mother. He had enlisted as a private in the infantry at seventeen, fought in Cuba and the Philippines, experienced the Mexican Punitive Expedition, and endured the trenches of World War I. He would become the first U.S. soldier to advance in rank from private to four-star general.

In his book *Crusade in Europe*, written shortly after the conclusion of World War II, Eisenhower wrote, "General Krueger himself was one of the senior officers of the Army. A private, corporal, and sergeant in the late 1890s, he had an Army-wide reputation as a hard-bitten soldier. But through more than forty years of service, he kept pace with every military change, and few officers had a clearer grasp of what another war would demand of the Army; few were physically tougher or more active. Relentlessly driving himself, he had little need of driving others—they were quick to follow his example."

Many found Krueger, who still spoke with a thick German accent, stern and intimidating. In reality, he was a modest man with a good sense of humor, and Ike had no difficulties in assuming his role as Krueger's chief of staff. Ike wrote in a letter to George Moseley, "Luckily I've spent most of my life in large headquarters, so am not overpowered by the mass of detail." In *Crusade*, Ike added, "I was brought closer to the problems of the Army of the United States as a whole." Ike and Krueger quickly formed a team dedicated to the study and execution of modern warfare innovations and requirements.

Krueger, Eisenhower, and the Third Army faced a daunting task. General Marshall had called for maneuvers to begin in September 1941 with the Third Army opposing the Second Army in war games stretching from East Texas to the Mississippi River. Known as the Louisiana Maneuvers, the exercise would field more than four hundred thousand men—both on the ground and from a parachute regiment—as well as tanks and aircraft. To members of Congress, who complained about the staggering cost of the maneuvers, Marshall replied, "I want the mistakes made down there in Louisiana; not over in Europe."

During July and into early August, the Third Army prepared for the Louisiana Maneuvers. In a letter to General Joyce on July 25, Eisenhower wrote, "The opening date of the maneuvers is rushing toward us, and with each passing day it seems we discover new problems that must be solved before the shooting starts. This army of eleven divisions stretches from Arizona to Florida and concentration plans are not easy to perfect. But, I'm hopeful that we'll get the job done, possibly well."

The letter was also used to thank Joyce for "the generosity of your final report on me" and to express his admiration for his former commander. He added that he hoped those higher than the clerks at the War

Department and Adjutant General would see the efficiency report "not only because of what you said, but more importantly because you said it."

The Third Army, headquartered at Lake Charles, Louisiana, began assembling in mid-August for internal training and maneuvers prior to the official opening of the exercise. Ike noted in *At Ease*, "Old Louisiana hands warned us that ahead lay mud, malaria, and mosquitoes. Their description was accurate. But they didn't add to such attractions the fact that we would also meet head-on the problems of 400,000 men moving into relatively unsettled country, where the road net was designed for a car or two at a time, not an army, and a climate that seemed calculated to produce exhaustion. But the work was gripping."

Despite an approaching hurricane moving inland, the Louisiana Maneuvers officially began on September 15. This would be the first—but certainly not the last—time when Ike had to make or recommend orders based on the weather. When he later faced the question of whether to launch the assault on Normandy in the midst of dark clouds and stormy weather, he must have recalled those days back in Louisiana.

To his friend Gee Gerow, Ike wrote, "The Army got a good drenching. Yet when the problem started . . . everybody was full of vim and ready to go. I do not know how long this problem will last, but I can assure you that in the Armies of about a quarter million you don't do things in a hurry."

The maneuvers were designed to take place in two phases. Initially the Blue Army under Krueger would attack the Red Army commanded by Lieutenant General Ben Lear. Despite Ike's claim that things were not done in a hurry, Krueger advanced quickly, attacking on line with divisions deployed to exploit gaps in the Red Army's defenses. After only four days, with the Blue Army surrounding the Red Army, the exercise umpires called an end to Phase One.

Phase Two of the exercise commenced with the roles of the two armies reversed. The results, however, were the same. Krueger's army quickly stopped Lear's force and began a counterattack. George Patton, now a major general in command of the 2nd Armored Division, almost turned the tide for the Red Army with a night maneuver and attack. The exercise umpires ruled that his move was not allowed, as Patton had paid for the needed fuel at local gas stations rather than receiving it through normal supply channels. Patton was disappointed with the decision. He likewise regretted his inability to secure Ike as one of his regimental commanders, but that did not stop him from offering a reward of $50 for "a certain s.o.b. called Eisenhower." The bounty went unpaid, and although there was no official winner of the exercise, everyone considered the Blue Army the victor.

Ike wrote that the exercise revealed the army's lack of experience and the pressure on its leaders "to transform textbook doctrine into action." He also noted that the training exposed unfit officers who had to be replaced, "some of whom," he lamented, "were good friends."

In expanding his observations, Ike concluded, "After each stage of the maneuvers, we tried to assemble the principal officers for a critique. In these morning chats we emphasized everything that went right; encouragement was essential to the morale of men tiring physically. At the same time, we had to uncover and highlight every mistake, every failure, every foul up that in war could be death to a unit or an army. With every one of these critiques the self-confidence of each participant seemed to grow."

General Marshall arrived from Washington to observe the maneuvers. By the time he departed, he had added more positive points about Ike to his mental checklist for potential candidates.

"During the maneuvers," Ike continued, "my tent turned into something of a cracker barrel corner where everyone in our army seemed to come for a serious discussion, a laugh, or a gripe. These visitors prolonged my hours and considerably reduced sleeping time. But I never discouraged those who came to complain for I was often astonished to see how much better they worked after they had unloaded their woes; and, of course, the harder they worked the smoother things went for us at Army headquarters."

As Ike noted, humor often made its way into the discussions. His favorite story was about an umpire who flagged a bridge as having been destroyed and no longer usable. According to Ike, "Shortly, a corporal brought his squad up to the bridge, looked at the flag, and hesitated for a moment; then resolutely marched his men across it. The umpire yelled at him: 'Hey don't you see that that bridge is destroyed?' The corporal answered, 'Of course I can see it's destroyed. Can't you see we're swimming?'"

Doubtless, Ike appreciated the humor of the story. The inclusion of it in *At Ease* is but another demonstration of his admiration for the intelligence and ingenuity of the American soldier.

Media correspondents from across the country converged on Louisiana to cover the maneuvers. Krueger, with his gruff personality and heavy accent, could not woo the press, but easygoing, self-effacing Eisenhower—who conducted twice-daily briefings for them—made such an impression that he became "the face of the Third Army." Reporters also stopped by Ike's tent to join in the after-hours discussions. Early in the exercise, *Time-Life* reporter Robert Sherrod welcomed fellow newsmen Eric Sevareid of CBS and Hanson Baldwin of the *New York Times* with the advice that they should look up Colonel Eisenhower because he "makes more sense than any of the rest of them."

In *Crusade*, Ike elaborated on his first important introduction to the press and its cameras. He also confirmed that he was still an "unknown," writing, "During the critique at Camp Polk a group shot was made of General Krueger, Major A. V. Golding, a British military observer, and me; in the caption my two companions were correctly identified, but I appeared as 'Lt. Col. D. D. Ersenbeing'—a least the initials were right."

Syndicated columnist Drew Pearson got the name right: "Colonel Eisenhower . . . conceived the strategy that routed the Second Army. . . . Krueger's Chief of Staff has a steel-trap mind plus unusual vigor. . . . To him the military profession is a science."

Sherrod later wrote:

In 1941 I became a military reporter, an embryo war correspondent, and one of my first assignments was to the swamps of Louisiana in the summer of 1941. Down there, I heard that the brightest young fellow around was a colonel named Eisenhower. I've forgotten who directed me to him, but I did go down and had quite a long and enlightening talk with Colonel Eisenhower, who was very articulate . . . so much more articulate than any other officer I encountered during the Louisiana Maneuvers. . . . He was a deeply impressive man. He was very forceful, altogether, as I've said, the most impressive man I've seen.

Correspondent Sevareid also lauded Eisenhower in his reports. In his postwar book *Not So Wild a Dream*, he modestly credited Sherrod with "discovering Eisenhower."

In a matter of weeks, Ike went from being a relatively unknown soldier to being quoted and acclaimed in newspapers across the nation. In *At Ease*, he continued to play down the media attention: "Shortly afterward [conclusion of the maneuvers], I was given unsought publicity in a newspaper column whose author attributed credit to me that should have gone to General Krueger. I still have no idea why I became the target for praise."

Ike summarized the impact of the Louisiana exercise in *Crusade*. He ruminated, "The maneuvers provided me with lessons and experience that I appreciated more and more as subsequent months rolled by."

He followed that statement with a brief and unheralded declaration: "At the end of the maneuvers I was promoted to the temporary grade of brigadier general." In *At Ease*, he wrote, "The maneuvers ended. I got, instead of a command, the star of a brigadier general." To Gee Gerow, he wrote, "Things are moving so rapidly these days that I get almost dizzy trying to keep up with the parade. One thing is certain—when they get clear down to my place on the list, they are passing out stars with considerable abandon."

Mamie more directly said that Ike's promotion to brigadier general was her "proudest moment."

Not everyone supported Ike's promotion. Lieutenant General Lesley J. McNair, General Marshall's chief of staff, observed the Louisiana Maneuvers and provided a list of officers to his boss who he thought had potential for division command. Ike was not on the primary list but was included in an annex of "others." McNair, an artilleryman and 1904 graduate of West Point, did not think an officer who had such little troop experience and no commanded experience above the level of battalion deserved promotion. If not for the support of Brigadier General Mark Clark, a friend from West Point and earlier assignments, as well as General Marshall's operations (G-3) officer, Ike might not have made the list at all.

Clark exerted other influences as well. During Marshall's visit to the maneuvers, he asked Clark for recommendations for his replacement as the G-3 when he was reassigned. There would be only one man on the list, Clark replied—"The name: Ike Eisenhower." Clark continued, "If you have to have ten names, I'll just put nine ditto marks below."

Ike had served for sixteen years as major before being promoted to lieutenant colonel and another five before becoming a full colonel. A mere five months later, he advanced in rank to brigadier general. As his brother had pointed out some years earlier, suddenly Ike "was going places."

CHAPTER 15

War Department and General Marshall

WITH A STAR ON EACH COLLAR, IKE RETURNED TO FORT SAM HOUSTON from the Louisiana Maneuvers with the Third Army staff. There was no stand-down or time for rest. Ike wrote, "October and November were as busy as the months preceding maneuvers. Measures to correct defects revealed in Louisiana were begun at unit level; in many cases the return movement offered an immediate opportunity. Some officers, both Regular and National Guard, had of necessity to be relieved from command; controversies and rumors, following on this step, required quick action to prevent injury to morale among officers and troops."

At the beginning of December, Ike accepted an invitation to speak at the graduation of Kelly Field aviation cadets on December 12. In his initial draft of the speech, Ike wrote, "I am highly honored in having been invited to welcome this class into the commissioned ranks of the army. This day is an important one to each of you; it is likewise important to our government and our army, because it witnesses an appreciable reinforcement in our flying personnel, and marks another definite step toward attainment of the country's objective in military preparation."

In *Crusade in Europe*, Ike wrote, "On the afternoon of December 7 at Fort Sam Houston, Texas, tired out from the long and exhausting staff work of the maneuvers and their aftermath, I went to bed with orders that under no circumstances was I to be disturbed. My dreams were of a two weeks' leave I was going to take, during which my wife and I were going to West Point to spend Christmas with our plebe son, John. But even dreams like these—and my strict orders—could be shattered with impunity by the aide who brought the news that we were at war." The next day, the United States declared war against the Empire of Japan. Three days later, it did likewise against Japan's Axis allies, Germany and Italy.

The Third Army staff immediately began receiving orders from the War Department to transfer antiaircraft units to the West Coast to counter a possible Japanese attack. Troop units were also alerted for deployment. Volunteers were recruited. As Ike wrote in *Crusade*, "It was a period of intense activity."

Despite the turmoil and anxiety, Ike found time to rewrite his Kelly Field cadet graduation speech. One paragraph now stated:

> Within the past few days our beloved country has found itself involved, with bewildering speed, in a war against the most powerful combination of ruthless military force ever known upon this planet. Once again America's call has gone out to all her sons to rally to the common defense. They are answering by the thousands. There is no need for us to concern ourselves with the basic patriotism of our young men. But patriotism, though indispensable, is not enough! Love of country cannot, alone, produce the skill, the hardihood, the training and the techniques that are necessary to make the modern warrior.

Ike never delivered the speech. Draft copies lay in dusty files for years before being recovered and added to the Eisenhower Library in Abilene. Instead of congratulating the graduates, Ike was on his way to Washington. On the morning of December 12, Ike received a telephone call from Colonel Walter Bedell Smith, General George Marshall's secretary of the general staff, who said, "The Chief [Marshall] says for you to hop a plane and get up here right away. Tell your boss that formal orders will come through later."

Mamie hurriedly packed him a bag while he requisitioned a plane and pilot from Kelly Field. Forced down by weather in Dallas, Ike transferred to a train and arrived in Washington on the morning of December 14. His brother Milton met him at the station and took him directly to the War Department. It was a Sunday, but Marshall and the staff were on a full-time schedule with no weekend breaks. Ike stayed at his brother's home in Falls Church but never saw the house in daylight. In his diary entry for Sunday, January 18, 1942, Ike noted, "Just another day. Grind away."

Ike correctly reasoned that he was summoned to Washington for his expertise on the Philippines, which had by now been attacked by the Japanese as they had assaulted Pearl Harbor. Although honored to be called on, he recalled in *Crusade*, "The message was a hard blow. During the First World War every one of my frantic efforts to get to the scene of action had been defeated—for reasons which had no validity to me except that they all boiled down to 'War Department orders.' I hoped in any new war to stay with troops. Being ordered to a city where I had already served a total of eight years would mean, I thought, a virtual repetition of my experience in World War I."

Eisenhower had met Marshall on only three previous occasions and for no more than a few minutes each time. Now he would be with the general every day. Remote, cold, austere, and formal, Marshall had few friends and little interest in anything outside the army. He expected and demanded total dedication and rarely gave anyone a second chance. Many an officer ended up assigned to some remote, irrelevant post for the sin of crossing or failing Marshall. Except for his wife, no one—including President Franklin Roosevelt—called him George. He was indeed General Marshall to everyone else. Marshall, likewise, reciprocated the formality with his staff, referring to his assistant as Eisenhower, never as Ike.

In an interview published in *The Atlantic* in 1964, Ike had only positive reflections about Marshall. "A few of his characteristics are uppermost in my memory, and on these I shall dwell," he said. "They include his consideration for others; his clear, direct, and logical approach to any major military problem; his complete, single-minded dedication and loyalty to his country and government; and his selflessness and objectivity in making decisions and in courageously discharging his vitally important duties."

Marshall immediately began briefing Eisenhower on the situation in the Pacific. After explaining all the threats and vulnerabilities in the vast area, Marshall asked, "What should be our general line of action?"

Ike put on his best poker face and asked for a few hours to formulate his response. When the general agreed, Ike went in search of a desk in the War Plans section of the Operations Division (ironically headed by Gee Gerow), where he could gather his thoughts. In *Crusade*, Ike wrote, "If I were to be of any service to General Marshall in the War Department, I would have to earn his confidence: the logic of this, my first answer, would have to be unimpeachable, and the answer would have to be prompt."

"A curious echo from long ago came to my aid," Ike continued. He recalled the advice given by Fox Conner, who cautioned, "We cannot escape another great war. When we go into that war it will be in the company of allies. Systems of single command will have to be worked out. We must not accept the co-ordination concept under which Foch was compelled to work. We must insist on individual and single responsibility—leaders will have to learn how to overcome nationalistic considerations in the conduct of campaigns. One man who can do it is Marshall—he is close to being a genius."

With that memory in mind, Ike decided that his response "should be short, emphatic, and based on reasoning in which I honestly believed. No oratory, plausible argument, or glittering generality would impress anyone entitled to be labeled genius by Fox Conner."

Three hours later, Ike returned to the general's office with a three-hundred-word memorandum containing his concise thoughts and conclusions. Verbally he briefed Marshall, saying:

> It will be a long time before major reinforcements can go to the Philippines, longer than the garrison can hold out with any driblet assistance, if the enemy commits major forces to their reduction. But we must do everything for them that is humanly possible. The people of China, of the Philippines, of the Dutch East Indies will be watching us. They may excuse failure but they will not excuse abandonment. Their trust and friendship are important to us. Our base must be Australia, and we must start at once to expand it and to secure our communications to it. In this last we dare not fail. We must take great risks and spend any amount of money required.

Marshall merely replied, "I agree with you. Do your best to save them."

Before dismissing Eisenhower, Marshall gave him instructions that he later recorded: "The department is filled with able men who analyze their problems well but feel compelled always to bring them to me for final solution. I must have assistants who will solve their own problems and tell me later what they have done." Eisenhower remembered the dictum, about which he said, "I have never forgotten."

Marshall's remarks made an impression. Ike later recalled, "As I left the room, I resolved then and there to do my work to the best of my ability and report to the General only situations of obvious necessity or when he personally sent for me."

In coordination with army units, logistical centers, and U.S. Navy transports, Ike began directing men and matériel to Australia. Meanwhile, a system of blockade runners and submarines was organized to provide supplies to the beleaguered Philippines. Just who would oversee the buildup in Australia was solved when former secretary of war and colonel in the reserves Patrick J. Hurley arrived at the War Department offering his service. Ike prepared orders promoting him to brigadier general, pinned one of his own stars on Hurley's uniform, and had him on an airplane bound for Australia by midnight.

President Roosevelt and Prime Minister Winston Churchill met in late December. After much debate, they agreed that they would combine their headquarters and that each theater would have a single supreme commander. They also agreed, in coordination with the Soviets, that the European theater would be the priority before turning all their might against Japan. Ike wrote much of the agreement approved by the two leaders.

To prepare the U.S. military, Marshall restructured the War Department as he eliminated the multiple branches and bureaus into a streamlined system of three commands: ground, air, and logistics. The internal War Department staff was also reorganized, with the War Plans Division becoming the Operations Division. While Gerow departed to command an infantry division, Eisenhower moved into the position of the chief of the Operations Division.

Humorously, Gerow's departing words to his old friend were that he had Pearl Harbor on the book and had lost the Philippines, Singapore, Sumatra, and all of the Dutch East Indies north of the barrier. Then he said, "Let's see what you can do." On a more serious note, Gerow wrote in Eisenhower's officer efficiency report that he was "the best officer of his rank in the entire Army" and that he should be entrusted with "the highest command."

Along with Eisenhower's new position came a massive walnut desk that had belonged to General Philip H. Sheridan when he was the army's commanding general in the 1880s. Originally including a horseshoe from Winchester—the mount General William Tecumseh Sherman had ridden on his famous 1864 Civil War ride to victory at the Battle of Cedar Creek—the desk was but one perk of the new assignment. Another was housing on Generals Row at Fort Myer. Mamie joined him in DC at the huge brick home, which offered a panoramic view of the Washington Mall. Their quarters, Number 7, were just down the street from Marshall's at Number 1.

On March 10, 1942, Ike's brother Roy called Mamie to inform her of the death of family patriarch David Eisenhower. She wrote to her parents, saying, "One of the hardest things I had to do was telephone Ike and tell him. He is a wonder. People said he worked right on and no one could have known. Guess it was his salvation (work). Poor fellow, I've felt so sorry for him."

In his diary, Ike recorded, "Father died this morning. Nothing I can do but send a wire." After receiving the call from Mamie, Ike continued to draft a message for President Roosevelt to send to Chinese leader Chiang Kai-shek. Ever dedicated to the task at hand, Ike then, in the same entry, also recorded what he thought were the "three musts" for the Allies: "Hold open the line to England and support her as necessary; keep Russia in the war as an active participant; hold the India–Middle East buttress between the Japs and Germans. All this assumes the safety from major attack of North America, Hawaii, and Caribbean area."

The next day, Ike lamented, "I feel terribly. I should like so much to be with my Mother these few days. But we're at war. And war is not soft, it has no time to indulge even the deepest and most sacred emotions. I loved my Dad. I think my Mother the finest person I've ever known. She has been the inspiration for Dad's life and a true helpmate in every sense of the word. I'm quitting work now, 7:30 P.M. I haven't the heart to go on tonight."

"My father was buried today," Ike wrote on March 12. He continued:

> I shut off all business and visitors for thirty minutes, to have that much time, by myself, to think of him. . . . He was a just man, well liked, well educated, a thinker. He was undemonstrative, quiet, modest, and of exemplary habits—he never used alcohol or tobacco. He was an uncomplaining person in the face of adversity, and such plaudits as were accorded him did not inflate his ego. . . . His finest monument is his reputation in Abilene and Dickinson County, Kansas. His word has been his bond and accepted as such; his sterling honesty, his insistence upon the immediate payment of all debts, his pride in his independence earned for him a reputation that has profited all of us boys. . . . I'm proud he was my father. My only regret is that it was always so difficult to let him know the great depth of my affection for him.

Putting his grief aside, Eisenhower continued to add to his own reputation as the consummate staff officer with his unique ability to write memos, letters, and orders in the voice of his boss, Marshall, as well as that of President Roosevelt. Ike always excelled at his task—even knowing that the better his performance on staff, the lower his chances for promotion and troop command. Marshall reinforced these conclusions, telling Eisenhower that too many staff officers in the last war had been promoted ahead of field commanders. He confided to Ike, "The men who are going to get the promotions in this war are the commanders in the field, not the staff officers who clutter up all the administrative machinery in the War Department and in higher tactical headquarters. The field commanders carry the responsibility and I'm going to see that they're properly rewarded so far as promotion can provide a reward."

Marshall, aware of Eisenhower's desire to return to field duty, continued, "Take your case. I know that you were recommended by one general for a division command and by another for corps command. That's all very well. I'm glad they have that opinion of you, but you are going to stay right here and fill your position, and that's that! While this may seem a sacrifice to you, that's the way it must be."

Ike took the statement as a declaration that he "was completely condemned to a desk job in Washington for the duration." Whereas Ike would usually think over his responses with care and measure them for their effect on the recipient (especially if it was his superior), this time he lashed out in frustration and impulsively declared, "General, I'm interested in what you say, but I want you to know that I don't give a damn about your promotion plans as far as I'm concerned. I came into this office from the field and I am trying to do my duty. I expect to do so as long as you want me here. If that locks me to a desk for the rest of the war, so be it!"

Having had his say, Ike rose from his chair and started toward the door. By the time he reached the exit, he began, according to his writings, "feeling sheepish about the outburst." Realizing his explosion "did nothing to help either of us," he turned to find Marshall eyeing him intently. Ike recalled, "I had to grin a bit at my own childishness. A tiny smile quirked the corner of his face. I left the office."

A few days later, Marshall made an exception to his promotion policy when he forwarded a recommendation for the advancement of Eisenhower to major general over 162 senior brigadier generals. Marshall wrote that Eisenhower was not really a "staff officer," but rather his "subordinate commander" responsible for "all dispositions of Army forces" worldwide.

In his diary on March 28, 1942, Ike wrote, "I made major general yesterday. Took the oath of office today. Still a permanent lieutenant colonel, but the promotion is just as satisfactory as if a permanent one. I suppose one could call it the official 'stamp of approval' of the War Department." He made no mention of the fact that he had spent a mere seven months with one star before earning the second.

Two days later, Ike made another journal entry recognizing receipt of official orders for his promotion. He added a note that revealed he still had no idea of the destiny that awaited him: "This *should* assure that when I finally get back to troops I'll get a division!!!"

Ike's brief remarks on his promotion reflected a combination of modesty and the intense work environment of the time. Not until *At Ease* did he elaborate on the advancement as he thought back to his angry response to Marshall:

> A question arose in my mind that I have never been able to answer satisfactorily. Had the years of indoctrinating myself on the inconsequential value of promotion as a measure of an Army man's worth influenced my reply to him? Certainly, in the years past, knowing that I was locked in because of my age and grade, I had known a wonderful sense of freedom from awe when in the presence of superior officers. But without my outburst I often wonder whether General Marshall would have had any greater interest in me than he would have in any other relatively competent staff officer. In any case, I was now a major general.

There have been many attempts to define the dynamic between Marshall and Eisenhower. Master-protégé, mentor-student, teacher-pupil, and even father-son dichotomies have been used to describe their relationship. Each has merit, but Marshall had himself provided the best definition when he earlier declared Ike his "subordinate commander."

The two were an indomitable duo even as each presented himself in an understated manner. Eisenhower and Marshall were similar in their physical stature as well as their selfless devotion to duty. Neither flaunted his authority or participated in the petty quarrels or egotistical mannerisms that marked many other senior commanders. They shared some common interests. Like Eisenhower studying Gettysburg, Marshall had hiked over the Civil War battlefields near his college, the Virginia Military Institute. The two also held a great appreciation for the friendship and tutoring of Fox Conner.

Even so, their relationship was more traditional than not. Marshall was Eisenhower's headmaster in every way. Marshall's large, air-conditioned, blue-walled office became the finishing school for Eisenhower's education and growth as a senior commander. Marshall's organizational and planning skills were rivaled only by Eisenhower himself. Marshall viewed everything as black or white with no shades of gray as he demanded truth and integrity from his subordinates. He got along well with political leaders as well as Allied commanders. The press trusted his briefings and admired his openness and honesty.

While Ike and Marshall continued to solidify their relationship, the U.S. Armed Forces worked nonstop to mobilize, arm, and train. Meanwhile, in Europe, the Germans pushed deep into Russia, threatening Moscow itself, while other of their troops, supported by Italian and Vichy French allies, occupied much of North Africa. Russia pressed the Americans to go on the offensive to relieve pressure on the eastern front. President Roosevelt promised the foreign minister of the Soviet Union a second engagement in the west, where he favored an English Channel assault against the occupied French coast. The British, who had the only veteran fighters in the Allied forces, were reluctant, declaring that neither their troops nor the Americans' were prepared for such an offensive.

After several cross-oceanic negotiations, an American delegation prepared to meet directly with British leaders. On May 21, 1942, Eisenhower recorded in his journal, "I'm taking off the twenty-first with General [Henry H. 'Hap'] Arnold, [chief of Army Air Forces,] and others for a trip to England."

Arnold was to the air war what Eisenhower was to tank warfare, each having made innovative contributions in their respective arenas. The two met with senior British officers to discuss the opening of a second front. As usual, Ike impressed the Allied leadership and began forming professional and personal relationships with the British leaders, who found him likeable and easy to work with, as did his American counterparts. As pleased as Eisenhower was with the Brits, he was unimpressed by the American commanders stationed in England, whom he found to be lacking in a sense of urgency.

On May 28, Ike wrote in his diary about a meeting of the combined Allied chiefs of staff to determine the overall command organization for Operation Roundup—the code name for a cross-channel assault—then in the early stages of planning. Ike wrote, "I outlined the American position, as explained to me by General Marshall before I left Washington, so far as it applied to the subject of discussion. I stated that in principle the Americans believed that single command was essential and that committee command could not conduct a major battle."

Ike returned to Washington, DC, on June 4, where he noted in his journal that he had spoken with senior British as well as American commanders, writing, "Our own people are able but do not quite understand what we want done. It is necessary to get a punch behind the job or we'll never be ready by spring 1943 to attack. We must get going."

Eisenhower outlined this urgency in a memo to General Marshall and recommended that his West Point classmate, Major General Joseph McNarney, the current army deputy chief of staff, be promoted to lieutenant general and given the command.

Marshall read the memo with no comment and then instructed Eisenhower to prepare a draft directive specifying the responsibilities and duties for the commanding general of the European theater of operations (ETO). By this time, Eisenhower had more than one hundred staff officers and noncommissioned officers working under him in the Operations Division, but he personally prepared the document, closely adhering to the advice from Fox Conner about keeping such directives concise and brief. He wrote, in what he later called "the Bible," "The mission of the commanding general, European Theater, will be to prepare for and carry on military operations in the European theater against the Axis powers under the strategic directives of the combined U.S.-British Chiefs of Staff as communicated to him by the Chief of Staff U.S. Army."

On the morning of June 11, Eisenhower stood by while Marshall glanced through the document. After only a few minutes, he asked, "Does the directive suit you? Are you satisfied with it?"

"Yes, sir," Ike responded, "but you may have some suggestions."

"I'm glad it suits you," Marshall continued, "because these are the orders you are going to operate under. You are in command of the European Theater."

Even before reading Eisenhower's document, Marshall had already determined whom he wanted to command the ETO, and in conversations with President Roosevelt and Prime Minister Churchill, the three had come to consensus that Eisenhower was their choice. Not only could Ike coordinate and command a large staff, but he also had unique abilities to work with egotistical Allied commanders such as Bernard Montgomery and Charles de Gaulle.

Eisenhower was completely surprised. Although Marshall had mentioned a few days earlier that he was considering him for a leadership role, Ike had never presumed it would be the top European position, especially because he had never commanded any unit larger than a battalion. This promotion meant that he would skip over regiment, brigade, division, corps, and army commands to lead the entire European force.

At dinner that evening, he casually said to Mamie, "Looks like I'm going to London next week. Not just a trip this time. I'm to be in command over there."

"In command of what?" asked Mamie.

"Of the whole shebang," replied Ike.

Mamie helped Ike pack, knowing that she would now have to make her own plans because, with her husband assigned overseas, she would no longer merit the general officer quarters at Fort Myer. Her parents wanted her to return to Denver, but she preferred to remain in Washington to be close to friends. She would find an apartment in Wardman Park, where she would reside for the duration of the war.

Ike, never comfortable with public displays of affection, asked Mamie not to see him off at the airport. Instead, he asked her stand by the flagpole at Fort Myer, where he would have a final glimpse of her as his plane lifted off from nearby Bolling Field on June 23.

Ike made no mention in his diary about the elation he must have felt at his selection, merely and modestly stating, "The chief of staff says I'm the guy." In *At Ease*, he wrote, "General Marshall sent me to London to command the European Theater of Operations. This brought me up closer to the war—and the desk job in Washington was behind."

Although he never ceased to learn from his contemporaries, his subordinates, and even his enemies, Ike was no longer the student or protégé. The boy from the wrong side of the tracks in a small Kansas town was well on his way to becoming the supreme Allied commander. The people of Abilene, his parents, the cadre at West Point, John Pershing, Bernard Baruch, Fox Conner, Douglas MacArthur, George Moseley, Charles Thompson, Kenyon Joyce, Walter Krueger, and George Marshall—all had all contributed to Ike becoming Eisenhower. Now it would be he who formulated the ultimate strategies, issued the operational directives, and assumed responsibility for the outcome in the European theater of World War II.

CHAPTER 16

War and Postwar Eisenhower

TIME MAGAZINE FEATURED LIEUTENANT GENERAL DWIGHT D. EISENhower on its November 16, 1942, cover as the commander of European forces. Promoted to the rank of three-star general shortly after his arrival in England, the once obscure soldier named Eisenhower was now known around the world, not just among a small group of army officers. As the first non-British officer to command Gibraltar, he led the Allied offensive into North Africa. On February 11, 1943, he was pinned with a fourth star and raised to the rank of full general. On July 9, Ike, from his headquarters on Malta, directed the invasion of Sicily and the drive toward Rome by soldiers from the United States, Great Britain, and Canada.

Eisenhower wrote to West Point classmate Major General Vernon Prichard, "I have developed almost an obsession as to the certainty with which you can judge a division, or any other large unit, merely by knowing its commander intimately. Of course, we had pounded into us all through our school courses that the exact level of a commander's personality and ability is always reflected in his unit—but I did not realize, until opportunity came for comparisons on a rather large scale, how infallibly the commander and unit are almost one and the same."

Military and political leaders privy to strategic plans assumed that General George Marshall, *Time*'s "Man of the Year" for 1943, would be the general to command the cross-channel invasion of France, renamed Operation Overlord, when it was launched. Others thought Marshall was too valuable in his current position (directing the entire war effort as the army chief of staff) for him to leave. Marshall himself expected to command Overlord, and Ike, who frequently expressed his admiration for the chief, assumed the same.

In late November 1943, Allied leaders—including President Franklin Roosevelt, General Marshall, and Eisenhower—had met in Tehran and Cairo to determine future operations. Ike had had lengthy conversations with both Americans. Roosevelt had proclaimed that "by all rights" command of Overlord should go to Marshall and told Eisenhower, "I hate to think that fifty years from now, practically nobody will know who George Marshall was. That is one of the reasons why I want George to have the big command—he is entitled to establish his place in history as a great general."

Ike could only presume that he would return to Washington for the remainder of the war. The British, however, as well as several senior U.S. leaders, thought differently because it was now Eisenhower who had the more recent experience on the ground at the front and his superior, Marshall, who was more valuable performing desk duties in Washington. After a December meeting with Winston Churchill and Soviet leader Joseph Stalin in Tehran, Roosevelt told Eisenhower, "Well, Ike, you are to command Overlord."

President Roosevelt then informed his fellow Allied leaders of the decision. The news quickly spread. In a handwritten note "from the President to Marshal Stalin," the writer declared, "The immediate appointment of General Eisenhower to command of Overlord has been decided upon."

Marshall secured the directive after its translation for the Soviet leader and graciously forwarded it to Ike with a note reading, "I thought you might like to have this as a memento. It was written very hurriedly by me as the final meeting broke up yesterday. The President signed it immediately."

On Christmas Eve, President Roosevelt announced in a radio broadcast to the public that Eisenhower would lead Overlord with the title of supreme commander, Allied Expeditionary Forces. Ike returned to London to plan for the operation. On June 6, 1944 (the same day his son, John, graduated from West Point), the first Allied troops went ashore on the Normandy beaches. Before they departed England, Ike issued a message to the troops, declaring, "You are about to embark upon the Great Crusade, toward which we have striven these many months. The eyes of the world are upon you. . . . We will accept nothing less than full Victory! Good Luck!"

The invasion of the French coast was an extremely risky endeavor. Chances that the Germans would push the Allies back into the sea were high. While Ike expected victory, he, in the manner of his mentors, prepared for the worst and would accept full responsibility if the invasion failed. He prepared a message in the event of such catastrophe: "Our landings in the Cherbourg-Havre area have failed to gain a satisfactory foothold and I have withdrawn the troops. My decision to attack at this time and place was based upon the best information available. The troops, the air and the Navy did all that bravery and devotion to duty could do. If any blame or fault attaches to the attempt, it is mine alone."

The Normandy beaches and cliffs were deadly, but the Allies held on and then broke out to attack toward Paris. There would be setbacks—such as the failure of Operation Market Garden, the near catastrophe in the Ardennes, and the brutality of Battle of the Bulge—but by the end of 1944, the Allies were poised to invade Germany.

On December 15, 1944, the U.S. Senate voted to promote Ike to the rank of general of the army—designated with five stars. Named "Man of the Year" for 1944 by *Time* magazine, he was now the best-known military man in the United States—if not the world.

Fame, however, did not impact his demeanor. Eisenhower recognized that he commanded his seventy-three divisions "from afar," never wearing the steel combat helmet or otherwise pretending to be a frontline soldier even when he visited combat units. For this reason, he appears in all wartime pictures wearing a simple overseas or garrison cap.

On May 7, 1945, Eisenhower accepted the surrender of the German army at Rheims, France. In a message to General Marshall, President Roosevelt, and the world, Eisenhower simply reported, "The mission of this Allied force was fulfilled at 0241 local time." In *At Ease*, Ike recalled that he and his staff were so tired from the negotiations that there was no celebration. Before going to bed, Ike, wrote, "I issued the final and climactic order of the war in Europe, 'Make sure the firing stops at midnight of the eighth.'"

Ike then pivoted to command of the occupation forces in Europe and began preparations for the transfer of units to the Pacific theater. In June, he received honorary citizenship of the City of London and, in his acceptance speech, said, "Humility must always be the portion of any man who receives acclaim earned in the blood of his followers and sacrifices of his friends." During the same month, he flew to the States.

Mamie met Ike when he first landed in Washington. *Life* magazine covered the arrival, and under their photograph, it reported, "Mrs. Eisenhower greets the general as he steps from his plane at Washington's airport. Photographers missed the long kiss Eisenhower gave his wife. He refused to pose for another."

The *New York World-Telegram* edition that lauded Ike's homecoming also had a separate article about Mamie. It revealed just how little they and the public knew about her: "Mrs. Mamie Eisenhower, good-natured housewife from Abilene, Kansas, today shared New York's tumultuous acclaim for the homecoming commander of the Allied Forces. But Gen. Ike's lady was retiringly modest and tried to keep in the background."

While Eisenhower's purpose for the trip was to brief Marshall, he also received a hero's welcome with victory parades in Washington, DC, Kansas City, Abilene, West Point, and New York City. On June 19, after Ike's ticker tape parade, the *New York World-Telegram* headline read, "6,000,000 Salute Eisenhower; the City Roars Out Its Mightiest Welcome." In the nation's capital, Eisenhower addressed a joint session of Congress.

About her husband and his fame, Mamie would later say, "He belonged to the world and not to me anymore."

Even after Ike returned to his headquarters in Frankfurt, where he oversaw America's demobilization in Europe, he continued to receive honors and accolades, even joining Stalin atop Lenin's Tomb in Moscow for the Soviet victory parade.

On November 19, 1945, Ike returned to the States to replace General Marshall as the army chief of staff. Ike's office was in the newly built Pentagon, which was already well known for its complex rings and corridors. In *At Ease*, he admitted to not being able to find his own office and having to ask a group of stenographers for directions.

Once established, Ike continued efforts to demobilize the army with the objective of having "all the boys home by Christmas." He wrote, "The job ahead was not pleasant. The demobilization of a wartime army is a dreary business." His work hours continued to be long, but he and Mamie now occupied Quarters Number 1 at Fort Myer.

As America's foremost war hero, Eisenhower inevitably became the focus of political operatives. He discouraged any talk of his running for president, but the press closely followed his actions and also began to report on Mamie more in depth. Her granddaughter Susan Eisenhower later wrote, "Her ready wit surprised many, and as her public visibility grew, she had many occasions on which to display her ability to respond publicly, with forthrightness and humor."

Ike's relief at being home and his satisfaction at occupying the army's highest position were dampened by the death of his mother on September 11. Ike mourned her not only because she was his mother but also because Ida Stover Eisenhower had been Ike's first and one of his most influential role models. He wrote of her, recalling, "Many such persons of her faith, selflessness, and boundless consideration of others have been called saintly. She was that—but above all she was a worker, an administrator, a teacher and guide, a truly wonderful woman."

On May 2, 1948, Ike retired from the army and assumed the presidency of Columbia University in New York City. He found the logistics of managing the Ivy League college similar to running an army post, overseeing its multiple departments, visiting classrooms, and talking with and listening to professors and administrators. In his journal, he wrote, "I accepted, after long urging, the presidency of Columbia in belief that in this post and with the help of these great facilities I could do more than anywhere else to further the cause to which I am devoted, the reawakening of intense interest in the basis of the American system."

As one of the most respected men in America, Eisenhower was called on to attend many civilian affairs as well as to continue to advise Pentagon officials. Despite his hectic schedule, Ike managed to take up oil painting and to write his war memoir, *Crusade in Europe*, which was published in November 1948 by Doubleday. He collected a flat fee of $635,000—the equivalent of nearly $8.3 million in today's value.

In December 1950, President Harry Truman asked Eisenhower to take a leave of absence from Columbia and return to active duty to lead the newly formed North Atlantic Treaty Organization (NATO), which he did until May 1952. At that time, he relinquished his command of NATO, returned home, retired from the army, and resigned his Columbia presidency. Then and only then did Eisenhower address the growing call for him to run for the presidency of the United States. Initially reluctant, Ike earned the Republican nomination on the convention's first ballot. In accepting the nomination, Eisenhower said, "I know something of the solemn responsibility of leading a crusade. I have led one. I accept your summons. I will lead this crusade."

On November 4, 1952, he won the presidential race in a landslide. In his inaugural speech on January 20, 1953, Ike opened his remarks by declaring, "We are called as a people to give testimony in the sight of the world to our faith that the future shall belong to the free." He concluded, "Patriotism means equipped forces and a prepared citizenry. Moral stamina means more energy and more productivity, on the farm and in the factory. Love of liberty means the guarding of every resource that makes freedom possible—from the sanctity of our families and the wealth of our soil to the genius of our scientists."

Eisenhower was reelected to a second term on November 6, 1956—again by a huge majority of votes. At his inauguration the following January 21, he said, "May we pursue the right—without self-righteousness. May we know unity—without conformity. May we grow in strength—without pride in self. May we, in our dealings with all peoples of the earth, ever speak truth and serve justice."

Time magazine again named Ike its "Man of the Year" in 1959. In his farewell speech to the nation on January 17, 1961, Ike displayed the melding of his military and political selves:

> In the councils of government, we must guard against the acquisition of unwarranted influence, whether sought or unsought, by the military-industrial complex. The potential for the disastrous rise of

misplaced power exists and will persist. We must never let the weight of this combination endanger our liberties or democratic processes. We should take nothing for granted. Only an alert and knowledgeable citizenry can compel the proper meshing of the huge industrial and military machinery of defense with our peaceful methods and goals, so that security and liberty may prosper together.

On leaving the highest office in the nation, Ike and Mamie retired to a small farm adjacent to the Gettysburg, Pennsylvania, battlefield—located a mere seventy miles from where the Eisenhower family had first settled after immigrating to America in the eighteenth century. For the first time in their nearly half century of marriage, Ike and Mamie had their own home—one that came with no threat of pending transfer orders.

Dwight David Eisenhower died on March 28, 1969, of congestive heart failure. Mamie lived for another decade before her death on November 1, 1979. Both are buried with their son "Icky" in the Place of Meditation Chapel on the grounds of the Dwight D. Eisenhower Presidential Library, Museum & Boyhood Home in Abilene.

President Richard Nixon, Eisenhower's former vice president, said at his funeral, "Some men are considered great because they lead great armies or they lead powerful nations. For eight years now, Dwight Eisenhower has neither commanded an army nor led a nation; and yet he remained through his final days the world's most admired and respected man, truly the first citizen of the world."

Epilogue

Army Industrial College: By the outbreak of World War II, the college had trained about one thousand officers. In 1946, the school changed its name to the Industrial College of the Armed Forces and moved to Fort McNair. Two years later, the secretary of defense moved its administration from the army and reorganized the college "as a joint educational institution under the direction of the Joint Chiefs of Staff." The college moved into new facilities at McNair, including Eisenhower Hall, in 1960. In 1993, the college began awarding master's degrees to its graduates. Renamed the Dwight D. Eisenhower School for National Security and Resource Strategy in 2013, it today is more commonly known simply as the Eisenhower School. Its official mission is to "prepare selected military officers and civilians for strategic leadership and success in developing national security strategy and in evaluating, marshalling, and managing resources in the execution of that strategy."

Baruch, Bernard Mannes (1870–1965): President Franklin D. Roosevelt appointed Baruch as a special advisor to the director of the Office of War Mobilization. His innovative ideas shortened the start-up time for production of airplanes, tanks, and other war materials. In 1944, he led a group of physicians in formulating a plan to expand rehabilitation programs for wounded soldiers that was adopted by the Veterans Administration. In 1946, President Harry S. Truman appointed Baruch as the US representative to the United Nations Atomic Energy Commission. Prime Minister Winston Churchill considered Baruch a personal friend and spent time at his massive Hobcaw Barony estate in South Carolina. Baruch continued to advise political leaders until his death in New

York City at age ninety-four. He is buried in the Flushing Cemetery in Queens, New York.

Belle Springs Creamery: The creamery moved from Belle Springs to Abilene, Kansas, in 1892. By 1903, the company had grown so much that it erected a new brick building and incorporated the Drover's Cottage, which had been the town's largest hotel during the cattle-drive days. It produced ice, ice cream, and cheese in addition to processing eggs and poultry. It was best known, however, for butter, its biggest-selling product. Fifty-four-pound tubs of butter, enclosed in tin containers full of crushed ice, were shipped throughout the state and to Arkansas and Texas. At its height, the creamery produced nearly three million pounds of butter a year. It continued processing dairy products until 1958, when regional farmers ceased dairy operations to concentrate on growing milo and wheat.

Brett, Sereno Elmer (1891–1952): Born in Portland, Oregon, Brett graduated from Oregon State University in 1916 and earned a commission as a second lieutenant in the U.S. Army. After service along the border with the 3rd Infantry Regiment during the Mexican Punitive Expedition, he quicky advanced to the rank of major in the Tank Corps of the American Expeditionary Force in France. There he commanded the 326th Tank Battalion before taking over command of the 1st Tank Brigade from Colonel George Patton when the future legend suffered wounds at the Battle of Saint-Mihiel in September 1918. Before the war ended, Brett had earned the Distinguished Service Cross, second only to the Medal of Honor, as well as the Distinguished Service Medal for noncombat actions. He was also awarded two Silver Stars, the third-highest valor award, and had paid the price as shown by the three Purple Hearts he received. Brett remained in the army, advancing to the rank of brigadier general in World War II. He retired in 1943 because of medical issues. His extensive diaries, reports, and other papers are in the University of North Dakota library. Brett died in 1952 and is buried in Arlington National Cemetery. His headstone is topped by the image of a World War I British M-4 tank.

Brooks, Gladys Harding (1892–1959): Gladys Harding never revealed why she did not accept Ike's proposal of marriage, but friends later reported that she had expected them to marry someday. While Ike courted Mamie, Gladys quit her travel with the Apollo Concert Company and returned to Abilene. She soon began a relationship with Cecil H. Brooks (1886–1944), a well-to-do widower from nearby Enterprise. On June 10, 1916, the two married—sixteen days before the wedding of Ike and Mamie. Gladys and Ike had no direct contact until 1943, when she sent correspondence to him congratulating him on the victory in North Africa. Ike answered with a full-page typed response on Allied Force Headquarters, Office of the Commander in Chief letterhead. He included an update on the campaign and family news. He finished the letter by signing, "Special good wishes to you and Cecil. Cordially, Dwight." A week after D-Day, Ike again answered a brief letter from Gladys about a trip she had taken to New York. This time under the letterhead of Office of the Supreme Commander, he wrote, "This is going to be a few lines, but I know you will understand that right now I am up to my eyes in work. Am feeling fine and in good spirits." Four months later, Ike sent Gladys a note of condolence upon the death of her husband. Ike wrote his final letter to Gladys the following October concerning their mutual friends in Abilene. He closed by saying he had a great desire to get the war over quickly and to get home, concluding, "It is a fearful thing of waste and destruction and it is pity that the human race has to go through it so often." Ike's last contact with Gladys came shortly after his election to the presidency. During a visit to Abilene, Ike halted his motorcade when he spotted Gladys on the sidewalk. According to the news media, he stopped his convertible—decked out with flags on the fenders and Secret Service men all around—and "leaned out, embraced her, and gave her hardy kiss."

Class of 1915, U.S. Military Academy: A quarter century after their graduation, 115 of 164 graduates of the Class of 1915 remained on active duty. By the end of World War II, fifty-nine had been promoted to general officer. Members of the "Class the Stars Fell On" included Eisenhower and Omar Bradley, who earned five stars. There were also two full generals (four stars), seven lieutenant generals (three stars), twenty-four major generals (two stars, fifteen of whom commanded infantry or armor divisions), and twenty-four brigadier generals (one star).

Command and General Staff School: The Command and General Staff School, now known as the Command and General Staff College, continues to be an important (if not essential) step in an officer's advance in rank and selection for promotion. Its official mission statement is that it "educates and develops leaders for full spectrum joint, interagency and multinational operations; acts as lead agent for the Army's leader development program; and advances the art and science for the profession of arms in support of Army operational requirements." Today it graduates about eleven hundred students annually, including many Allied officers, from Eisenhower Hall. The number one U.S. graduate is awarded the General George C. Marshall Award. The distinguished international officer receives the General Dwight D. Eisenhower Award.

Conner, Fox (1874–1951): Conner departed Panama in late 1924 to become the army's chief of staff for logistics. Promoted to major general on October 20, 1925, he advanced to deputy chief of staff of the army the following March 9. He commanded the 1st Infantry Division in 1927, the Hawaiian Department in 1928, and the First Corps in Boston in 1930. General John Pershing would have preferred Conner for army chief of staff in 1930, but the position went to Douglas MacArthur. Conner took command of the First United States Army in 1936 before retiring on November 4, 1938, after forty years of active duty.

Conner suffered a severe head injury in the Adirondacks while attempting to free his car stuck in mud on November 17, 1941. He spent three months recovering in Walter Reed Army Medical Center in Washington, DC. He regularly corresponded with Eisenhower, George S. Patton, and George C. Marshall during the war, and they often sought his opinions and advice. Conner died on October 13, 1951, and his ashes were spread in the Adirondacks. Per his instructions, with no reason given, his personal papers were burned. He left no memoir or writing about his career and famous pupils. In a 1964 interview, Ike said, "In

sheer ability and character, he was the outstanding soldier of my time."
Virginia Conner died on May 15, 1960, and is buried in Ossining,
New York.

EISENHOWER BROTHERS

Arthur Bradford Eisenhower (1886–1958): The oldest of the Eisenhower brothers dropped out of high school and moved to Kansas City,
where he roomed with future U.S. President Harry Truman. He found
employment at a bank with a beginning salary of $5 per week. He
advanced in responsibility and title, proud of never missing a day of work
due to illness, to become vice president and then director of Commerce
Trust Company, one of the largest banks in the Midwest. His brothers
admired him as a trailblazer for leaving Abilene for better opportunities.

Edgar Newton Eisenhower (1889–1971): Edgar Eisenhower earned his
bachelor's and law degrees from the University of Michigan and then
established a successful legal practice in Tacoma, Washington. He also
served as the director of a bank and a paper manufacturing company
to become the most financially successful of the Eisenhower brothers.
Edgar was so extremely conservative in politics that he criticized Ike's
progressive leanings as president.

Roy Jacob Eisenhower (1892–1942): After high school, Roy Eisenhower began working in drug stores, first in Abilene and then in Ells-
worth, Kansas, before attending pharmaceutical school in Wichita. In
1919, he purchased a drug store in Junction City, just outside the gates
of Fort Riley, Kansas, which he operated for the next two decades. More
gregarious and outgoing than his brothers, he became a prominent citizen who sponsored several civic organizations.

Paul Dawson Eisenhower (1894–1895): Paul Eisenhower was a sickly
baby and died of diphtheria before his first birthday. Although the early
death of a son and sibling must have had a significant impact on the
family, neither Ike nor his parents recorded the effects of it. The only

records of Paul are the dates of his birth and death in the Eisenhower family Bible and his headstone that stands in the Belle Springs Cemetery.

Earl Dewey Eisenhower (1898–1968): Earl Eisenhower moved to Tacoma after high school graduation, where his brother Edgar paid for his attendance at the University of Washington. After earning a degree in electrical engineering, Earl sailed to the Far East as an engineer aboard the passenger liner SS *President Grant*. On his return, he worked for a public utility company in western Pennsylvania and then moved to Illinois, where he managed a newspaper before purchasing several radio stations. In 1965, he was elected to the Illinois State Legislature.

Milton Stover Eisenhower (1899–1985): Milton Eisenhower graduated from Kansas State University and then relocated to Washington, DC, to work for the federal government. He served in the Department of Agriculture before becoming the deputy director of the newly formed Office of War Information. Following the attack on Pearl Harbor, he served as head of the War Relocation Authority before resigning in protest over the mass internment of Japanese Americans. Then he headed Kansas State, Pennsylvania State, and Johns Hopkins universities as president. He was a close confident of Dwight during his presidency and later served Presidents John F. Kennedy and Lyndon B. Johnson.

Eisenhower, Doud David "Icky" (1917–1921): The first-born son of Ike and Mamie, Icky Eisenhower died at the age of three in 1921. In 1966, Ike—accompanied by his brother Milton and his longtime military aide General Robert Schulz—arrived via a military airplane on a night flight to Denver and had Icky's body exhumed. Mamie was unable to join them, as she was hospitalized with shingles at Walter Reed Army Medical Center in Washington, DC. The body was then flown to Manhattan, Kanas, where it was met by a local undertaker and transported to the Eisenhower Presidential Library and Museum Chapel (also known as the Place of Meditation) in Abilene. The casket was placed in a grave at the foot of the location where his parents were to be buried. A brief service was held, officiated by a local Presbyterian minister, Reverend

John Kellison, and an army chaplain from nearby Fort Riley. Workers filled the grave, placed the same headstone transported from Denver over it, and cleaned the area so the chapel was available to the public the next morning. The entire operation had been done clandestinely. Having no desire to reveal the grief he still felt, Ike received the privacy he demanded. A brief Associated Press article on June 5, 1966, stated simply, "Former President Dwight D. Eisenhower brought the exhumed body of his first-born son to Abilene Friday night for re-burial in the family cemetery plot. Eisenhower was accompanied by his brother, Milton. The first-born child, Doud Dwight Eisenhower, died of scarlet fever in 1921 at the age of 3. He had been buried in a Denver, Colo. cemetery. The recommittal service was private."

Ike rarely made any mention of his son's death other than to express his condolences to others who experienced similar losses. In 1947, he wrote to correspondent John Gunther—who had covered Eisenhower's headquarters in the Sicily Campaign in 1943—on learning of the death of his son: "I am deeply shocked to learn of your son's sad passing and know well that neither success nor words of solace can much lighten the grave loss that is yours. A similar experience of my own, years ago, makes me particularly sensitive to the pain you will continue to bear."

Two years later, Ike also wrote to actress Helen Hayes after the death of her daughter from polio: "We were once in that same black pit, and if these words can help you out of that pit, I will consider writing them worthwhile."

Eisenhower, John Doud (1922–2013): John Eisenhower, Ike and Mamie's surviving son, continued to serve in the army after World War II and saw combat in the Korean conflict. He left the regular army as a lieutenant colonel in 1960 but remained in the reserves until 1975, when he retired as a brigadier general. In his later years, he wrote several well-received books about the Mexican War and World War II. On December 22, 1968, John's son David married Julie Nixon, the daughter of sitting president Richard Nixon, former vice president to his father. John was the oldest surviving child of a president when he died on December 21, 2013. He is buried in the West Point cemetery.

Gerow, Leonard Townsend "Gee" (1888–1972): Gerow commanded the 29th Infantry Division and then V Corps in World War II. He assisted in the planning of Operation Overlord and became the first corps commander to land on the Normandy beachhead. He was also the first American major general to enter Paris after its liberation. He assumed command of the Fifteenth Army in early 1945. After the war, he returned to Fort Leavenworth to become the commandant of the Command and General Staff School. He later led the Second Army before retiring in 1950, after almost forty years of service. In 1954, the U.S. Congress passed an act promoting him to full general. He died on October 12, 1972, and is buried in Arlington National Cemetery.

Hazlett, Edward E. "Swede" (1892–1958): Born on February 22, 1892, Hazlett went on to graduate from the U.S. Naval Academy. He served thirty months aboard the USS *Leonidas* during World War I and was present at Spalato, Dalmatia, for the surrender of the Austro-Hungarian battleship *Srinyl*. Hazlett transferred to the submarine service after the war, where he advanced to the rank of captain before a heart condition forced his retirement in 1939. Recalled to active duty during World War II, he taught at the Naval Academy and then served as a professor of military science for the navy at the University of North Carolina before retiring again in 1946. He died at Bethesda Naval Hospital in Maryland on November 2, 1958, and is buried in Arlington National Cemetery. Eisenhower was one of his final visitors at the hospital.

Helmick, Eli A. (1863–1945): Helmick continued to serve as the army's inspector general until his retirement on September 27, 1927. He then resided in Hawaii until his death on January 13, 1945. He is buried in Arlington National Cemetery.

Hodgson, Paul Alfred (1891–1955): Hodgson graduated eighteenth in the 164-member Class of 1915. He was commissioned as a member of the Corps of Engineers on graduation, but his unit did not deploy to France during World War I. He served on the West Coast as well as in Washington, DC, and graduated from the Command and General Staff

School at Fort Leavenworth before becoming seriously ill with arthritis in 1941. He retired only to soon be recalled to active duty as the executive officer of Fort Sam Houston, Texas, at the outbreak of World War II. Promoted to colonel, he served in that position until the end of the conflict, when he once again retired. He lived in California until his death at Letterman General Hospital in San Francisco on October 7, 1955. Hodgson and Ike maintained a regular correspondence until his death.

Krueger, Walter (1881–1967): In late 1942, Krueger wrote to a friend, "There's nothing that I should like better than to have a command at the front. I should love to try to 'rommel' Rommel. However, I am sure that younger men will be selected for tasks of that nature, in fact for all combat commands. I shall be 62 this coming January [1943] and though I am in perfect health, can stand a lot of hardship, and people tell me I look and act ten years younger, I do not delude myself." Krueger's prediction proved incorrect. Unlike most senior officers of his age, who were assigned to training positions during the war, Krueger joined Douglas MacArthur in the Pacific as commander of the Sixth Army. Krueger's plodding, careful approach to fighting the Japanese was a perfect match for MacArthur's fast-paced strategy, making for a synergetic team. MacArthur later wrote of Krueger, "History has not given him due credit for his greatness. I do not believe that the annals of American history have shown him superior as an Army commander. Swift and sure in the attack, tenacious and determined in defense, modest and restrained in victory—I do not know what he would have been in defeat, because he was never defeated." Krueger retired to San Antonio after the war and wrote a book about his campaigns in the Pacific. His retirement years did not go well. His son, James, was dismissed from the army in 1947 for conduct unbecoming an officer and gentleman after an alcohol-related incident. In 1952, his daughter, Dorothy, fatally stabbed her husband in their officer quarters in Japan. Sentenced to life in prison, she was released five years later and went to live with her father. Krueger died on August 20, 1967, and is buried in Arlington National Cemetery.

MacArthur, Douglas (1880–1964): President Franklin Roosevelt recalled MacArthur to active duty in July 1941, as the Supreme Allied Commander Southwest Pacific Area. Although he failed to have his units in the Philippines on alert after notification of the Japanese attack on Pearl Harbor, he rallied his troops to defend Bataan and Corregidor. On Roosevelt's orders, he escaped the islands by PT Boat to Australia, where he made his famous "I shall return" speech. Roosevelt, at a time when America was desperate for heroes, awarded MacArthur the Medal of Honor for his defense of the Philippines. He did indeed return to the islands in October 1944 and then led the American forces across the Pacific to accept the Japanese surrender aboard the USS *Missouri* in Tokyo Bay in August 1945. For the next five years, he supervised the demilitarization of Japan and the reformation of its economic and political systems. In June 1950, he assumed command of United Nations forces to oppose North Korea's invasion of the South. The UN armed forces turned back the North Koreans as well as an intervention by the Chinese. MacArthur, however, clashed with President Harry Truman, who thought the general was too outspoken and that his actions risked an even greater escalation of the war. Truman relieved him of command in April 1951. MacArthur returned to the United States to a hero's welcome and took up residence in New York's Waldorf Hotel. After an unsuccessful run for the presidency in 1951–1952, he assumed the chairmanship of the board of Remington Rand and spoke for conservative causes. MacArthur's "old soldiers never die; they just fade away" speech to a joint session of the U.S. Congress on April 19, 1951, and his "duty, honor, country" farewell speech to the cadets at West Point on May 12, 1962, are among the greatest examples of American oratory. The general died on April 5, 1964, and is buried in Norfolk, Virginia—his mother's birthplace and the place his parents married.

Marshall, George C. (1889–1959): Prime Minister Winston Churchill called George Marshall "the organizer of victory" of World War II. Marshall resigned his position as army chief of staff in November 1945 and went to China as President Harry Truman's special representative to mediate the Chinese Civil War. Both the Nationalists and the Communists rejected his peace proposals. Marshall returned to the United States, where President Truman appointed him secretary of state. In June 1947, Marshall proposed the European Recovery Plan (known as the Marshall Plan) to aid in the reconstruction of war-torn Europe. He also led the effort to recognize Israel as a sovereign nation and initiated the discussions that led to the North Atlantic Treaty Organization. In 1950, President Truman once again recalled Marshall to become his secretary of defense in order to prepare U.S. Armed Forces for the Korean War. Marshall officially retired in September 1951, but he continued to chair the American Battle Monuments Commission. In that position, he oversaw the construction of fourteen cemeteries in eight countries to memorialize those killed or missing in World War II battles. Marshall died on October 16, 1959, and is buried in Arlington National Cemetery.

Moseley, George Van Horn (1874–1960): Moseley left the War Department in 1933 to command the V Corps for a year and then headed the IV Corps from 1934 to 1936. His final assignment was as commander of the U.S. Third Army. He continued his vitriolic speech against Jews, saying there was a Jewish Communist conspiracy to take over the government. After the attack on Pearl Harbor, he alleged that the attack was a conspiracy of the Jews and the British government to bring the United States into the war.

Moseley was not unaware that his relationship with Ike might be detrimental to his former subordinate's future. On September 29, 1943, he wrote to Ike, stating, "You must always keep me far in the background and unknown as far as our friendship is concerned. As you know, I spoke over the country in '38 and '39 attacking the subversive and un-American elements and attempting to show how peace could be maintained. I made many enemies. Thus, I am a liability and must not be mentioned in any way in connection with your brilliant career."

Despite his father's beliefs, Moseley's son, George Jr., graduated from West Point in 1927 and became a career army officer. As a colonel, he led the 502nd Parachute Infantry Regiment in the invasion of Normandy in 1944. The senior Mosely lived out his last years in Atlanta's Biltmore Hotel. He died in 1960 and is buried in the West Point cemetery.

Parker, Charles W. (1864–1932): Born on April 26, 1864, in Griggsville, Illinois, Parker moved with his family to Dickinson County, Kansas, three years later. As a youth, he dug water wells, built stone fences, and worked as a janitor in the county courthouse in Abilene. In 1882, he went out on his own with the purchase of a portable shooting gallery. Over the next decade, he added various mechanical entertainment devices before purchasing a simple merry-go-round. He improved this device and began shipping his merry-go-rounds across the United States. In 1902, he organized the Parker Amusement Company, the first amusement park of its scope in Kansas. Parker formed C. W. Parker Shows, consisting of a vast range of mechanical amusement facilities, along with actors and entertainers, that toured across the United States aboard thirty-five rail cars. In 1911, Parker moved his merry-go-round factory to Leavenworth, Kansas, where it became the largest producer of the devices in the world. Parker died in 1932. His son ran the business until it finally closed in 1955. Surviving Parker merry-go-rounds are on exhibit in towns across North America—including one in Abilene.

Thompson, Charles F. (1882–1954): Thompson left the 3rd Infantry Division in August 1941 to assume command of the Infantry Replacement Center at Camp Croft, South Carolina. In October 1942, he transferred to the Pacific theater, where he was responsible for the defense of Fiji and Tongo as well as the administrative, logistical, and training requirements for arriving U.S. units. After a brief assignment to the War Department's Operations Section in the spring of 1944, he became the deputy commander of the Second Army at Memphis, Tennessee. From September 1944 to July 1945, he headed the Military District of Washington. Prior to his retirement on November 30, 1945, his final assignment was as commander of the Patient Detachment at Walter Reed General Hospital. He died in Washington, DC, on June 15, 1954, and is buried in Arlington National Cemetery. Ike and Mamie attended the funeral.

Appendix A

Family Background

The Eisenhowers had no tradition of military service even though research into the Eisenhower family tree could conceivably be traced to medieval warriors who fought along with Charlemagne in the eighth century. By the early 1740s, however, the family had become pacifists following the Mennonite movement that believed the Bible and personal conscience, not man or government, offered the only religious or political leadership. The Eisenhowers and their fellow Mennonites suffered persecution for their beliefs and from general lawlessness across their homeland of the Rhineland, Germany.

Internal wars between the German provinces and with neighboring countries threatened conscription of young Eisenhower men into the military despite their professed pacifism. Finally, the opportunity for German Mennonites and other groups to improve their lives came because of recruitment efforts by representatives of the British colony of Pennsylvania in North America. Established by William Penn as a Quaker refuge for all persecuted religious groups, the colony offered free and low-cost lands to potential immigrants. Germans accepted the opportunity and began to pour into Pennsylvania.

Dwight Eisenhower's first ancestor to arrive in American was Hans Eisenhauer, who landed in 1741. He settled with other German Mennonites from the Rhineland in the Susquehanna Valley of Pennsylvania, where he prospered. First as Eisenhauers and then, by the 1860s, as Eisenhowers, the family became prominent farmers and landholders.

When patriarch Hans died, he willed the farm to his oldest son, John Peter. John also thrived, and when he passed away at age seventy-eight, his seventeenth child had just been born. This son was Frederick, Ike's great-grandfather, and he married Barbara Miller in 1816.

Frederick, with the generous dowry Barbara brought to the marriage, was an extremely successful farmer. Their son Jacob, Dwight's grandfather, who was born in 1826, became the spiritual leader of the River Brethren, a Mennonite offshoot. It was he who encouraged this flock of several hundred to emigrate to Abilene, Kansas, in 1878, when Pennsylvania suffered hard times after the War between the States.

There, on the Great Plains, Jacob Eisenhower and his parishioners were able to find financial success. In 1886, they established a co-op creamery near Belle Springs, where they converted the milk from their dairy herds into butter and other marketable products. The creamery became a major source of income, as well as employment, for the Brethren sect members. Proceeds allowed Jacob to open a bank in Hope, Kansas, a River Brethren commercial center twenty-five miles southeast of Abilene. As well as operating the creamery, the brotherhood purchased additional land.

Appendix B

Abilene, Kansas

Abilene, Kansas, was established as a stagecoach stop named Mud Creek in 1857. As its population grew, the settlement took on the more idyllic name of Abilene, meaning "grassy plains," from the biblical passage Luke 3:1. In 1867, the Kansas Pacific Railway (Union Pacific) reached the town.

Joseph G. McCoy, an Illinois farmer who came west to make his fortune, built a hotel for drovers, stockyards for cattle, and a stable for horses and began to advertise in Texas that he would purchase cattle for shipment to slaughterhouses back east. Herds began to arrive from what was known as the Chisholm Trail. The first eastbound shipment of cattle left Abilene on September 5, 1867.

More and more cattle and drovers arrived over the following months. Cowboys with their pockets full of cash and their thirst for alcohol and other entertainment quickly turned Abilene into the first "cow town." Well deserving of its Wild West reputation, sections of the village along the railroad were called the "Valley of Perdition," "Hell's Half Acre," and the "Devils Addition."

On February 11, 1870, the *Western News* reported, "In the last three years there have been murdered in Abilene seventeen men, seven of these were murdered through the influence of fancy women and six were slaughtered through intemperance and drunken rows, the remaining four being murdered outright in cool hand-to-hand fights. Murder, lust, highway robbery and prostitutes run the town day and night. Decent women dare not walk the streets, and men who made the town dare not appear on her sidewalks."

An article in the *Topeka Record* on August 5, 1871, noted the differences in the two sections of Abilene. The story stated that the town north of the railroad tracks was "literary, religious, and commercial," while the south side contained gambling dens, houses of ill repute, and other evils. It concluded that north of the tracks you were in Kansas, where you could hear sober and profitable conversations. However, "when you cross to the south of the tracks you are in Texas."

A series of town marshals attempted with varying success to keep the peace. Thomas J. "Bear River Tom" Smith, a former New York City policeman, wore the town's lawman badge before being killed by two men whom he attempted to arrest in November 1870. Famous lawman James Butler "Wild Bill" Hickok then became Abilene's head law enforcer. He later left town after accidently killing one of his deputies in a shootout with a rival for the affections of a saloon worker. Wyatt Earp and William Bonney (Billy the Kid) also briefly called Abilene home with no known record of violence.

For four years, Abilene shipped as many as a quarter million cattle annually. However, its rapid rise as a cattle center and one of the most wicked towns in the West came to an end almost as quickly as it had begun. By the end of 1871, new railways extended farther west and south, and the Texans turned to the closer markets. With no more cattle herds and their drovers, Abilene returned to being a farming community and encouraged immigration from the east, which brought Jacob Eisenhower and the River Brethren to Kansas. By the time the River Brethren arrived in 1878, Abilene was so peaceful that it no longer employed a town marshal.

Appendix C

Eisenhower Ancestral Religion

AMONG THE RELIGIOUS IMMIGRANTS TO ARRIVE IN NORTH AMERICA was Hans Nicholas Eisenhauer, who landed in Philadelphia in 1741. He began farming in the Susquehanna Valley and practiced his belief in adhering to the Bible and answering to personal conscience rather than man or government.

Hans prospered and, on his death, willed his farm to his oldest son, John Peter. By the time John died at age seventy-eight, the same year his seventeenth child, Frederick—Ike's great-grandfather—was born, the family had become Lutheran. They remained such until Frederick married Barbara Miller in 1816 and joined her church of River Brethren.

The River Brethren, a Mennonite offshoot, adopted their name from the nearby Susquehanna River. The several hundred Brethren believed the scriptures and the Bible to be the true word of God and practiced baptismal immersion. They adhered to plain dress, head coverings for women, avoidance of alcohol and tobacco, and rejection of military service. Despite their conservatism, the Brethren embraced prosperity and the accumulation of property.

Frederick, with the generous dowery Barbara brought to the marriage, became an extremely successful farmer. Their son, Jacob, was born in 1826 and would eventually become the spiritual leader of the Brethren, delivering sermons in both English and German.

While several Eisenhowers served in the Union Army during the Civil War, Jacob (despite being such an admirer of President Abraham

Lincoln that he named a son Abraham Lincoln) followed the Brethren belief in pacifism and did not take part in the conflict.

Although the Brethren prospered, new opportunities began to dwindle in postwar Pennsylvania. In 1877, in response to newspaper articles and advertising brochures about the fertile land and bountiful crops in Kansas, the Brethren dispatched several of its flock to see the potential of the state for themselves. These representatives returned with high praise and the recommendation that the sect relocate to Middle America. In addition to rich land, two factors influenced the Brethren's decision. First, newly built railroads provided fast and cheap transportation. Second, the Homestead Act of 1862 offered a grant of 160 acres to each new settler.

In 1878, the Brethren sold their farms and other holdings in Pennsylvania and moved en masse to Kansas. Departing from Harrisburg, they occupied fifteen freight cars, carrying their personal possessions, farming equipment, and twelve heavy wagons drawn by eight horses. Dwight's paternal grandparents moved west to answer the call; they arrived in Dickinson County, Kansas, located twenty miles from the geographic center of the United States, and settled in and around Abilene along the Smoky Hill River.

Sources

Primary sources are thousands of documents, photographs, and other materials from the Eisenhower Presidential Library, Museum, and Boyhood Home in Abilene, Kansas, as well as the U.S. Military Library Archives and Special Collections. The best source of Eisenhower's own observations and feelings on the influences that led to his successes is his book *At Ease: Stories I Tell to Friends*. Unless otherwise specified, quotes from Eisenhower are from *At Ease*. Ike's book *Crusade in Europe* and *The Eisenhower Diaries*, edited by Robert H. Ferrell, provide additional insights.

Although this book includes much biographical information, it is not intended to be a biography; rather, it recounts the people and incidents that developed Ike's identity and ideas and led to his "becoming Eisenhower." Of the many biographies, several were most helpful. The earliest, *Soldier of Democracy* by Kenneth S. Davis, published in 1946, is noteworthy because Davis interviewed Ike, as well as his family, Abilene neighbors, and fellow soldiers—many of whom were dead by the publication of more contemporary biographies. Also helpful were biographies by Carlo D'Este, Michael Korda, and Jean Edward Smith.

Lastly, the author's more than twenty years of experience as an officer in infantry and mechanized units in the United States, Vietnam, and Germany assisted in the understanding of Ike's difficulties and challenges.

Secondary Sources

Adams, Sherman. *Firsthand Report: The Story of the Eisenhower Administration*. New York: Harper & Row, 1961.

Ambrose, Stephen E. *Duty, Honor Country: A History of West Point*. Baltimore: Johns Hopkins Press, 1966.

————. *Eisenhower: Soldier and President*. New York: Touchstone, 1990.

————. *Ike: Abilene to Berlin*. New York: Harper and Row, 1973.

American Battle Monuments Commission. *American Armies and Battlefields in Europe: A History, Guide, and Reference Book*. Washington, DC: U.S. Government Printing Office, 1938.

————. *A Guide to the American Battlefields in Europe*. Washington, DC: U.S. Government Printing Office, 1927.

Ballard, Jack. *Fort Logan*. Charleston, SC: Arcadia Press, 2011.

Bender, Mark C. *Watershed at Leavenworth: Dwight Eisenhower and the Command and General Staff School*. Fort Leavenworth, KS: Command and General Staff College, 1990.

Beschloss, Michael R. *Eisenhower: A Centennial Life*. New York: Harper and Row, 1990.

Bischof, Gunter, and Stephen Ambrose. *Eisenhower: A Centenary Assessment*. Baton Rouge: Louisiana State University Press, 1995.

Blumenson, Martin. *Eisenhower*. New York: Ballantine Books, 1972.

————. *The Patton Papers: 1885–1940*. Boston: Houghton Mifflin, 1972.

Boyle, Peter. *Eisenhower*. New York: Pearson/Longman, 2005.

Brandon, Dorothy Barrett. *Mamie Doud Eisenhower: A Portrait of a First Lady*. New York: Scriber, 1954.

Brands, H. W. *Bound to Empire: The United States and the Philippines*. New York: Oxford University Press, 1992.

Branigar, Thomas. "No Villains, No Heroes: The David Eisenhower–Milton Good Controversy." *Kansas History* 15, no. 3 (autumn 1992).

Brendon, Piers. *Ike: His Life and Times*. New York: Harper and Row, 1986.

Brown, Charles H. "Fox Conner: A General's General." *Journal of Mississippi History* 49, no. 3 (August 1987).

Bruscino, Thomas. *Developing Strategists: Dwight D. Eisenhower and the Interwar Army War College*. Carlisle Barracks, PA: U.S. Army Heritage and Education Center, 2019.

Burk, Robert Frederick. *Dwight Eisenhower: Hero and Politician*. Boston: Twayne Publishers, 1986.

Butcher, Harry. *My Three Years with Eisenhower: The Personal Diary of Captain Harry C. Butcher, USNR, Naval Aide to General Eisenhower, 1942–1945*. New York: Simon and Schuster, 1946.

Cadden, Vivian. "Mamie Eisenhower Talks about Fifty Years of Marriage." *McCall's* (September 1966).

Calkins, Ken. "Ike the Pilot." *Boeing Magazine* (January 1954).

Childs, Marquis. *Eisenhower: Captive Hero*. New York: Harcourt Brace, 1958.

Chynoweth, Bradford G. *Bellamy Park*. Hicksville, NY: Exposition Press, 1975.

Clausewitz, Carl von. *On War*. Princeton, NJ: Princeton University Press, 1976.

Cobb, Kirkpatrick. *Ike's Old Sarge*. Dallas, TX: Royal Publishing, 1964.

Coffman, Edward M. *The American Army: 1898–1941*. Cambridge, MA: Belnap Press, 2004.

Conner, Virginia. *What Father Forbade*. Philadelphia: Dorrance and Company, 1951.

Cooling, Benjamin Franklin. "Dwight D. Eisenhower at the Army War College, 1927–1928." *Parameters: Journal of the U.S. Army War College* 5, no. 1 (1975).

Cox, Edward L. *Gray Eminence: Fox Conner and the Art of Mentorship.* Stillwater, OK: New Forums Press, 2011.

D'Este, Carlo. *Eisenhower: A Soldier's Life.* New York: Henry Holt, 2002.

Dastrup, Boyd L. *The U.S. Army Command and General Staff College: A Centennial History.* Manhattan, KS: Sunflower University Press, 1982.

David, Lester and Irene. *Ike and Mamie.* New York: G. P. Putnam's Sons, 1981.

Davis, Kenneth S. *Eisenhower, American Hero: The Historical Record of His Life.* New York: American Heritage, 1969.

———. *Soldier of Democracy: A Biography of Dwight Eisenhower.* Garden City, NY: Doubleday, 1945.

Dodd, Gladys. "The Early Career of Abraham L. Eisenhower, Pioneer Preacher." *Kansas Historical Quarterly*, no. 3 (autumn 1963).

Donovan, Robert J. *Eisenhower: The Inside Story.* New York: Harpers and Brothers, 1956.

Eisenhower, Dwight D. *At Ease: Stories I Tell to Friends.* Garden City, NY: Doubleday, 1967.

———. *Crusade in Europe.* Garden City, NY: Doubleday, 1948.

———. "George Catlett Marshall." *The Atlantic* (August 1964).

———. "A Tank Discussion." *Infantry Journal* 17 (November 1920).

Eisenhower, John D. *General Ike: A Personal Reminiscence.* New York: Free Press, 2003.

Eisenhower, Mamie. "My Memories of Ike." *Reader's Digest* (February 1970).

Eisenhower, Susan. *Mrs. Ike: Memories and Reflections on the Life of Mamie Eisenhower.* New York: Farrar, Straus and Giroux, 1996.

Ferrell, Robert H. *The Eisenhower Diaries.* New York: W. W. Norton, 1981.

Field, Rudolph. *Ike, Man of the Hour.* New York: Universal, 1952.

Frye, William. *Marshall: Citizen Soldier.* Indianapolis: Bobbs-Merrill, 1947.

Gabel, Christopher R. *The U.S. Army GHQ Maneuvers of 1941.* Washington, DC: U.S. Army Center of Military History, 1992.

Goodman, Herman. "The Anti–Venereal Disease Campaign in Panama." *Western Medical Times* 42, no. 1 (July 1922).

Grant, James L. *Bernard M. Baruch: The Adventures of a Wall Street Legend.* Hoboken, NJ: Wiley, 1997.

Greene, Douglas. "Ike: The Human Side." *American Legion Magazine* (May 1983).

Griffith, Robert, ed. *Ike's Letters to a Friend: 1941–1958.* Lawrence: Regent's Press of Kansas, 1984.

Gunther, John. *Eisenhower: The Man and the Symbol.* New York: Harper & Brothers, 1952.

Hansen, Laurence J. *What It Was Like Flying for Ike.* West Largo, FL: Aero-Medical Consultants, 1983.

Harger, C. M. "Abilene's Ike." *New York Times Magazine*, November 22, 1942.

Hatch, Alden. *Red Carpet for Mamie.* New York: Henry Holt, 1954.

Hertzler, J. R. "The 1879 Brethren in Christ Migration from Southeastern Pennsylvania to Dickinson County, Kansas." *Pennsylvania Mennonite Journal* (January 1980).

Hobbs, Joseph P. *Dear General: Eisenhower's Wartime Letters to Marshall.* Baltimore: Johns Hopkins University Press, 1971.

Hoffman, Paul D. *Chronicle of the Belle Springs Creamery Company.* Abilene, KS: Abilene Printing Company, 1975.

Holland, Matthew. *Eisenhower between the Wars.* Westport, CT: Praeger, 2001.

Holt, Daniel D., and James W. Leyerzapf, eds. *Eisenhower: The Prewar Diaries and Selected Papers, 1905–1941.* Baltimore: Johns Hopkins University Press, 1998.

Howard, J. Woodford. *Mr. Justice Murphy: A Political Biography.* Princeton, NJ: Princeton University Press, 1968.

Huff, Sid, and Joe Alex Morris. *My Fifteen Years with General MacArthur.* New York: Paperback Library, 1964.

Humes, James. *Eisenhower and Churchill: The Partnership That Saved the World.* Roseville, CA: Forum Books, 2001.

Ingersoll, Ralph. *Golden Years in the Philippines.* Palo Alto, CA: Pacific Books, 1971.

Irish, Kelly. "Dwight Eisenhower and Douglas MacArthur in the Philippines: There Must Be a Day of Reckoning." *Military History* (April 2010).

———. "Dwight Eisenhower and the 1930 Industrial Mobilization Plan." *Journal of Military History* (January 2006).

Jameson, Henry B. *They Still Call Him Ike.* New York: Vantage Press, 1972.

Killigrew, John W. *The Impact of the Great Depression on the Army.* New York: Garland Publishing, 1979.

Kingseed, Cole C. "Eisenhower's Prewar Anonymity: Myth or Reality?" *Parameters* 21, no. 1 (1991).

———. "Mentoring General Ike." *Military Review* (October 1980).

Kinnard, Douglas. *Eisenhower: Soldier-Statesman of the American Century.* Washington, DC: Brassey's, 2002.

Korda, Michael. *Ike: An American Hero.* New York: HarperCollins, 2007.

Kornitzer, Bela. "The Story of Ike and His 4 Brothers." *U.S. News & World Report*, July 1, 1955.

Lanning, Michael Lee. *The Military 100: A Ranking of the Most Influential Military Leaders of All Time.* New York: Citadel Press, 1996.

———. *Patton in Mexico: Lieutenant George S. Patton, the Hunt for Pancho Villa, and the Making of a General.* Essex, CT: Stackpole Books, 2023.

Lee, R. Alton. *Dwight D. Eisenhower: Soldier and Statesman.* Chicago: Nelson-Hall, 1981.

Lovelace, Delos W. *General "Ike" Eisenhower.* New York: Thomas Crowell, 1944.

Lyon, Peter. *Eisenhower: Portrait of a Hero.* Boston: Little, Brown, 1974.

Madden, Robert W. "The Making of a General of the Army." *Army* (December 1990).

Mahan, Dennis Hart. *A Complete Treatise of Field Fortification: With the General Outlines of the Principles Regulating the Arrangement, the Attack, and the Defense of Permanent Works.* Goleta, CA: Praeger Press, 1969.

Major, John. *Prize Possession: The United States and the Panama Canal.* Cambridge: Cambridge University Press, 1993.

Manchester, William. *American Caesar: Douglas MacArthur, 1880–1964.* Boston: Little, Brown, 1978.

Massow, Rosalind. "Ike and Mamie Talk about 50 Years of Marriage." *Parade*, June 26, 1966.

McCallum, John. *Six Roads from Abilene: Some Personal Recollections of Edgar Eisenhower.* Seattle, WA: Wood and Reber, 1960.

McCann, Kevin. *Man from Abilene.* Garden City, NY: Doubleday, 1952.

McKeogh, Michael, and Richard Lockridge. *Sgt. Mickey and General Ike.* New York: G. P. Putnam's Sons, 1946.

Medhurst, Martin. *Dwight D. Eisenhower: Strategic Communicator.* Westport, CT: Greenwood Press, 1993.

———. *Eisenhower's War of Words: Rhetoric and Leadership.* East Lansing: Michigan State University Press, 1994.

Miller, Edward, and Betty Jean Mueller. *The Dwight D. Eisenhower Library.* New York: Meredith Press, 1966.

Miller, Francis Trevelyan. *Man and Soldier.* Philadelphia: John C. Winton, 1944.

Miller, Merle. *Ike the Soldier: As They Knew Him.* New York: G. P. Putnam's Sons, 1987.

Miner, Craig. *West of Wichita: Settling the High Plains of Kansas.* Lawrence: University Press of Kansas, 1986.

Moos, Malcolm. *Dwight D. Eisenhower.* New York: Random House, 1964.

Morin, Relman. *Dwight D. Eisenhower: A Gage of Greatness.* New York: Simon and Schuster, 1976.

Murray, G. Patrick. "The Louisiana Maneuvers: Practice for War." *Louisiana History* 13 (1972).

Neal, Steve. *The Eisenhowers.* Lawrence: University Press of Kansas, 1984.

———. *The Eisenhowers: Reluctant Dynasty.* Garden City, NY: Doubleday, 1978.

Nenninger, Timothy K. "Leavenworth and Its Critics: The U.S. Army Command General Staff School, 1920–1940." *Journal of Military History* 58 (April 1994).

———. *The Leavenworth Schools and the Old Army: Education, Professionalism, and the Officers Corps of the U.S. Army, 1881–1918.* Westport, CN: Greenwood Press, 1978.

Nevins, Arthur S. *Gettysburg's Five-Star Farmer.* New York: Carlton Press, 1977.

Odom, Charles B. *General George S. Patton and Eisenhower.* New Orleans: Word Pictures Productions, 1985.

Parker, Jerome H. "Fox Conner and Dwight Eisenhower: Mentoring and Application." *Military Review* (July-August 2005).

Parmet, Herbert S. *Eisenhower and the American Crusades.* New York: Macmillan, 1972.

Patton, George S. *War as I Knew It.* Boston: Hughton Mifflin, 1947.

Payne, Frederick H. "Fundamentals of Industrial Mobilization." *Army Ordnance* (July-August 1930).

Perret, Geoffrey. *Eisenhower.* New York: Random House, 1999.

———. "MacArthur and the Marchers." *MHQ* (winter 1996).

Peterson, Elmer T. "Mother Eisenhower Talks about Her Most Famous Son." *Better Homes and Gardens*, June 21, 1943.

Petillo, Carol Morris. *Douglas MacArthur: The Philippine Years.* Bloomington: Indiana University Press, 1981.

Pickett, William B. "Eisenhower as a Student of Clausewitz." *Military Review* (July 1985).

Rabalais, Steven. *General Fox Conner: Pershing's Chief of Operations and Eisenhower's Mentor.* Havertown, PA: Casemate Publishers, 2021.

Reynolds, Quentin. "Eisenhower of Kansas." *Collier's*, December 18, 1948.

Robere, Richard H. *The Eisenhower Years.* New York: Farrar, Status, and Cudahy, 1956.

Rockenbach, Samuel D. *The Rockenbach Report: Operations of the Tank Corps A.E.F.* Silver Springs, MD: Dale Street Books, 2016.

Russell, Donald B. *Invincible Ike: The Inspiring Life Story of Dwight D. Eisenhower.* Chicago: Successful Living Publications, 1952.

Sevareid, Eric. *Not So Wild a Dream.* New York: Alfred A. Knopf, 1969.

Shavelson, Melville. *Ike.* New York: Warner Books, 1979.

Sixsmith, E. K. G. *Eisenhower as Military Commander.* New York: Stein and Day, 1973.

Smart, Vaughn. "1919: The Interstate Expedition." *Constructor* (August 1985).

Smith, Gene. *Until the Last Trumpet Sounds: The Life of General of the Armies John J. Pershing.* New York: John Wiley & Sons, 1998.

Smith, Jean Edward. *Eisenhower in War and Peace.* New York: Random House, 2012.

Snyder, Marty, and Glen D. Kittler. *My Friend Ike.* New York: Frederick Fell, 1956.

Taylor, Allan, ed. *What Eisenhower Thinks.* New York: Thomas Y. Crowell, 1952.

Tonkin, R. G. "I Grew Up with Eisenhower." *Saturday Evening Post*, May 3, 1952.

Vandiver, Frank. *Black Jack: The Life and Times of John J. Pershing.* College Station: Texas A&M University Press, 1977.

Verckler, Stewart. *Cowtown Abilene: The Story of Abilene, Kansas, 1867–1875.* New York: Carlton Press, 1961.

Vexler, Robert, ed. *Dwight D. Eisenhower: 1890–1969.* Dobbs Ferry, NY: Oceana Publications, 1970.

Vivian, James D., and Jean H. Vivian. "The Bonus March of 1932: The Role of General George Van Horn Moseley." *Wisconsin Magazine of History* (autumn 1967).

Weaver, John D. "Bonus March." *American Heritage* (June 1963).

Weintraub, Stanley. *15 Stars: Eisenhower, MacArthur, Marshall: Three Generals Who Saved the American Century.* New York: Free Press, 2007.

Weyand, Alexander M. "The Athletic Cadet Eisenhower." *Assembly* (spring 1968).

Wicker, Tom. *Dwight D. Eisenhower.* New York: Times Books, 2002.

Wickman, John E. "Ike and the Great Truck Train." *Kansas History* (autumn 1990).

Wilson, Dale E. *Treat 'Em Rough! The Birth of American Armor, 1917–1920.* Navato, CA: Presidio Press, 1990.

Wukovitz, John F. *Eisenhower.* New York: Macmillan, 2006.

INDEX

ABOUT THE AUTHOR

Michael Lee Lanning was the author of thirty nonfiction books on military history, sports, and health. More than 1.1 million copies of his books are in print in fifteen countries, and editions have been translated into twelve languages. He appeared on major television networks and the History Channel as an expert on the individual soldier on both sides of the Vietnam War.

The *New York Times Book Review* declared Lanning's *Vietnam 1969–1970: A Company Commander's Journal* "one of the most honest and horrifying accounts of a combat soldier's life to come out of the Vietnam War." The *London Sunday Times* devoted an entire page to a review of his *The Military 100: A Ranking of the Most Influential Military Leaders of All Time*. According to the *San Francisco Journal*, Lanning's *Inside the VC and NVA* is "a well-researched, groundbreaking work that fills a huge gap in the historiography of the Vietnam War."

His more recent books include *The Court-Martial of Jackie Robinson*, *The Blister Club: The Extraordinary Story of the Downed American Airmen Who Escaped to Safety in World War II*, and *Patton in Mexico: Lieutenant George S. Patton, the Hunt for Pancho Villa, and the Making of a General*.

A veteran of more than twenty years in the U.S. Army, Lanning was a retired lieutenant colonel. During the Vietnam War, he served as an infantry platoon leader, reconnaissance platoon leader, and infantry company commander. In addition to having earned the Combat Infantryman's Badge and Bronze Star with "V" device with two oak leaf clusters, Lanning was Ranger qualified and a senior parachutist.

Lanning was born in Sweetwater, Texas, and had a BS from Texas A&M University and an MS from East Texas State University.